Arctic Son

Fulfilling the Dream

Jean Aspen

ALASKA
NORTHWEST
BOOKS®

Arctic Son was originally published in 1995 by Dell Publishing in New York.

Library of Congress Cataloging-in-Publication Data
Aspen, Jean.
  Arctic son : fulfilling the dream / Jean Aspen.
     pages cm
  Originally published: Birmingham, Alabama : Menasha Ridge Press, 1995.
  ISBN 978-0-88240-920-7 (paperback)
  ISBN 978-1-941821-00-8 (e-book)
  ISBN 978-1-941821-22-0 (hardbound)
  1. Aspen, Jean. 2. Aspen, Jean—Family. 3. Pioneers—Alaska—Brooks Range—Biography. 4. Brooks Range (Alaska)—Biography. 5. Brooks Range (Alaska)—Description and travel. 6. Alaska—Description and travel. 7. Frontier and pioneer life—Alaska—Brooks Range. 8. Wilderness areas—Alaska—Brooks Range. 9. Wilderness survival—Alaska—Brooks Range. I. Title.

  F912.B75A77 2014
  979.8'70092—dc23
  [B]
  2013050352

Cover Design by Jean Aspen and Vicki Knapton
Interior Design by Vicki Knapton
Illustrations by Jean Aspen

Published by Alaska Northwest Books®
An imprint of

GRAPHIC ARTS
BOOKS®

P.O. Box 56118
Portland, Oregon 97238-6118
503-254-5591
www.graphicartsbooks.com

For Luke

And his children's children,

And for every child

Who dreams of Freedom, Beauty, and Adventure;

And for Tom Irons and Laurie Schacht

Who made my dreams come true.

Our wilderness family, October 1992.

CONTENTS

We chose our cabin site on a 1990 canoe trip. Luke was four.

ACKNOWLEDGMENTS

The first time I set off for the Arctic I had just turned twenty-two. It was a perfect age for testing myself against hardships and the unknown. I felt the need to do it on my terms and sought little help. Two decades later, proving myself was no longer the issue. At forty-two I was comfortable with my physical limitations. As a mother, I wished to ensure the safety of our journey. As a seeker I was learning to accept life's gifts.

I was therefore deeply moved by the number of friends and even strangers who stepped forward with offers of assistance when Tom and I announced we were returning to the Brooks Range to build a cabin and live alone for a year and a half with our young son, Luke. Were it not for this help, our undertaking would have been far more difficult.

Apart from the love these gifts represented, there was sometimes a wistful quality. I felt rather like an astronaut, setting forth where few will go but many will follow in their hearts. In receiving, I discovered a nobility of human spirit, a desire to contribute and be a part of something beyond our daily lives, and so came to see our venture not in terms of us alone, but as something greater. This odyssey then belongs not only to me and mine, but to all who stood and waved good-bye and to any our story may touch and inspire.

I apologize to anyone I fail to mention by name. The oversight is not intentional. I am grateful to each of you for your contribution, your love, and for teaching me that it is also good to receive.

In the order they come to mind and not in importance, I wish to thank and acknowledge the following individuals:

- Mark and Denise Wartes were our safety lines. They collected our mail, organized supply flights, kept our truck, and gave us a loving home base in Fairbanks.
- My sister, Ann Helmericks and her husband, John Louder, built our stovepipe oven and gave us numerous items. My Aunt Janet and

Uncle Bert Cutler provided the stove and helped purchase video-tapes. Tom's brother and wife, Fred and Sally Irons, helped us buy video equipment.

- My father and stepmother, Bud and Martha Helmericks, and my brothers Jim, Mark, and Jeff Helmericks and their families, were kind to us.

- Tom's family: Alice and Larry Irvin, Frances Putman, Mary-Eva Irons, Nancy and Charlie Weatherman, and Richard and Barbara Irons supported us with love, despite their concerns.

- Vic and Judy Michael rekindled the dream.

- Stan and Ruth Brown supported in countless ways with joy and enthusiasm. Luke's sleeping bag was a present from them. Barb and Bill Dantzler championed us with clothing, food, and much else. Neighbors Joyce Mattson and Debbie Gonzolez often took on an extra child to leave me free to prepare.

- Jeffrey and Nicole Ureles and Jennifer Barnacastle took care of our Arizona home with assistance from Joe Burns and Keven Mulkins. Peg Hausler, Robert Fleming, and Bea Carter handled our affairs.

- Alaskan bush pilots who greatly deserve our thanks: Stephen Ruff and Ken Howard of Brooks Range Aviation, Steve Porter of Transporter Air, Don Ross of Canning Aviation, the Alaskan Civil Air Patrol, and the Fairbanks-based US Air Force Medevac Team.

- Drs. Georgie and Jack Boyer were our medical advisors and Dr. J. Rokey set us up with an emergency dental kit, as he had twenty years before. Dr. Christopher Demas, Mr. Rogers, PA, and Dr. Stephen Moore deserve our thanks as well. Our pharmacists, Rich Howard and Mary Sparling, also guided us.

- We couldn't have made the video without technical help and encouragement from Chris Knight of The New Film Company. Kate Bandos of KSB Promotions was indispensable in handling my books.

- When Arizona schools turned us down, several individuals contributed materials and ideas for Luke's first grade. Among these were Sue Clemans, Peggy Clemans, Jennifer Vemish, Jane Chittenden, Ruby James, Beth Zona, Susan Kraft, David Anderson, Marie Tsaguris, and Amelia Warner and her children.

- Robert Morgan located a canoe for us and gave Luke a pair of skis. Ralph Griest donated his knives as did Eugene Brown. Eugene Brown and Betty Brown drove three hundred miles to clean our carpets as a parting gift. Friends and neighbors offered to help us pack.

- My spiritual teacher, Frederick Patchen, has altered forever the quality of our lives.
- The Indian people of Venetie, Beaver, and Steven's Village treated us like family.
- The cooking staff at the University of Arizona Student Union saved empty food containers. Susanne Loeper of Back to Basics in Payson, Arizona, special ordered dried foods.
- Special thanks goes to my editors, Budd Zehmer and Kathy Howard, for keeping my creative style within acceptable bounds, and to Barb Wieser, Mike Jones, Stephen Reynolds, and Doug Pheiffer for believing in me. Jacob Hoye, Scooter MacMillan, Angela Zbornnik, and Vicki Knapton also contributed.
- And finally we are thankful to everyone who loved and supported us, including: Duane and Jenny Durham, Mark and Jane Fraze, Don and Ginny Fisher of Papillon Glass, Denny Genzman of Snoopy's Flight School, Hugh and Claire Wingfield, Ralf and Celia Webber, Michelle Polis, John Callentine, Valina Cutler, Albert Cutler III, Chris Vemish, George and Fredi Young, Jake Cadzow, Jay and Sandy Dominic, Philip Fergione, Charlotte Cardon, Gayle and Richard Carter, Bob and Jean Rupkey, John Lacoma, Sally Steven-Towne, Bob Stauffacher, Terrel Miedaner, Lillian Fisher, Michael Zanders, Troy Mattson, and Darlene Schacht.

I personally wish to acknowledge Laurie Schacht for her suggestions on this manuscript and my husband, Tom Irons, for his considerable help in creating this book. Above all, I am deeply grateful to Tom, Luke, and Laurie for their love and trust.

Tom, Jeanie, Laurie, and Luke the summer of 1992.

PROLOGUE

Luke shifted sleepily in my arms, and I realized that he was still awake. The steady rocking of our chair had lulled me into a dream state, but as I looked down, I could see his large, brown eyes watching me. Eyes like forest pools dappled in sunlight, I always thought, liquid and deep.

"Sing," he commanded with the quiet assurance of a two-year-old. Thoughtfully, he tucked the frayed corner of his blue blanket into his mouth, snagged his front teeth on it, and pulled. Then came a happy sucking sound.

I searched my memory for something different and began an old Howard Halsey song that Johnny Horton had made famous.

Snowflakes fall as winter calls,
And time just seems to fly . . .

Again my thoughts drifted out the window, North. Snowflakes. Wind in the dark treetops. The call of migrating geese. Alaska. Autumn was upon the high country five thousand miles away, while in Arizona the thermometer still registered in the hundreds. The ceiling fan droned quietly on, Luke sucked his blanket, and I sang and dreamed.

Many years before, I had set out to live on the land in the wilderness of the Brooks Range of Alaska with my first husband, Phil Beisel. We were college kids with little money and no strings to hold us back. It seemed the perfect time of life for a Grand Adventure.

This wasn't my first expedition. My parents, Constance and Bud Helmericks, were arctic adventurers and authors of a dozen books on the wilderness. I had traveled with them as a toddler, following the caribou herds by dogsled and flying in our Cessna over the vast distances between our Brooks Range cabin and the arctic coast. My sister, coming along eighteen months after my birth, was left with grandparents in a small town in Colorado. Grandpa ran a gun shop and delivered mail over mountain roads with little Annie propped between the mail sacks. Leaving her was the price my mother had paid for the Arctic.

My parents were divorced when I was quite young, and our mother brought my infant sister and me to live in Arizona. It wasn't until I reached fourteen and Ann turned twelve that our mother returned with us to the wilderness. The three of us canoed three thousand miles through Canada to the Arctic Ocean on the Peace, Slave, and Mackenzie Rivers, a journey spanning two summers. This adventure resulted in my mother's seventh book, *Down the Wild River North*, and opened a door for me. From the Mackenzie delta, I continued north to spend the winter on the Alaskan tundra with my father and his new family.

I was headed into medicine and my senior year at the University of Arizona when the memory of Alaska caught up with me. I would sit on the third floor of the library and try to study, but my eyes drifted out the window where the white-crowned sparrow sang in the treetops. He had stopped briefly on his way to the great northern tundra, and his voice called to me. Perhaps if I had studied without a window, I would be a doctor today.

So the spring of 1972 found Phil and me floating our canoe, laden with all we could carry, down the Yukon River. On board were snowshoes, a sheet metal stove, books, clothes, Plexiglas windows, axes, and food. There wasn't much, for a canoe doesn't hold much, but it was all we needed to build a home in the wilderness. When we reached the mouth of our chosen tributary, we turned north, walking the beaches as we pulled our craft up the tumbling rapids and into the mountains of the Brooks Range.

Autumn found us thin and worn as we neared tree line of the Arctic Continental Divide. We unloaded our canoe and set to work with axes, building a cabin. It wasn't an easy time, facing hardship and starvation as winter rapidly descended, blanketing the North and locking the river. We walked the freezing banks hunting moose and shared the intimacy of plans around our fire at night. The rest of the world seemed very far away and unreal. Who was president? What was happening in Vietnam? It didn't really matter. It was a time of quiet, of reflection, of growing up.

In the end, we spent nearly four years in our valley, calling it home. I was twenty-six when I remembered the outside world. A feeling had been growing that there was something back there that I needed, and I didn't know what. Phil and I returned to Arizona for me to complete my biology degree. Eventually we were drawn in different directions. This adventure became the basis for my book *Arctic Daughter: A Wilderness Journey*, first published by Bergamot Books in 1988.

I became an artist and in time married again. My husband, Tom Irons, had left the fast lane of California where he worked in aerospace to build a home in the Arizona desert and live simply. He was also an artist, and we worked together creating a home and business on our natural five acres. Our time was filled with construction and the labors of the self-employed. It was as mainstream as I was likely to get. I was almost thirty-six and Tom was nearly forty when Luke was born. Of all my adventures, this was the grandest.

My life seemed full and busy, but as I rocked my baby to sleep, singing songs that my mother sang to me, I couldn't help but gaze out the window, North. Sometimes at the change of season, just at twilight, I would catch a certain note of birdsong or a half-remembered scent on the breeze, and see the northern forests stretching unpeopled and free before me. I wished that I could share them with Luke.

I smiled down at the sleeping child. Always big for his age, he now sprawled across my lap, putting my arms to sleep. He was worth any price, my Luke. He was still now, but I continued to rock and hum softly. He had fallen asleep with his eyes partly open and I resisted an impulse to close them. Glossy, chestnut hair fell limp over his damp forehead in the heat. He twitched and startled, eyes opening wide for a moment and then slowly closing.

The familiar rapping sound of Tom building a stained glass panel came from the studio beyond the closed door. We created large, unique pieces for churches and homes, each of us performing a different aspect of the work. It was a good life, but demanding too—never off the economic treadmill, rarely time to relax, especially since Luke. Life had become a funnel necking down instead of expanding my options. I couldn't see a way out.

I stopped rocking and rose and carried Luke to his crib. He gave a long shuddering sigh as I lowered him onto his back.

"Someday," I whispered to him. "Someday."

However, it didn't seem very likely just then. My youthful days of adventure were over. I was middle-aged, soft, respectable, established. I had a business, property, and commitments. I had a small son and no extra cash. It seemed a time for prudence, a time to buy insurance, put money away for college, collect IRAs. And I thought of Tom. As an Ohio farm boy, he had a good deal of common sense but had never spent time in the wilderness nor shown any desire to do so.

Still, there was a restlessness growing in each of us that had no real name. Art, I was finding, is not something you do, but a way of living. Being an artist means being willing to explore new paths, to risk and to let go of form.

The summer of 1990, we set out to canoe my familiar old river. The opportunity had arisen out of nowhere. A producer who had followed my family through their books wanted to film a return voyage. He and his wife arranged the trip and, although they were unable to accompany us at the last, it was the impetus that turned us North. Luke was four.

I wasn't sure how my family would take to wilderness, or even how I would. Eighteen years is a lifetime of change. Still it was returning home for all of us; it was not just a place, but a remembering of who we were.

After the trip we spoke of Alaska as a treasured family bond. It gave me joy that Tom now shared my dream. In some inexplicable way I felt that he could never really know me without loving the Arctic. I smiled when I heard Luke at play with his friends pretending to catch fish or set up camp. As I did errands about town, Luke would fly our car back to Alaska, and whenever someone asked him what he really wanted, he said, "to live in the Arctic."

The love of wild places and the courage to explore one's dreams was a legacy from my mother, now mine to pass on to Luke. It hadn't been an easy gift, this restlessness to see the next mountain, but it was the most important thing I had to give. It was living life fully awake, and in the end, what else mattered?

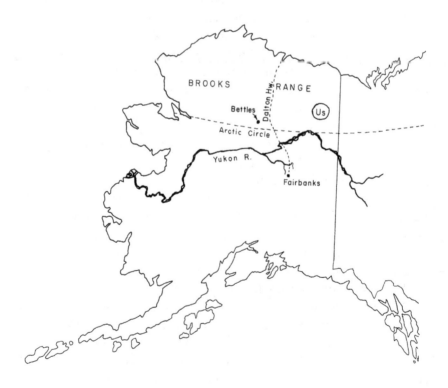

CHAPTER 1

R OAD CLOSED AHEAD,'" I read aloud anxiously. "'4:30 PM to 4:30 AM.'
I didn't catch at what mile post . . . did you?"

"I have to keep my attention on the road," Tom answered grimly. We were careening down a steep grade, our small Toyota one-ton pickup truck loaded with fifteen hundred pounds and pulling another five thousand, as it had for the past month. I clenched my jaws, feeling the load sway and wallow dangerously as it pushed us down the bumpy dirt strip at seventy miles per hour.

This was the last leg of Tom's long journey from Arizona: the Dalton Highway. Called "the Haul Road" by locals, it was built to connect oil fields on the Arctic Ocean with cities far to the south. Tom had left Arizona while Luke and I made last-minute preparations. We had joined him in Fairbanks and added another eight hundred pounds of supplies and a new puppy to the load.

"When will we get there?" Luke asked again. He was bobbing his head up and down, playing a pretend video game between bug splats on the window and the rushing scenery. His restless six-year-old legs drummed against the seat.

Low western sunlight streaked the dirty windshield and illuminated rooster plumes of dust that hung in the still air above the winding gravel road. Beside the road, the great silver tube of oil pipeline snaked on pylons or plunged occasionally beneath the ground. The land had opened from the more southern forest of spruce and birch and now stretched in a vast rocky upland, green and gray beneath a deep blue sky. It was a land of horizons, a place boundless and eternal. But my attention, like Tom's, was riveted to the road.

"Perhaps we can get more information at the Yukon River," I said. The hill bottomed abruptly and climbed just as steeply on the far side. One by one, Tom dropped through the gears as the engine lugged down. A sign crawled up on the right side: 12% GRADE. He shifted into first gear and I tried to think light. Good old truck, only a few more miles.

"We haven't seen any traffic for a while," I said nervously. What would we do if the road was really closed? A chartered floatplane was scheduled to meet us at a little lake the following morning for our final jump into the mountains.

Tom was leaning forward, urging the engine as if his will could give it that extra boost.

"Why can't I sit by the window?" Luke asked.

"We've been through this," I answered shortly. "Just sit still so that Daddy can drive."

The front seat was crowded, and I pulled Luke against me and leaned into the window to give Tom room to maneuver. "I know you're tired and hungry, Honey," I said smoothing Luke's head against my chest.

"When will we get there?" he persisted.

I sighed and answered tenderly, "When we do. It's still a long way. But we'll stop for dinner at the Yukon and be able to stretch our legs a bit," I promised. "Do you remember driving across the bridge the summer you were four when we took that long canoe trip?"

Luke thought a moment and shook his head. "No."

"Well, the Yukon is big. I mean really big. And I want you to remember it, because this is where we'll end up next summer when we paddle from our cabin all the way down out of the mountains. It'll take much of the summer to get here, for it's several hundred miles."

This information did not seem to impress him.

"Do you remember the poem I read you that talks of a land where the mountains are nameless?"

"Uh-huh."

"Well, that's where we're going."

"Do you mean we can name them?"

"Well, for us maybe. Nobody else will use those names, but then nobody else will be there."

"Can we call the creek, 'Luke's Creek?'" he asked with renewed interest.

"I think that's a dandy idea. What do you think, Tom?"

But Tom clearly wasn't thinking about naming creeks. My thoughts returned to the road and I picked up the topo map for a clue about the conditions ahead. "It looks like the hills smooth out on the other side of the Yukon," I said by way of encouragement.

"That would be nice," he replied dryly.

"What'll we do if we can't get through?" I wondered aloud. "I suppose we could sleep in the truck until the road opens in the morning, then drive on." My stomach tightened. So much to pull together. It seemed like our lives had been a continuous marathon of details and timing for months.

HOPING TO PULL TOGETHER financing for our trip, we had waited until the day after Christmas to make the final decision. America was experiencing an economic decline, and as self-employed artists it was harder on us than many. The sensible thing to do was to put it off another year.

I remember sitting at the table over dirty dishes that December evening. Luke had just been put to bed. I was tired and discouraged. It was dark outside, and the warm light of stained glass and wood suffused the dining nook. It gave me a feeling of comfort to view the surroundings we had designed and built. Our home was an outgrowth of our lives and fitted well into its natural desert surrounding where quail, coyotes, and bobcat came to drink in the shade of trees.

"Well," Tom asked, "are we going to do it?"

I looked up, head on hand, and asked, "How?" That had been the question last year when we had postponed our trip. Here it was again. How? I had written countless letters seeking money to film a documentary, but they had come to nothing. So here we sat, just the two of us and the question.

"You say that the Universe supports choice," he answered, "perhaps it's time to live by it."

I nodded slowly. Tom was often a teacher for me. While I spoke of personal growth, he was apt to put the ideas into practice. The truth was that change scared me to death, and letting go of security was like prying my fingers free from a ledge.

Tom took a napkin and was scratching out figures with a pen. I watched him, my mind quiet. Through the years I had come to know him as a man of integrity, solid as bedrock in what he stood for, yet flexible and kind. I knew I could count on him to do his best at anything he undertook. He was of modest height, an inch or two taller than me, and a bit heavy. We had the same sized feet. His hands were neat and competent. Salt-and-pepper chest hair protruded from the neck of his shirt. He had fair skin that looked fragile and tended to freckle. His face was slightly asymmetrical with a slender nose that drifted off to one side where a high school football coach had broken it trying to force him off the team. It was a quiet reminder of his determination, for though he was small, Tom had refused to quit.

I studied him as he bent over the table. His collar-length hair was the rich brown color of Luke's but balding on top. There was a curious tuft remaining in front, a dark island marooned in the sea of forehead and scalp. He wore a full beard punctuated with bold streaks of white, like whipped cream swirled in chocolate pudding. Though unfashionably dressed, Tom was fastidiously neat and his fingernails were always clean. Behind thick glasses his large, hazel eyes were gentle, observant, and apt to twinkle with mischief. There were wrinkles at the corners of his eyes and across his forehead. He was not what most people would think of as a mountain-man type.

And me? Hardly your typical arctic explorer either. As a child I needed surgery to correct bone problems in my feet, and only the summer before had undergone carpal-tunnel operations on both hands. I wasn't certain how well my extremities would hold up to the heavy work of building another cabin. I was definitely on the soft and chubby side, though sturdily built and of average height. My skin was brown, and while not yet wrinkled, tended to look weathered if I spent too much time out-of-doors, which I often did. I had long, honey-blond hair that I cut myself and wore loose. My direct, gray-green eyes slanted up at the corners under arching brows, giving me almost an Indian look. My mother used to call me a Viking, and I undoubtedly hail from Nordic stock. My features were angular: strong jaw with high cheekbones, full lips, and even teeth. No one had ever called me cute. Handsome I have heard, sometimes even beautiful, but I had never learned (as they say) "to do anything with it."

I looked around the cozy room, so safe and familiar. My eyes climbed to the shelf opposite the loft where three pair of snowshoes rested, dusty from years of waiting. One I had used twenty years before, the other two came from my grandfather, my father's father. He was in his eighties, still a big farmer of a man with gray beard and faded overalls, when he came to visit Annie and me. I can see him now, gripping the wheel of his old Ford pickup, going twenty-five miles per hour down the middle of the road all the way from Colorado. He wouldn't let the traffic hurry him. I have only three memories of Grandpa, but he had many of me. He was not a sentimental man, and it was several years later that I realized he loved me.

"I saved these for you," he had said, matter-of-factly. "Kept them mukluks and baby snowshoes in the freezer." The little fur boots and the tiny snowshoes had been mine, made by my "Eskimo Grandparents," George and Nanny Woods. The work was delicate and fine. "These big snowshoes were given to me by your dad," he went on, "when I visited them back in the fifties. And here are some little towels and such I saved for you when your Grandma Abby died."

He had stayed two days, then climbed into his old truck and driven back to Colorado at twenty-five miles per hour. I only saw him alive one more time. I was en route to Alaska with Annie, her infant daughter, Faith, and my three huskies in a broken-down VW wagon. Grandpa seemed embarrassed when our mob showed up. Perhaps overwhelmed is a better word.

"Oh, we don't want to bother you," we had told him.

"Whatever you wish," was his answer. "This is your home." He was laying out home-canned plums (no sugar, because of his diabetes). He wasn't a great cook, but he was proud of his independence. His drinking glasses were tin cans.

We stayed the night in his old, wood-paneled home, and in the morning, although Grandpa was his usual gruff self, there were tears in his eyes at our departure. "Well, good-bye," he said shortly, giving me a clumsy hug and turning away.

And good-bye it was. Colorado was out of the way, and I didn't go through there again until the funeral—which of course is like not going at all.

My thoughts returned to Tom, who had finished his figures. He scooted around to show them to me.

"We have a lot of equity here," he began, "and few debts. Let's use what we have to get where we want to go. You've said you're tired of doing glass. Let's sell the business. Your car is old—we can sell it too. We'll worry about getting another when we come back. I think we can extend the mortgage on the house. There must be a few things around here we can sell. For that matter, we can sell the whole place."

I swallowed. We had worked years to build up the business. To just throw it away seemed reckless. How would we make a living when we came back? And my car! Sell the whole place?! He had a way of springing these impossible schemes on me, and I had a way of freezing up when he did.

Tom was watching me, a curious light in his hazel eyes. "Look," he prompted, "I'm almost forty-six. If we wait much longer, we'll be too old for the physical labor of this trip. Life is an adventure. You always say that. So let's go for it."

I collected my thoughts and addressed the hardest item first. "I don't think we should sell our home. We'll need a place of stability when we come back. I can't handle too many changes at once. Letting the business go is hard, but I can agree. And you're right about the car. There's no point in storing it.

"We'll need the truck to get up there," he said with excitement. He had already reached for another napkin to start a second list. We both loved lists.

I was thinking now too. "I like your idea about the mortgage," I told him. "That would probably get us in—and like Scarlett O'Hara, I can worry about paying for it when I get home. They certainly won't come looking for us." I found myself smiling. "We're going to do it, aren't we?"

We looked at one another and grinned.

"I thought you didn't like snow," I teased. "Something about Ohio winters, as I recall."

"I'm willing to change," he replied simply.

I shook my head and smiled. "I know. That's what I love about you."

Once the decision was made, we had five months to orchestrate a major expedition. We rapidly passed the point of no return. All that did not serve our purpose was turned into cash. With the apprehension and thrill of a canoeist who commits his life to white water on a one-way ride, we put all our resources— the security of business and home gained slowly through years of uphill work— into this one effort. We burnt our bridges and never looked back. It felt like riding the crest of a giant wave: exhilarating, frightening, unreal.

Risk is the price of freedom: there are no guarantees. The nature of life is change. Living your dreams involves risk, but what are the alternatives? Life is transitory, no matter how careful we are. Security is a myth, and a very expensive one if we pay for it with our dreams. Still, taking risks never gets easy. By definition, it requires moving into new territory where you can never be sure of the outcome.

We sold our business and spent hundreds of dollars each week. It was a giddy sensation buying on credit things we would never need unless we went to the Arctic. Our studio (now empty of equipment) began to fill up with tools, food, and the necessities of wilderness life. Night after night I sat at my computer revising endless lists. I dug through my old journals and located inventories of twenty years before on lined notebook paper with items outlined into groups like "medical kit," "sewing kit," "cabin building tools," and "camp equipment."

In truth, I had begun the process in my mind some time before, chafing for the final decision. All fall I had been buying small items or things that might prove hard to locate: pieces of a giant puzzle that we could afford without commitment. Tom and Luke had received new jackets for Christmas. After discovering that mountaineering catalogs charged up to $52 for a single long underwear top, I haunted the Goodwill and Salvation Army stores for long underwear, wool shirts, sweaters, socks, mittens, and pants. Gradually, I accumulated a mismatched assortment of used clothing and packed it away in large, plastic garbage cans, which would serve to keep out the weather and could later be used for storing water.

I ran Tom's ancient sewing machine, refitting clothing and making parkas, mukluks, and equipment. I found old fur pieces—mink capes and rabbit skin jackets at the Goodwill—and made them into fur caps and ruffs for our parkas. One treasure was a down jacket for $12 that I refitted for Luke, making a hood with down from pillows. I reduced woolen navy pants to size six for him, sewed the buttons shut and put in zippers.

Tom spent time in his shop creating items we couldn't buy. Daily, we traipsed out in different directions to acquire a peculiar array of treasures, which we proudly displayed after each trip to town. We would leave home with lists and return excited about our acquisitions: augers, axes, stovepipe, dried eggs, candlewicks, used five-gallon plastic buckets and jugs, fishing tackle, toothpaste, notebooks, life preservers, a trailer. We already had a nineteen-foot freight canoe in our hope chest.

We found renters for our home-studio, put our affairs in the hands of our lawyer and accountant, and arranged for neighbors to help the tenants with any problems that might arise. Slowly, we began to say good-bye.

Tom's family was alarmed and couldn't understand what we sought in the Arctic. His brother, Fred, was the only one with enthusiasm for the project. Thirteen years older, Fred was of another generation. With neatly cropped hair, rosy complexion, and blue eyes, he was an engineer, a methodical thinker, and a perfectionist. After viewing the documentary my parents had filmed when I was a toddler, Fred insisted that we should record our journey. With his help and encouragement, we invested $12,500 in state-of-the-art, Hi-8 video equipment and took on one more project: learning to use the cameras and taping our daily lives.

We were fortunate to contact a producer, Chris Knight, who was experienced in teaching adventurers to film themselves in a professional manner. He purchased the best equipment for our needs, even having some designed for our unique problems, and then flew from Massachusetts to give us intensive training. Week by week we sent off cassettes to be critiqued and spent nights on the phone updating our skills as he reviewed our work.

Early in our planning, we had put out the word among friends that we were seeking a third adult for the adventure, a sort of "wilderness nanny," we said, tongue-in-cheek, someone to add a safety factor. Two could haul logs or hunt without dragging Luke back and forth over the muskeg. We were committed regardless, but such a person would add a great deal, and from the standpoint of a six-year-old boy with only his parents for fourteen months, would also lend a needed social dimension.

We had about given up on the idea when Laurie Schacht, the twenty-eight-year-old daughter of our friend, Darlene, called from Seattle.

"What if she doesn't like kids?" Luke had asked with obvious concern when I told him.

"We all have to agree or we won't take her," I assured him. "She'll be flying down next weekend to meet us."

Laurie arrived late Friday night. Tom picked her up at the airport, and she made herself at home on the top bunk in Luke's room. I didn't meet her until the following morning.

The first thing that struck me about Laurie was her down-to-earth presentation. Luke took to her immediately. We all crawled into his play-loft in our nightgowns and shared a blanket while watching the sun rise over the Catalina Mountains. It was a good beginning.

❧

"IT'S RATHER LIKE AN arranged marriage," I told my sister a few days after Laurie had visited us. "It's a very intimate and mutually dependent life we're embarking on."

Annie and I were sitting on her large, covered deck sipping coffee. Her yard, a jungle of trees and flowers, was host to flocks of wild birds. Behind us were stacks of large paintings and easels of more underway, testimony of a passion for art shared with her fiancé, John Louder. Even the chairs were whimsically painted. Annie was small-boned and of average weight, with fair skin that burned easily and steel-blue eyes in an oval face. We were close in age and height, though different in build.

"Well, what did you think of her?" she asked.

"I liked her very much," I confessed. "We're similar in many ways. She even looks like I did at her age. Sturdy, too. I told her she had 'good haunches.' She can pull logs, of that I'm sure. A sight better than I can."

"How did she respond to that?"

"Well, that's the important thing. She's open and it's easy to talk with her."

We sat for a moment in silence. John was tending his flowers, and the faint sound of running water came up to us. The late afternoon sunlight glinted off a stained glass window in the chicken house. Fat hens crowded by the fence, talking.

"I figured we are going to be living in a little tent together with no privacy," I continued, "so I asked the difficult questions and she was reassuringly candid in her answers. For example, I asked how she felt being the single adult with a married couple."

"And?"

"She said she envisioned herself in the role of older sibling to Luke, not (as she was quick to tell us) that we were as old as her parents. She's good with kids, treating them like real people. Incidentally, she and Luke got on famously. She's willing to set boundaries without being condescending."

"Why are you going back?" Annie asked suddenly. "I can see what Tom and Luke would get out of it, but you've done it before. Why give up everything you've built to wash clothes by hand and carry water at your stage in life?"

I was inclined to say, "If you have to ask, there's nothing I can say that would make you understand," but it sounded too glib, so I sat and pondered what Alaska really meant to me. Wilderness. Unspoiled and uncluttered wilderness. My night dreams swimming in crystal rivers among big fish. My daydreams free from clocks and telephones, clients and doctor appointments, schedules and bank statements.

In the end all I could say was, "I didn't think it would ever happen to me again. I thought I was all settled and respectable, and that my wild, free days were only memories."

I knew she understood. She had said the identical thing to me two years before when Tom and I invited her to join our summer canoe trip. She knew the place we were going. She also remembered the Mackenzie and Peace Rivers where puberty had overtaken her amid the mud and mosquitoes of Canada's Northwest Territories.

We were silent, watching the sunset. Inside the house, her two pubescent kids were watching a *Batman* video.

"I wish I could share it with them," she said sadly, inclining her head toward the house.

"I was shopping for paddles today," I told her. "One of those big supermarket places. Lines of people. I was standing in one with my paddles, and in front of me was a harried mother with a boy, about eight. He had his eye on a fishing pole. I could see that it meant a lot to him. His mother turned on him and yelled, 'Will you shut up about the fishing pole?!' I felt like crying, looking at that little boy. 'Why am I going on this wonderful odyssey?' I wondered. 'I've been there. It will always be part of me. This child should be going.'"

"I understand these things," she said, "but what's in it for you? You know better than anyone that the romantic ideal of wilderness can be bitterly hard. If you've forgotten, I suggest you go back and read your first book."

"I don't know," I answered simply.

"Frankly, I'm concerned about your hands. What if they don't hold up?"

"I've been wondering about that too," I confessed. "I have lost strength in my thumbs, and the fingers aren't so strong, either. I've always taken my body for granted and it's damned annoying."

"It's also a serious drawback for an artist," she replied, rubbing her own hands together. Annie had rheumatoid arthritis and had undergone the same surgery I had, but for different reasons.

"So what are you going to do if they give out?"

"Isn't it funny," I mused. "I'm the only person I know who's had surgery on both hands and both feet. Not a likely candidate for arctic explorer. Though wasn't it Peary who walked to the North Pole in his fifties with no toes?"

She was studying me, blue eyes unblinking. "You haven't answered my question. Are you aware that whenever you hit a question you don't like, you go off on some oblique pathway into a swamp somewhere?"

"I've heard it said. Tom, I believe, has brought it to my attention. A totally unconscious habit, I assure you."

"Your hands?" she prompted.

"Well, Dr. Demas told me they wouldn't be as strong. When I asked if I could use an ax, he laughed and said that most of his patients wanted to use their computers. Anyway, he didn't see harm in it, though I got the feeling it wouldn't be his first choice of lifestyles for me."

"Believe me," she stated, "I know what I'm talking about. Take care of your hands." She flexed her pale, slender fingers through the limited range they would go.

I took her hand and held it between my sturdy, brown ones. "Annie, you only get a few years on this planet. I look at my body like my car. I change the oil regularly and do my best to respect it, but its job is to get me around. If I use it up in the process, so be it. If I sit home and be careful for eighty years, it still goes in the end. I'll protect my hands as well as I can, but I'm not building my life around them."

"You will if they fail you."

"Well," I smiled, "it may be that I'll end up as the nanny and Laurie will be Wonder Girl of the Arctic. It would probably be more fitting. It seems to me that when one has mastered something, the next step is to give it away. There's growth for both parties, and it keeps you from getting stuck in your own script. Like Mother did."

We grinned knowingly at one another. Our mother, the paradox. Connie had never given up the role of lecturer and "Arctic explorer," even years after it had ceased to play any part in her life, defining herself by it as some women do by motherhood. Yet she was often strangely helpless in the face of physical challenges. When Annie and I were young, our eccentric mother—who packed thirty extra pounds, wore sensible shoes and unfashionable used clothing with a flourish, and dyed her gray hair red—had maneuvered an eight-thousand-dollar advance from her publisher to finance the crazy dream of canoeing the Mackenzie River System with her two young daughters.

That adventure had changed my life. An awkward and unhappy teenager, I discovered my own value on the long expanse of those rivers. I was cast (for better or worse) in the role of "man of the family" at the age of fourteen by a mother, who despite her courage, was inept with anything more complex than a safety pin, and at fifty was not a strong person. In this role, I discovered that I could be sensible and effective.

"She had guts, you know, Jeanie." Annie's gaze was far away. Twilight bathed the backyard while the sky was a flame of orange silhouetting giant saguaro cactus. The birds were making bedtime twittering sounds, and from the henhouse came the truculent voices of chickens arguing over perches.

"We didn't give her much slack, did we?" I said, breaking the silence.

"No, we didn't."

"It's good that life usually lasts a lifetime. It gives you an understanding and appreciation of the other side."

"She gave us a lot," Annie said. It was a generous admission, for she had been cast in a less expansive role by our mother, who saw everyone as characters in a script. It had taken my sister many years to realize that she, and not another, wrote the lines.

"You ought to come," I told her suddenly.

"Not winter with my arthritis. Besides, I need light. I can't imagine a dark cabin at fifty below. Yuck! How depressing," she shuddered. "Besides, Tom would never have me. There'd be open warfare."

"You're right," I said. "I'm sure Laurie will work out best."

"Do you think she knows what she's getting into?"

"Well, we did our best to tell her. She's really excited about it, but she's never even car camped! No hiking, nothing."

"She's got courage," my sister admitted. "Lots of courage. And trust in you."

"Or maybe just trust in life," I answered. "There's a deep wisdom in her."

"Is Tom gonna pick her up on the way north?"

"She's attending a wedding at the last minute, so she'll fly up. Alaskan logistics always boggle me. I don't know how we'd manage without Mark and Denise Wartes in Fairbanks. We can't fly from there because a small plane eats up most of the payload in gasoline at that distance. We're chartering out of Bettles, but there's no road, so we'll drive the Haul Road north to where the plane can land on a lake. Luke and I will fly in first. Tom will take the truck back to Fairbanks and pick Laurie up at the airport. They'll fly commercial to Bettles and charter in."

❧

OUR LITTLE RED PICKUP crested a hill and Tom, Luke, and I gazed down upon the Yukon River. The only Alaskan bridge to brave that mile of moving chocolate-colored water stretched across the canyon below us. The bridge sloped oddly down as it made the leap to a lower hill on the north shore. We crossed slowly, the passage restricted to a single lane by construction. On the far bank stood a dusty collection of mobile units hooked together to form a restaurant-motel-service station that served truckers, hunters, and the occasional tourist. It was a no-nonsense sort of place created for the dusty, greasy needs of the road. The large parking lot hosted a collection of heavy vehicles, their windshields cracked and nearly opaque with mud.

"Why don't you and Luke order something while I walk the dog?" I suggested as we pulled to a stop in front of the restaurant. After the incessant bang and bump of the gravel road, the silence seemed unnatural, and I yawned to clear my ears.

"Maybe the truckers will know if the road is closed," Tom said. "Come on Luke, let's go get a last hamburger."

I stretched, feeling stiff and old. In the camper shell our new, nameless puppy had been throwing up. She'd been acquired as a companion for Luke the day before from a dog musher, and at four months old had experienced little human contact. She was a husky, fawn-colored with black guard hairs and dark ears that lopped forward. Her chest and big feet were snowy, her toe pads a mixture of pink and black. She was a thin, gangling animal with obvious misgivings about life in general and people in particular. As I reached for her, she backed into the boxes, eyeing me wildly from the end of her rope.

A fine layer of dust coated everything, and I felt sorry for the frightened creature. "Come on little girl," I coaxed, pulling on the leash. "How about a drink of water and a walk?" I have always had an affinity with animals, but it was going to take some time to win this one's heart.

The pup clearly preferred to cower in the truck, and after a brief attempt to walk her, I settled her there again, pushing the boxes back to give her more room. I wanted to leave the camper open, but a large yellow dog seemed to regard the yard as his property, and I deemed it unsafe.

"Don't worry," I told her. "This is the hard part. Soon, you and your new boy will have all the Brooks Range in which to play. With love, you'll grow to trust and enjoy us. I hope." I had once owned a dog with this wild look, and she never did settle down. I wondered if I hadn't made a mistake, but we had only found three available pups to choose from in Fairbanks.

"The road is closed for the night," Tom informed me as I seated myself beside Luke at the table. They were already working on large platters of excellent food.

"Where?" This was the really important question.

"Nobody knows. It seems they're replacing the bridges, and it depends on where they're working just now. Some of the truckers say about fifty miles north of here."

I helped myself to Luke's French fries, dipping them in catsup. "I think we should drive as far as we can. If they stop us, we can sleep in the truck until the road opens."

"These are my fries," Luke said, pulling his plate closer. "Why don't you get your own?"

"I figured you wouldn't finish it all . . . I hate to waste . . . you wouldn't deny your own mother?" I tried to look pathetic and hungry.

"You can get your own," he assured me, unmoved.

"We can afford it," Tom added with a lift of one eyebrow.

Twenty minutes later, our last hamburger consumed, we were on our way again. "You're clear," I called, sticking my head out the window to see the long, sloping bridge. Our little red truck threw herself against three tons of weight and we bumped up the shoulder and back onto the Dalton Highway, headed North.

The hour grew late and Luke fell asleep, his head cradled in my lap and his feet in Tom's. He had given himself up with the total abandon that only a sleeping child can. I held him as we bounced along, mostly in silence now. At one point, we turned into an improvised camping area where the other traffic had stopped for the night. Here families stood about fires on a large open hillside, talking and swatting mosquitoes in an almost festive mood. The evening sun made the truck uncomfortably hot for sleeping. At this time of year it would probably not set at all on the exposed ridge.

"I think we should just go on," I said to Tom as he reentered the truck and closed the door on the swarm of pests. Luke was still sleeping.

He nodded and started the engine. "Nobody seems to know about the road. But we'd be miserable here unless we put the tent up, and I'm not even sure I can find it."

Evening drew on and the arctic sun disappeared from time to time behind mountains as we journeyed. We had the road to ourselves now and watched each curve with a sense of apprehension. We were cresting a hill when the dreaded sign appeared: ROAD CLOSED 1000 YARDS.

"What do we do now?" Tom asked. There was no place to turn our awkward rig about on the raised gravel highway. We slowed to a near stop before the ominous sign.

"Might as well go on," I answered with resignation. I felt guilty, the naughty child who has disobeyed and is about to be caught. I found myself mentally rehearsing excuses for the angry earthmovers. There would be a foul-up of major proportions when we got to the heavy equipment.

As promised, the road was blocked some little way ahead, but we noticed that there was enough room between the barricades for our outfit to squeeze by.

"Keep going," I insisted. Might as well hang for a sheep as a lamb, as my Grandmother Winnie used to say. "We can park on the road if we need to." We began our descent into a shadowed valley. "At least we'll find out what's ahead."

So we pulled between the barriers and down into the valley. We proceeded slowly. There was activity ahead, trucks and people, but it was hard to see in the shadows. Then a cheerful young woman in an orange Day-Glo vest and hardhat stepped forward. She looked about twenty with sunburned face, blond hair in braids, and dancing blue eyes.

"Where you headed?" she asked, leaning down to look in the window. She smiled and lowered her voice when she saw Luke.

"We've got to get up to Grayling Lake tonight," Tom told her. "A charter is meeting us there first thing in the morning."

"Oh, really?" She glanced back at the tandem-wheeled, utility trailer piled six feet high with gear and lashed with the dusty blue tarp. "That's a lot of stuff."

"We're headed up into the Brooks for a year and a half," Tom continued by way of explanation.

"Yeah?" she asked in excitement. "Say, I just read a book by a woman who did that. Built their own cabin and everything. Lived on moose meat and fish. You'd really like this book . . . Arctic something."

"*Arctic Daughter?*" I said helpfully.

"Yeah! That's the one. You read it, too?"

"My wife wrote it," Tom told her proudly.

"Really? No kidding?! Gosh, wait 'til I tell my parents. They're reading it now. So you guys are going back and all? Wow, that's a kick. I've always wanted to do something like that."

I tried not to look fat, middle-aged, and worn-out. I hoped I wasn't a disappointment. "It was twenty years ago," I said by way of apology. About the time she was born. "Now we're going back to share it with our son. Do you think we can get through?"

"Yep. Won't be long now. See that crane? As soon as he off-loads those I beams, we'll get you across." She moved toward the bridge to ensure our passage.

I breathed a deep sigh and smiled at Tom. "We're gonna make it," I said.

He stroked my cheek with the hand that rested on the seat back. "You bet we are."

I closed my eyes and my head swam. I seemed to be still jostling down that endless road. "I'm tired, and we still have a marathon before us."

"One hill at a time. Tomorrow we'll get you and Luke into the mountains. Then take it easy. Don't feel like you have to do anything. Set up camp and rest awhile. Relax until Laurie and I get there."

I opened my eyes and grinned. "Well, I'll have to handle five thousand pounds of gear and get it out of the weather."

"Yes," he admitted. "But then you can rest."

"When do you think you and Laurie will fly in?"

"Well, you fly tomorrow. Then a day to drive back to Fairbanks. I pick Laurie up at the airport. A day to get her hunting-fishing license and any other gear she needs. Then we'll fly in to Bettles and Steve Ruff will bring us in to you. Say four to five days. But don't worry if it's longer. It'll take as long as it takes. You know."

"I know. And we have all we need." I have always believed it foolish to go into this country without being prepared to live there and walk out if necessary. "I just hope we can land near the creek," I said for the hundredth time.

That was the next hurdle and the big unknown. All our plans of getting the cabin up before winter hinged on being able to land on the river. The nearest lake of any size was three miles away. It would take a month to carry everything to the cabin site if we had to land there.

Our conversation was interrupted as the cheerful girl in orange returned. "You can go through now," she told us. "And good luck!"

Tom started the truck and we pulled across the bridge, the sole piece of traffic that June night, and headed up the opposite hill.

"People up here always seem so kind," I observed as we topped the ridge. "It's like a secret society."

"Uh-huh," Tom commented, shifting gears.

In just over an hour we were pulling off the highway at Grayling Lake. It was a long oval, cupped by a rim of peaks that rose almost from the water to occlude the evening sun. The pipeline road curved along the western shore, and a pullout lay within a few feet of the glassy lake where (true to its name) fish popped the still surface after clouds of mosquitoes.

The haunting beauty of an arctic summer night greeted us when we shut off the engine. The perfect stillness was broken by the call of nesting birds and the drone of countless bugs. Stunted spruce broke the swampy ground and seemed to offer firewood to ward off mosquitoes. I plunged through the familiar muskeg, wet moss to my knees, my nose alive with remembered smells: spruce, Labrador tea, and cranberry bog. The area was well picked of firewood, and it took considerable time to round up a modest pile of dead sticks, which I set aside for the morning.

Meanwhile, Tom unloaded several boxes from the pickup to give us a retreat. We left Luke asleep in the closed cab, but I found him drenched in sweat. He couldn't stay there, so Tom carried him to the back and we all climbed in, closing the shell behind us. Black clouds of mosquitoes swirled about the screen windows and soon began to seep, like water, around the tailgate. Bunched in a corner, I found the dog-vomit towel (borrowed from Denise Wartes, and later destined to become our table cloth) and used it to chink the cracks. The three of us, plus the miserable dog, curled up on the floor in the narrow space between the wheel wells. Hot on top and cold where we touched the metal of the truck, we slept like dead people for the brief remainder of the pastel arctic night.

CHAPTER 2

I awoke in a tangle of bodies and tried to sit up. My arms were asleep, my hands numb and tingling, and my head ached from fatigue. It was already hot inside the camper shell, and I could myopically see the sun sparkling off the nearby lake. The traffic had resumed early, and a big truck thundered past a few feet away. That was what had wakened me. But I could also hear the sweet song of my old friend, the white-crowned sparrow, who had called me North so many years before.

I rotated my shoulders and rubbed my hands, restoring sensation, then pushed my hard contact lenses from the side of my eyes to the center. It was a trick my ophthalmologist had shown me when I canoed the Mackenzie almost three decades before. It's not the method of choice, but there are times in the bush when removing contacts is nearly impossible. Through the years my eyes had changed and I could no longer see well with glasses. At least this way I could respond quickly to emergencies, and I imagined it would have to do for the summer.

At my movement, Luke opened his eyes and smiled exposing a white row of baby teeth behind rosy lips. His face was dirty and there were dark circles under his eyes. Already a few red welts speckled his soft skin and he scratched absently at his scalp. "Are we there yet?" he asked.

"Yes, we're there. Now wait. Put on your hat, boots, and mosquito repellent before you go outside or the bugs will eat you alive. You need to start protecting your body."

"But I have to go pee. Right now."

"Here, let me help you. Once we open the door they'll be everywhere. I'll build a fire as soon as I get out. I'm putting a match container and mosquito repellent in your shirt pocket."

Tom was curled away from the activity as we pulled on our boots. Luke spotted the dog and his face lit up. He began to crawl toward her, laces flopping. She cringed back and flattened into the corner behind Tom.

"Ow! Luke get off my hand," Tom yelped. "I'm waiting for you so I can get up."

"Leave the dog alone," I admonished. "You can't make friends with her by grabbing. Wait until we get to the river. Please."

I reached for the door and popped it up. The mosquitoes had abated somewhat under the morning sun, but a few dozen drifted in on the gentle breeze. I helped Luke over the tailgate. "Careful now," I told him. "Watch for traffic on the road. I'm going to bring the dog out, but you mustn't untie her. I let her go last night and it took me an hour to catch her again. When we get to the river, she can run free."

"Can I take her for a walk?" he pleaded. He was standing on the bumper tugging at her rope. The puppy backed away, eyeing him, one lip wrinkled in warning.

"No. She doesn't understand yet. And she's too frightened. Move back so I can get out. This is going to be a hard day, and I want you to handle yourself so Daddy and I can organize things. It's important."

I sighed and heaved myself over the tailgate. That's all the poor kid had heard for months now. "Just handle yourself, I'm busy." Part of the reason I was here was to get out of that cycle, but somehow I was in deeper than ever.

"I'm going to begin unpacking the trailer and making piles for trips," Tom said as he followed me into the bright morning. "Anything that won't fit in three flights I'll send back to Bettles with the pilot. It can come in with Laurie and me."

It was cooler outside and a breeze helped to blow the bugs away. Not a fish broke the ruffled, blue surface of the lake. Above us, the steep mountains hung, green on green beneath a flawless sky. I started a fire and dug out soggy luncheon meat, stale bread, milk, and Luke's cold French fries. My stomach was a knot of nerves and I could swallow little. Tonight, I promised myself, I'd cook a good meal for Luke. As I'd told him, we needed to care for our bodies, but everything depended upon today. I searched the sky, wondering when our plane would appear. Thank God we were here at last! And it wasn't raining. There's always a reason to be thankful.

Tom seemed almost cheerful, and I realized again the terrible strain he had traveled under for the past weeks—the weight of our entire expedition between his shoulders as he fought that load and worried about our open trailer over 4,500 miles.

We began unpacking the trailer. Every item had been weighed and labeled, for weight is critical in a small plane. I ran lists on a calculator as Tom organized the tonnage into four piles and Luke crawled under the trailer wanting to make friends with the strange puppy.

"Hey, Son," I called, trying to head off trouble, "look at the butterflies." The wet shore danced with small black-and-orange butterflies. They gathered in quivering clumps, tame enough to pick up. "Be gentle," I cautioned needlessly. This was the child who wouldn't let anyone kill a fly. I imagined he would come to feel differently about mosquitoes.

Most of the load had been packaged to keep the weather out. Food, consisting of dried staples in bulk, was stored in five-gallon plastic buckets, recycled cooking oil jugs, and square metal cans—each weighing around thirty pounds. We had a large, plastic grub box with small containers of dried food that would be refilled as needed. The thousands-of-little-bags alternative was too expensive and bulky for our needs.

I had calculated the nutritional requirements of four active people over fourteen months, allotting each three- to four-thousand calories a day. Despite his size, Luke already consumed nearly as much as I did. The dried carbohydrates and proteins gave us around eighteen hundred calories a pound, while fats have twice as much energy. I had figured out the proper balance of nutrients and chosen a wide variety within the range we could afford.

We had about thirty-two hundred pounds of food. There was rice, varieties of beans, different types of flour, dried milk, dried cheese, powdered eggs, dried potatoes (in different forms), pasta, beverages, premixed pan breads (of three types), oatmeal, cornmeal, sugar, textured vegetable protein, dried fruits and vegetables, puddings, seeds, nuts, candy, and granola. Smaller items that were somewhat watertight (like cans of dried fruit, peanut butter, margarine, coffee, and spices) were packed in cardboard boxes, as were last-minute purchases from Fairbanks. Two hundred pounds of dog food was still in paper sacks.

When Phil and I spent our first winter in the Arctic we had been able to carry only those items that fit in a canoe, and had of necessity hunted for the vast majority of our food. It's surprising how much an active person consumes: we ate five moose, a caribou, and a bear that year. I wasn't willing to impose again on this fragile country. We intended to live with the land, not off of it. In addition, I had no desire to place my family in the subsistence position of finding game or starving.

We had thirty-gallon plastic garbage cans full of clothes and five-gallon containers of books. There were wooden crates of various sizes containing tools wrapped in old blankets, Christmas presents, lamps and personal supplies, a stove, an oven, sleeping bags, tents, backpacks, a canoe, a washtub, paddles, and life preservers. Odd items were stowed in duffel bags or organized in some way for handling. There were camera and video cases, sewing and medical kits, cooking pots, tarps, Plexiglas for windows, a role of plastic for the roof, snowshoes, a chain-saw, white gas, and kerosene. The inventory had taken thirteen pages on my computer. Each pound would cost two dollars to transport, so items were chosen to be low in bulk as well as weight. Still, it made a sizable pile.

It was almost noon when the gold-and-blue Beaver came flashing over the lake, circled and landed. The pilot taxied up to shore and cut the engine. Steve Ruff, a lanky man in his thirties, hopped onto the floats and threw Tom a line. He was dressed in Levi's with hip waders and a long-sleeved cotton shirt. With short brown hair, observant gray eyes under heavy brows, a full mustache that drooped at the corners, and a ready smile, he had the alert appearance of a friendly hawk.

"Bet you wondered where I was," he called as he waded ashore and helped Tom tie the plane. "I got over-scheduled, as usual. I brought five hundred pounds of avgas for refueling, including a drum. I shouldn't have to go back to Bettles at all. Wish we could get in a bit closer to shore to unload. It's pretty shallow here. Did you see me hang up over there?"

The Beaver seemed big and strong compared to the little Cessnas I knew. Its bulky engine and blunt snout made it look like a real workhorse (which it was) and a gas hog. It could haul over fourteen hundred pounds of freight and still take off in less distance than the Cessna.

Steve removed the door and pulled can after can of gas from the crowded interior, handing them to Tom who passed them to me. Finally, came the fifty-five gallon drum, weighing around three hundred pounds. It seemed likely that one of us would lose a finger as we muscled it onto the metal skid and slid it out of the plane. It settled with a splash in a foot of water. Together we heaved it through the mud to shore.

"Well, we can get at it there," Steve said, giving me a hand pump. "Now let's see what you've got for a load."

"Here's the cargo list," Tom told him as we walked to the trailer. "We have it sorted into fourteen-hundred-pound piles, with a lighter load when you take the canoe." The canoe would be lashed outside and use up part of the payload in wind resistance. "It's a nineteen-footer and weighs 116 pounds."

"My goodness," Steve grinned, "you've got it all handled. You weighed all that stuff? I wish more of my clients would think like that. You should see some of the outfits I'm supposed to carry! They must think they hired a truck."

"How do you know what to take if it isn't weighed?" I asked.

"Well, in Bettles I'd weigh it, but you get pretty good at guessing. You can tell a lot by lookin' at how she sets on the floats."

Luke had stayed by the plane and was seeking a way to jump across to the floats.

"Jeanie and Luke will go with the first trip," Tom told him, "so she can help you unload and handle stuff on that end. I put all the survival stuff—food, rifle, tent, and such—in the first pile."

"That's always a good policy. You never know in this country. Clouds roll in and you can't make it back. Though I don't imagine we'll have any trouble today."

Luke had blundered out through the mud and onto a pontoon. He was soaked to the hips but already climbing the struts to the cockpit.

"Do you want him in there?" I asked. "He's muddy, I think."

"Aw, it's okay. He can't hurt much. I have four boys. Kids just love planes."

"Luke, don't touch the knobs!" I called, as I headed toward him with my arms full of gear. I could see the elevators moving as he happily tried the controls. "I'd have to tie him up to keep him away from the plane," I apologized. "He's always been into buttons and knobs. A high-tech kid in a low-tech family."

"How do you think he'll take to life in the bush?" Steve asked. "You can't get much lower tech than what you're doing."

"Well, he did fine two years ago. You and Dave Ketcher took us in to float the river. Maybe you don't remember." Steve had been working for the Ketchers and had later bought the operation. I have noticed a fairly high turnover in this business, often (though not in this case) from pilot death.

"Yeah. You had somebody else with you. A blond woman, pretty and very nice."

"That was my sister." People often remembered me as the one with the pretty sister. I tend to come across as more serious: your basic no-frills model.

Steve swung aboard and we handed up the load. With an easy sense of balance he stowed the cargo, filling a space not much larger than the family car with half a ton of supplies until only spots for Luke, the puppy, and me remained. Last aboard was the camera equipment. Documenting our lives in both video and 35 mm slides was turning into a full-time job.

I sat in the plane, camera braced on my knees, filming Tom through the open door as he hugged his son good-bye and zipped him into his life preserver. Luke crawled over my lap and was stuffed into the backseat of the Beaver and belted down. Steve carried our snarling, nameless dog out to the plane where she disappeared beneath the cargo at Luke's feet.

"Why can't I ride in front?" came the protest from the back.

"Because I need to show him where to go. After we're in the air, I'll let you wear the earphones and you can talk with the pilot." I was struggling with a mass of wires, seat belt, tripod, and camera straps. Steve explained the workings of the door handle and shut it firmly behind me.

He was saying a last few words to Tom as they cast off the line. Then he was aboard, all business as he started the engine and tested the controls. The smells of a small plane—plastic, upholstery, and fuel—combined with the engine noise to flood me with familiar, almost queasy feelings. We taxied onto the lake, lining up into the wind. Tom shrank to a tiny figure, fragile as a flower against the backdrop of mountains, as we must have seemed to him. Silently, I raised my hand in farewell. As his arm went up, I felt a connection greater than physical touch across the widening distance.

"Okay, I'm ready," Luke called imperiously from the crammed backseat.

Then came the serious roar of engine, that thrust across the dimpled waves, faster, faster, spray flying out from beneath the splayed pontoons. Beside me, Steve rode the rush, his attention focused as he rocked the plane to break the floats free from the water and onto the "step." The far shore was racing up to meet us at an alarming rate as he tested the load, and second by second our speed increased. Suddenly, we broke free, popping into the sky like a cork released from the bottom of the lake. Trees flashed past below, the sparkle of water transmuted to an abstract pattern of ripples and sunlight, receding. We banked and circled for elevation, then with a good-bye waggle of the wings to Tom so far below, were off, North, into an unknown future. For a moment, tears blurred my vision and I did not know why.

Steve handed me a map, creased and water spotted, indicating that I should navigate. I pressed my face to the side window; nothing but engine out the front. As always I wondered how pilots can see to land. I glanced at him, gauging if his greater height gave him more visibility, and decided that it probably didn't matter with the nose-up attitude of the plane. I studied the paper and looked again. He tapped me on my shoulder and pointed to a dot on the map. Yes, I could see now. That was Grayling Lake. So that must be this creek here . . . and there was that mountain. I scanned ahead, seeking recognizable landmarks. It always looked so different up here.

Luke's foot shoved against my elbow and I looked back. His face was intent and his mouth moved insistently. I leaned toward him and caught the words, "You promised!" He was pointing at the earphones. I untangled the wires and handed them back, twisting in the confines of my seat to help him adjust the headset and microphone, then returned to the map and sky. Ahead, spotty afternoon clouds clung to the ridges, curtains of rain obscuring parts of the landscape. The plane was beginning to pitch and yaw as it entered the invisible currents, jerking my unhappy stomach through arcs. I kept track as the green landscape unrolled beneath us, gray rock ridges following the looping creeks, land of a thousand lakes. Time and miles slid by to the loud drone of the engine.

"Better go up the river," I shouted at Steve about an hour later. He was headed along a large creek, following the contours below.

"I figured we'd go straight and drop into the river over there." He traced the direction on the map then pointed ahead through the gray mist of propeller.

I shook my head. "It'll box you in. Those mountains get high and there aren't any low passes." We couldn't see well through the transient showers. "I've hiked up there. We might have trouble getting through, especially if there's a downdraft. There's not much room to maneuver."

He nodded and adjusted our course to skirt the mountain mass and pick up the main river valley. This was an old friend; I had walked every foot of it. I watched it unfold with joy and excitement. How beautiful it still was! How wild.

"That's my old cabin!" I yelled again. Steve dropped the right wing for a better look at the familiar series of islands and bends. From our altitude we could see no trace of a structure, but there was no mistaking the area. The river looked high and muddy. It must have been a late spring, I thought. June 19 and snow still clung in swatches on the mountainsides. I had hoped the river would be on the way down by now, but this was not the case. I felt my stomach tighten again, wondering where we would land.

My beloved river scrolled by below us, revealing its bends in rapid succession, as it never did to one on foot. The sky here was mostly clouds, the air bumpy. Rain rattled against the windshield and the propeller droned. Luke had his nose pressed to the window and seemed to be involved in a conversation, via headset, with Steve. There was the lake we might land on . . . yes it was big enough, but what a walk! There was the creek, Luke's Creek, we would call it and the river bend. It looked tight at this speed. We were low and fast now, the country flashing by below. You can't hover in a plane.

Steve pointed and I yelled back, "Don't do anything you don't feel good about! We can always haul stuff from the lake." Three tons over miles of muskeg, but better than dying, I thought. I wouldn't ask this man to risk himself or his plane. It's a dangerous enough profession.

"Let's have a look upstream," he shouted over at me.

I nodded. We could float our outfit down in about six trips with the canoe. The river was an opaque flood of brown. I saw waves and could tell that the current was cutting right along. We rapidly ascended the valley, then Steve dropped the left wing and spun us about in a tight circle, avoiding the nearby mountain. I was already confused and wondered how he kept his bearing at this speed. I caught a glimpse of a slower stretch of water but we flew past, hurtling downstream. Again we circled, my stomach coming into my mouth as I viewed it with the camcorder.

"If you don't like it, go for the lake," I yelled again. Suddenly, the plane straightened and dropped. I wasn't sure where we were, but I knew we were going in. I tensed as he flared over the roiling, muddy river. The floats hit with a heavy smacking and geysers of spray. I could see trees and driftwood flying past out the side, but nothing to the front. I felt the skid and slew of the pontoons and hoped that Steve could see more than I could. I wanted to shut my eyes, but I was filming. Slowing, slowing, the great bird settled like a duck into the water, the pontoons plowing now rather than planing across the chocolate surface.

Miraculously, we had arrived. The propeller gently pulled us upstream a few yards, nosed into a shore eddy, and clattered to a stop. The abrupt silence left me feeling disoriented. My head ached with fatigue and tension, and my stomach was still bumping through the clouds. I let out my breath and looked about.

Steve swung open the door and dropped onto the floats in one easy motion, apparently unaffected by the long buffeting and noise. He tugged up his waders and stepped into the river, pulling the plane up shallow and tying it to the little willows there. I helped Luke with his headset and seat belt, then stiffly climbed onto the float and jumped for the bank.

We were out of the current in a backwater of revolving sticks by a willow bar. A few yards downstream was a ten-foot cutbank forested in mature spruce. Nearby, the bank seemed to drop abruptly to a timbered bench only a few feet above the river. This ran inland out of sight, as if the whole area had once been cut away by the river and then reforested. Upstream, a slough appeared to separate us from a wide gravel bar, partly under water.

Now I knew where we were! This had to be our creek! Steve had put us down at the very spot. A thrill of thanksgiving went through me. Yes! It was going to work. It was all going to work!

"I'll stay with the plane while you check about," he said.

"Okay. Be right back." Leaving Luke with Steve, I scrambled up the bank and inland, searching for landmarks among the tangle of vegetation. We had camped . . . somewhere. The river looked different this high, but I would find our old place back in the woods off the slough, which I now knew to be part of the creek. I paralleled the creek, crashing through brush without spotting signs of our camp. Reluctantly, I gave up and circled back toward the plane. There would be time for exploration later.

As I approached the river, my mental pieces twisted and fell into place and the land came suddenly into sharp focus. It's amazing how the world shifts when you align it differently. Here was our old camp within a few feet of the plane, much closer to the river than I remembered. Yes, that was where the campfire had been and there was the cabin of twigs that Tom and Luke had constructed, now fallen in a small pile of sticks among the spruce needles. We had taken pains to return each camp to nature, leaving little visible evidence of our journey but, unmistakably, this was home.

As I returned to the waiting plane, Luke came running through the willows toward me. I caught his arm in passing and stopped him for a hug.

"Don't go far," I admonished. He struggled free and was off up the bank. "There are bears out here and I want to be able to see you at all times," I called after him.

"Here's my little cabin!" he shouted in excitement. "Come see."

"I saw it already. I need to unpack the plane. We can look around together after Steve has gone. He has to get back to Daddy for another load."

"Just come for a second," he pleaded.

"Not now. And don't go far." I had never been able to convince him of the real danger of grizzlies for someone his size. He remained unaware of any peril, and considered my restrictions on his activities mere parental noise.

Steve was already unloading gear onto the strip of damp bar. He handed down items and I piled them a few feet away, slogging through mud and water in my wet nylon boots. We seldom wore rubber boots around the river, where we were often wet to the crotch. Soon the plane was empty and our precious supplies were heaped at random along the shore.

With a wave Steve cast off into the river, idling up current to warm the engine. Then he drifted downstream, engine chugging. At the bend he executed a tight turn against the cutbank and a moment later gunned the plane to life. I heard the distinctive, flat pitch of the Beaver's propeller. Ponderously, the plane roared toward us, outstretched floats sending up twin wakes of spray as it gathered speed like a giant goose in a very small pond. Luke had his hands over his ears and was singing at the top of his voice when the plane shot past us in a gold-and-blue crescendo, lifted, circled, and was gone. Slowly the blat of the engine became a buzz, a hum, and then silence. We were alone.

"I need your help," I called to Luke. "Come back, please, and help me carry things up the bank and make camp."

"I want to explore," he told me. "We can do those things later. Come on."

"You don't understand." I pointed dramatically up the valley where a high, flat ridge of mountain was darkened by a falling veil. "We have no place out of the rain that is coming. We have no home away from the bugs, no fire, no lunch. We need to get all our stuff up high and under a tarp. And Steve will be back with more soon. Come help."

"I can't. It's too heavy."

"Most of it is," I conceded, "but there are things you can carry. Here, take the life preservers. Camp is up there."

Reluctantly, Luke shouldered the sack and struggled up the bank. He, who could carry half his sixty-pound weight when it suited him, grunted miserably under this trifle. At the top, he dropped the sack and set off again.

"Don't wander away," I called hotly. I began breaking off dead spruce twigs to start a fire. Squatting over my pile of sticks, I held the match as the mosquitoes settled and bit through the material across my shoulders. One inevitably gets two or three hundred bites a day in this country in early summer, even wearing repellent and protective clothing. It's a fact you live with, and you become accustomed to it, but it wears you down. Soon my thin trickle of smoke puffed into a blaze and I could feel the hungry hordes giving ground, retreating beyond the smoke. A fire would help to thin their population in the immediate area and give us respite from their relentless probing.

For the first time I thought of the puppy. I had released her from the plane and she had promptly disappeared. She would come back though, I assured myself. Where else could she go? But what if the noise of takeoff had sent her panicked into strange country? If she had bolted up the creek, she couldn't even hear my call above the constant rush of the water. I should have kept her tied at least until this evening, I chided myself as I made trip after trip, puffing up and down the bank with arms aching. It would have been better to establish a home and then turn her loose. I'd been too quick to grant her freedom.

The rain clouds were streaming down the valley, diminishing the view in their dark, majestic progress. A wetting seemed inevitable. What to do? Protect the gear or put up the tent? I dithered a moment, my stomach still seething with the tension of holding all the pieces together. What if the river came up? Where were our rain jackets? "Luke! Where are you? Get back here!" I bawled.

He had made it across the backed up creek mouth and was working his way out onto the gravel bar, picking up rocks and throwing them into the river. Reluctantly, he turned back toward me and camp.

A fine mist began as I struggled to set up our tent. A dome shaped structure of gray-and-burgundy nylon, it required two people to erect. The collapsible rods needed to slide through external cloth sleeves, but their large metal collars hung up at each opening. Once the material was stretched, the poles were supposed to pop over metal pins attached to rings at the bottom of the tent, a task that was apt to badly pinch fingers. It was a poorly designed item, but had been a gift and would hold the four of us (provided I could get it up).

As the mist increased to rain, I felt desperate, pulling with all my strength to curve that mass of wet nylon into a home and snap the poles onto those wicked pins. The strain and fatigue of the past months washed over me in defeat.

"I think I can do it!" My eyes filled with helpless tears. The pole had lacked that final half inch of sliding home when I released the tension and the tent contracted, pulling back over the damnable collars. What had I gotten myself into? The dog had run off to die in the wilderness, it was raining, and I couldn't even get the stupid tent up!

"Yes, you can, Mama." Luke hovered close now, brown eyes wide and attentive, dark hair plastered to his head in tendrils. He reached his arms about my waist. I squatted and drew him onto one knee. Absently I pulled his hat, which trailed down his back on a chin strap, back over his head.

"Luke, I need your help," I pleaded. "I can't do it alone. There's no one else here. We're it. If we don't make a home for ourselves, we won't have one. Right now I feel very discouraged, tired, and a little scared. This country doesn't care. That river out there can float you in a canoe or drown you without a trace. It doesn't care. If we don't look after ourselves and each other, we won't last out here. This isn't a game, and it isn't me against you. We're on the same side."

He looked very serious as he blinked away the tears. "I care, Mama. I'm sorry I ran off." He smoothed the wet hair out of my eyes with a small, muddy hand.

I smiled. "Let's give it another try. I'm just so tense about all this. There's so much to do and it's all important."

J. ASPEN 94

Together, we tugged at the tent, and perhaps Luke's help made the difference, but this time I strained the pole over the pin and it shot home. The first one is always the hardest, and within a few minutes I had sent Luke inside, out of the rain, as I settled the fly over the tent and staked down the guy lines. He stayed there, huddled like a small cub in a thicket, until the storm blew past, but I continued carrying crates and stowing our supplies high and safe under a big blue tarp.

Twice more during that long first day the roar of Steve's Beaver broke the silence and I held my breath and filmed his balancing act with mountains, trees, and flooding river. Gear piled up and I kept hauling, sorting, setting up camp, gathering firewood.

Luke seemed subdued, and I forced myself to slow down and make him dinner. First I needed to find and empty the five-gallon water bucket. Down to the river for thirty pounds of muddy water and back to the fire. I dug through the cook gear and opened the grub box for macaroni, powdered onions, dried milk, and powdered cheese. This would do. Where did I put that box of margarine? Back to sort through the pile beneath the tarp. Our supplies had taken up a space five-by-six-by-twelve feet when carefully stacked in the trailer (plus those in the truck) and would cover more area on the lumpy ground between the trees—once I had it all up from the beach.

The day had turned uniformly gray and breezy. I looked about, trying to determine the time. At this season the sun would briefly pass behind the northern peaks around midnight. I decided it was somewhere between evening and midnight.

"Come sit with me," I called to Luke. He was squatting nearby, poking a stick into a hole in the ground. There were no snakes or poisonous insects this far north, and I didn't need to sound my usual warning about scorpions. An artistic driftwood "seat" still graced the bank, remnant of our former expedition, and I patted a spot next to me as Luke approached.

"What do you think lives in that hole?" he asked. He wrinkled his nose and threw back his head. "I don't like smoke."

"Well, get used to it. At least it keeps the bugs away."

"I don't mind them that much," he answered, awkwardly scratching one ear. It was red and swollen to twice its normal size. His cloth hat was askew and I automatically reached to straighten it. His dirty face was puffy with countless bites, his chubby hands, speckled and lumpy.

"Sit on my lap a minute. My, you're getting so big, you hardly fit." Luke nestled into my arms, trying to compress himself into the limited space and perhaps even return to the womb. I began a gentle rocking from my perch on the smooth, twisted log. He closed his eyes and sighed contentedly.

He was a tall child, sturdy and well formed, though somewhat clumsy after the manner of large children, as if his brain had not yet mastered the new dimensions. His body still held the soft contours of babyhood, but they were daily fading into the clean lines of a growing boy. Because of his size and vocabulary, it was easy to forget that he had only turned six this spring. His face, though masked in child form, had always been his own—a strong, clear-eyed, elfin face devoid of guile or meanness. I could see myself in the gentle slant of the eyes and the tanned color of his skin. Tom was there too, as was my father's cleft chin, but these influences were somehow superficial; it was the power of Luke that one noticed. He had always had his own ideas about life and did not readily accept instruction. It was as if he were embarrassed to be young.

We sat quietly, listening to the murmur of the river and the whisper of wind through the tall spruce. I let out a long breath, realizing that I had been holding it for hours. All day, in fact. Maybe weeks. The muted sky reflected, dappled gray, off the ever-changing patterns of the water below, while across the river a cone-shaped mountain cast its image on the swirling surface. The rushing sound of the distant creek came to us on sporadic gusts of wind, and a single bird called, sweet and clear as some forest spirit. Hermit thrush? I wondered. Why do we think naming something informs us? Mystery be thy name.

"I'm cooking macaroni and cheese," I said. "Your favorite."

"No, that used to be my favorite. Now it's pizza." He spoke with a soft lisp, unable yet to form certain letters.

"Is that so?"

"Uh-huh."

"I saw your puppy," I told him. "She's hiding in the willows across the slough." I could just make out her wary head from where I sat.

"Let's go get her." Luke started from my lap, idea instantly manifesting as action in his life.

I held on. "No, she'd just run away. She knows we're here and she's bound to get hungry. I'll try to get her later." I thought with compassion and irritation of the wild, skinny creature, trusting nothing but her own legs in a situation where we stood between her and death. She wouldn't last a week out here without us. I wondered if she knew it.

Which reminded me of something else. "Luke, do you remember me telling you about the Emergency Locator Transmitter?" I waited for his nod before continuing. "I want to show you where it is." I realized as I spoke that it was packed in a crate. He wouldn't be able to get at it, even if he could find the right one. I would have to remedy that. Tomorrow.

"You are not to touch it except in an emergency," I said as he wiggled off my lap and seated himself beside me on the log. He took a stick and began poking the fire and I went on, "It's something that airplanes use so that rescuers can find them if they crash. We brought it so we could get help in case of a life-or-death emergency." Here in this valley, beyond the range of radio, this small device would be our only contact with the outside world, a last ace to stack the deck in our favor.

"What if I broke my leg?" he asked, withdrawing the flaming stick and twirling it.

"I probably wouldn't use it. We have setting plaster, pain medicine, and antibiotics. I guess it depends on how bad it was. Just don't break your leg, all right? What I'm saying is that we would only use the ELT if it were really an emergency. Okay? And then Dad or Laurie or I would be the one to handle it. I only tell you this because we're here alone. You need to know how to get help."

"You mean if a bear ate you?" he asked, bluntly.

"Yes. Or if I drown or a tree falls on me or I have a heart attack or anything else. None of that is going to happen, but it's like carrying matches and mosquito repellent. They can save your life if you find yourself alone. If you get lost, build a fire and sit there. Listen. I'll be yelling. But the main thing is don't wander off."

Luke seemed preoccupied with his burning stick and didn't acknowledge my speech. We sat in silence a few minutes and I wondered if I had gotten in over my head. What was I doing out here, alone, with my priceless child? My hands ached from the heavy work of hauling freight and I felt a weight of discouragement at the monumental task of building a cabin before fall and getting in our moose for winter meat. Live your dreams, yes, but was this really mine? Bugs, danger, and hard labor followed by cold and dark? Being cooped up in a cabin all winter with a small child? It was a little late to ask.

I lifted the cooking pot from the grill, which was balanced on four rocks over the fire, and stirred a mixture of milk, cheese, and margarine into the macaroni and onions. Then I returned it to the edge of the grill. The blue enamel coffeepot was boiling and I poured a mug of tea for each of us and added sugar and creamer.

Luke seemed to be having second thoughts of his own for he suddenly said, "What if you die and then Dad dies and then Laurie dies and there is only me left?"

I put my arm about him and smiled. "That's not going to happen, Bukie." I stroked his hair and he leaned against me as we both watched the fire. "One of the reasons we have Laurie is to make sure you'll always have a grown-up around. It'll all be fine. It just takes time to pull everything together. Is that worrying you? That you'll be left all alone?"

"Uh-huh. It's different here than I thought it would be."

"I know. But Daddy and Laurie will be here in a few days," I reassured him. "In the meantime, when I finish with hauling all this junk up and protecting it from the weather, you and I can look around. Maybe tomorrow we'll explore and decide where to put the cabin. Then I'll get out a couple of books and we'll read to each other."

He glanced at me askance. "I can't read," he informed me. "You know that."

"Well . . . not yet. No. Nobody is born knowing how, but you're old enough to learn and I just happen to have some good books along to teach you."

It had been our most frequently asked question: what about Luke's school? I remembered my stepmother teaching my brothers at home in the wilderness, and they had succeeded in life. I saw no reason to be concerned. Homeschooled children are usually way ahead. True, I didn't have a certified program, but what could be so difficult about reading, writing, and basic math?

I took dinner off the grill and opened the pot, setting it on the ground. Then I scooped some into a white enamel bowl and handed it to Luke, balanced on a pie pan to protect his lap from the heat. He ate slowly, savoring the fat pasta and sucking the cheese from the center, his dirty face sticky with food and puffy from bug bites. We had not been out of our clothes since Fairbanks and Luke's were stiff with mud, soot, and various meals. Mine weren't much better.

After dinner I sponged his face, hands, and bottom with warm water in the protective smoke of the fire and hustled him into the tent away from mosquitoes that relish clean skin. Our sleeping bags were zipped together to form a quilt over blanket-covered pads. I had already laid out our pillows, my joggers, and Luke's footy sleepers. I crawled into the tent after him and zipped the screen door shut. He was cavorting in the bags, tunneling among the folds.

"Cut it out!" I snapped. "You're messing everything up." His face appeared, impish and dimpled with mischief, then disappeared as he wormed about the tent.

"I mean it! You need to be careful in here. If you tear the tent we'll have no place to sleep." This made no impression on him. "Here, sit up. I have medicine for you." It was a Benadryl to combat the cumulative effects of the bites. "It'll help you not to itch."

Obediently, he took the halved pill, tried to swallow it with water from a bottle, and ended up chewing it, his face a study of dislike. Raised on asthma medication, he accepted it. I was thankful that he seemed to have outgrown the asthma, but had brought a supply of capsules and inhalants in case the winter cold affected his lungs.

I helped him into his sleepers and zipped them. "Don't get my penis," he warned, his usual admonition since I had caught it once. "Will you stay with me? I don't want to be alone."

"For a while," I said. I was smashing a few dozen mosquitoes that had come into the tent with us and now clustered on the screen. "I won't be far away, but I still need to get the rest of our things up from the beach and I want to dig a toilet hole. By the way, you didn't go today, did you?"

"There are too many mosquitoes."

"Well, we'll spray your bottom with repellent. I'll help you. But we all need to go."

"Tomorrow."

"All right," I agreed, watching the cloud of insects swarm over the tent screen, "tomorrow. By the way, there's a loaded rifle in the corner of the tent. Don't touch it. Ordinarily I wouldn't have it anywhere around you, but we need to keep it within reach. Do you promise?"

"Yes." Luke might avoid giving his word, but he could be counted on to keep it.

I smiled and tucked the covers about him. "Here's old Oliver." I handed him the beloved small, white teddy and his ragged, blue baby blanket. He wrapped his arms about them as I began the ancient rendition of "Everything Is All Right in Our House . . . er Tent . . . Tonight," a song that catalogued the whereabouts of each family member and was created by my mother's mother, Winnie, for Annie and me.

Yes, for now, everything was all right in our tent tonight.

CHAPTER 3

I sang quietly to Luke as we settled down for yet another night alone in the tent. It had been five days since we'd been dropped off. Late sun dappled the gray nylon, twinkling low through the leaves, a change from the intermittent drizzle we had experienced much of the day. A blue tarp strung for shade over the tent lent a somber cast to the light. Somewhere, a bird I remembered only as the "cathedral bird" sang his wonderful solo of misty days and quiet evenings, his solitary voice slanting mysteriously between the trees. It was this sound, more than any other, that evoked an essence of arctic forests for me, a dream-like quality of forgotten memory.

"My mother used to sing," I told Luke, stroking his fine hair. "I hope in years to come you'll remember me as someone who sings."

They hadn't come today. I had watched for them since noon; a torment to listen for the sound of an airplane in the wilderness, ears ringing with the silence. Surely they would be here tomorrow. Meanwhile, Luke and I had begun exploring the area. We had found a good cabin site back from the river on a dry, rocky bench dotted with medium-sized spruce and carpeted in yellow-green lichen, sphagnum moss, and cranberry. White-and-yellow flowers of mountain avens peppered the ground. The place was high and looked well-drained and wholesome. An old creek channel cut along the bench, dividing it from the heavily forested lowland of our camp.

As our days alone wore on, we had busied ourselves with pushing a trail along the edge of this bench to a bend in the creek half a mile west of us. Luke was proving a game little companion, swinging the smallest ax to help clear brush from the path or trailing after me as I studied the land. Yet he was young and small, his legs no match for the distance or the rough terrain. Our nameless, wild pup did far better. Always out of reach except at night, when she sought refuge from the mosquitoes in the tent with us, she nevertheless kept track of our movements. Even at four months of age, she was strong, fast, and agile, perfectly at home as she followed her nose, her wolf ancestors watching behind inscrutable, golden eyes.

"Mama, is Daddy coming tomorrow?" Luke asked sleepily. He was burrowed against me under our shared cover of down. The dog rested uneasily at our feet, as far away from "her boy" as she could get, gangly legs braced against us. She had a neurotic habit of gnawing the fur from her knees leaving them patchy like a person with a poor haircut.

"I don't know," I answered truthfully. "Do you miss him?"

"Yes. I miss tickle time," he said, exposing his rounded tummy and arching his back to make it more appealing.

"They'll come," I assured him, smoothing the covers back over his ribs, "and life will be more fun. I thought they'd be here today, but don't worry, we have all we need for as long as it takes."

"Kiss Oliver," he said, holding up the small teddy whose black eyes were eternally fixed in a benign, myopic expression. "He's my bear-plane." To demonstrate, Luke flew Oliver in a loop above his head. I kissed the bear and tucked him in again.

The cathedral bird continued his melancholy trill against the omnipresent hum of mosquitoes. They were clustered in thousands against the tent screen, drawn by the delicious smells within like people to a banquet. There was constant movement as they stepped and probed, seeking entrance. I listened to the bird, feeling the pull of my two worlds—of wilderness and civilization—and wondering why I never quite belonged to either one. It seemed so easy for a bird to be itself; why was it so difficult for me?

"Mama?"

"Ummmm?"

"I wish my dog would love me. I love her."

"She's not a very good pet," I agreed. "I'm sorry it worked out this way. We brought her so you'd have a friend."

"I've been making a trap for her," he confided. "If I could just catch her, I would make her love me."

"I think she'll settle down in time. Don't try to grab her just yet. It will only make her wilder."

"She keeps stealing my magic sticks from my fort."

"Lie still, Little Toad," I crooned. "Let me smooth away the cares. All your daytime thoughts will be right here, with your clothes, when you wake up in the morning."

The cathedral bird was suddenly silent and I heard the warning "chit-chit-chit" of a squirrel. Animals tell you a good deal if you pay attention, but whether it was a weasel or a bear that alarmed him, I couldn't say. I continued stroking Luke's hair and peered through the tent screen. The dog's head had come up, watching me and sniffing. Luke noticed nothing. I could see little through the shelter of trees. If I went out, I would only inundate the tent with bugs, I decided, and I couldn't stay alert all night. At some point I had to release fear.

Bears, I thought. People always asked about them. These mountains were grizzly country. Grizzlies are hunters, greatly feared by moose and other animals. My mother said that they eat black bears where their ranges overlap, and it was true that I had never seen a black up here.

It helped that in my dozen close encounters with arctic grizzlies they had wasted no time in putting miles between us. They don't see well, and will often stand on their hind legs for a better look at you. It's a scary experience but not necessarily a threatening one. They read the world through their keen noses, and I imagine we must reek like strange carnivores to them. Some experts claim we smell distasteful, and all agree that we are never a preferred food. Still, ghastly tales abound of those who are less fortunate, for bears are notoriously unpredictable.

The Indians accord grizzlies a kind of mystique. They have told me that if one comes into camp where women are alone, you can ask him to go away, and he will. But if there is a man with a rifle, he will attack. I have twice seen one go after a dog, and know that they come in low with incredible speed and intensity. Far from being a deterrent, dogs may lure bears into camp, and I had weighed this fact in our decision to bring a pet. I hoped that she would prove to be cautious and quiet.

Grizzlies are magnificent animals: smart, swift, and powerful beyond your imagination. Yes, I decided, I respected them just as I respected that river, but there was no point in being afraid. Fear accomplishes nothing. When your home is a tent in the Arctic, you live with bears. My main concern was Luke. He was small enough to look like easy prey, and he often became so engrossed in life that he was unconscious of any danger. I had yet to convince him there was any. He had no idea how fast a bear could move. He resented my restrictions on his explorations and the plate-sized tracks in the mud were of no interest to him.

I heard my cathedral bird resume. From nearby, came the "clink-clink" of a junco and I could imagine the little gray bird busy among the fallen spruce needles. Luke had gone to sleep with his eyes partly open. Feeling chilled I scooted under the covers, enjoying the heat of his small body. He shifted and ground his teeth, a sound like cracking nuts that set mine on edge.

"Shhh, now shhhhh," I soothed, holding his jaw. Irritably he swung his head away and crunched again. Did he always do that? I wondered. Sleeping with a small child had not proved to be a restful experience. I thought of how it would be with Tom and Laurie packed in here. At least this time we had egg-crate mattresses, blankets to pad the floor, and real pillows. It was as cozy as I could make it.

THE CLOSE QUARTERS REMINDED me of our canoe trip two years before. Same tent and three adults, but at four years old, Luke had been smaller. When the film idea had fallen through, Tom, Luke, and I had paddled down the Koyukuk River to Bettles where our charter waited. There we impulsively called Annie over their satellite radio and invited her to join us.

"Don't bring anything more than your sleeping bag and clothes," we told my incredulous sister. "We'll diet, if need be. It's only five weeks. Any more weight and we'll sink."

Two days later, Annie stepped like Cinderella from the coach of a commercial aircraft, hefted her duffel bag, and joined us.

Although it was evening we had loaded into two Cessna 185s and were off to the headwaters of our river, the canoe strapped to the floats. I sat in front, reading the map for an affable young pilot, Steve Ruff, unfamiliar with this direction. I was going home.

It was an awkward outfit we inherited: seventeen-foot canoe towing an inflated raft laden with gear. While Tom and I paddled from the only seats, Annie and Luke were stowed like baggage. A small motor, which we rarely used in the fast shallow river, was mounted to the left side in the stern, greatly reducing the rear paddler's range of motion. Here Tom controlled our direction. This was his first experience canoeing a river, much less through rapids. It was my place in the bow to call the shots, and his to execute them. Luckily, he has an intuitive grasp of physics and soon understood the basic maneuvers. We learned rapidly to communicate and work together.

Tom and I are both strong-willed. We have come to laugh at how we invariably choose opposite ways of tackling any situation, but at times it is far from humorous. It often works best for each of us to take a different project, but in the canoe we had no choice. Someone had to lead, and I was obviously it. Unfortunately, I tend to play expert and that rubs Tom (also an expert) the wrong way. I compensate by being "tactful."

"Not tactful, ambiguous," he informed me bluntly at our first lunch break. "Don't worry about my delicate male ego. Just tell me where to go."

From this I discovered I could lead instead of trying to persuade others to go the way I thought best. Of course I, who never could tell my right from my left, would sometimes yell "right!" while frantically pointing left. Tom soon learned to follow the hand signals and I eventually gave up the shouting. From this experience we developed our "no-fault-marriage." When one of us makes a decision, the other doesn't affix blame if things turned out badly. It is astounding how much easier this made life.

I also learned that sometimes it's better to sit quietly and listen to the river, feel its subtle pulls and believe my intuition rather than my eyes. Allow the water to show the way. I learned that it's better to choose than to dither. A choice, any choice, has power; dithering puts one out of control and onto the rocks. And I learned that it was not too late for me. On that trip, Luke and Tom fell in love with wilderness and found that they could put up with bugs, dirt, and cold feet. How many people get a second chance at childhood, or would take it if it were offered?

Luke matured a good deal that summer. Just out of night diapers, he learned to be versatile, to nap between my knees slumped in the bow, granola bar clutched in his dirty hand. Each morning, I would give him a little bag of nuts, raisins, granola, and a few M&M's. We were not always able to pull over when he became hungry and this gave him a sense of security. By hoarding his treats carefully, he could savor them through the long miles.

One day I told him that we were almost out of M&M's. "Let's get more," was his reply.

I had gazed into the sun, down the glistening current and narrowed my eyes. "Look over there," I said pointing. He followed my finger. "Is that a Circle K?"

He peered ahead with consternation. "I don't see one," he told me. Then suddenly catching on, he grinned. "Mama, you're teasing me. There's no Circle K."

"That's right. There's no Circle K. And once the M&M's are gone, they're gone."

He had sat thoughtfully sucking his fingers and then dug through the little sack, sorting and counting. At our next stop, he presented each of us with a tiny, sticky pile of the precious candy, insisting that we take them, "to be fair."

Memories of that trip drifted sharp and frozen as slides before my closed eyelids. Tom, slender and wet to the armpits from retrieving a lure, holding up a big northern pike. True to my words, he and I had "dieted" to accommodate the extra person that trip, returning to civilization twenty-five pounds lighter. Each fish was a treasure to us. I remembered Luke, his face babyish and round, speckled with chicken pox and bug bites, a quiet smile outlined in milk as he tended his little white teddy, Oliver. Annie painting by the river. Me sitting cross-legged, a portrait of my mother in the smoke of a fire, my eyes peaceful. Then Luke again, a grayling gripped in each little hand as he proudly brought his dad's catch for me to gut.

I didn't fish, preferring a supportive role. I loved to watch fish, but no longer enjoyed catching them. Yet I ate them and willingly cleaned and cooked them for others.

Because I knew this country, I emphasized behaviors that would keep my family safe: take care of your equipment, keep a neat camp, watch the weather, protect your body, and stop when you're tired or hungry. In the constant daylight, it was easy to be lulled beyond sensible limits. I was beginning to sound like my mother. She once told me that accidents don't just happen— they are caused by carelessness. It is wise to remain humble and attentive, especially when you have no backup.

Each night I would study the map, planning a course should we capsize. We might walk out in two or three weeks. "If we sink," I told Tom, "you get the canoe if you can; I'll get Luke." On the upper river it was probable that a swamped canoe could be recovered, though lower down, just making it to shore would be chancy. I had capsized in this river more than once and held no illusions about it. The main danger was in losing one's outfit and facing weeks of cross-country walking with no trail, food, or equipment. It could be years before anyone happened by to help you out.

❦

IT HAD BEEN MISTING all morning and my son and I were again at work on Luke's Trail. With determination he flailed his way through the butt of a downed and punky tree, while I trimmed the bottom branches from a living one. The pup bounded insolently past, proud of her superior speed and agility. Although she was still shy of us, it wasn't fear as much as willful independence that now prevailed.

I stopped to sight the path ahead, choosing a route which would spare living plants. A trail would save random wear on the country as well as provide access inland to the creek. I pushed back the hood of my emerald rain jacket and listened, staring up at the wet, gray sky. Luke was imitating a chain-saw as he hacked the log, his voice as happy and unconscious as a bird's.

"Hush, Luke. All the world is silent except you!"

He looked up at me, offended, his face and hair wet where the blue slicker fell open. Our nylon boots and jeans were soaked from the glistening foliage, but we were both perspiring.

"An airplane!" we shouted happily together. In that instant the arctic quiet was shattered, and Steve's gold-and-blue Beaver shot by a hundred feet overhead. Grabbing up the tools, we raced back along our new path, arriving in time to video the final seconds of landing. Pontoons outstretched, the great bird plowed twin geysers toward us through the muddy water. Luke danced along the beach, both hands waving and high voice singing a welcome above the roar of the engine.

The propeller clattered to a stop as the craft swung in to shore and I caught the trailing wing rope. Steve Ruff was out on the left float, agile as a cat, before a grinning Tom and Laurie extricated themselves and began tossing gear ashore amid laughs and wisecracks.

"Twenty pounds!" Tom read from the top of a plastic jug as he lofted it to Laurie.

"No way! That was only nineteen," she shot back, keeping up the smooth rhythm of catch and stow.

"Thirty-five!" Tom called.

"Psych!" said Laurie, as she caught a light bucket.

I kept filming, but a sense of euphoria had come over me. It was all going to work out!

"Did you wonder if we were coming?" Tom asked as we moved toward camp in a festive spirit of camaraderie. "I hope you weren't worried." Unloading had gone swiftly with the extra hands. Even the drizzle had abated, but I threw a tarp over the pile that littered the beach.

"I figured you just got tied up," I answered. I felt shy, as I always did when we had been apart.

"We were scheduled to fly in last night, but Steve was too tired, and I certainly trust his judgment on that. He told me the dog ran off. Did you ever find her?"

I had forgotten the pup. I glanced over at the slough, hoping to catch sight of a small, skulking form. "Yeah, she's around here somewhere. We probably won't see her 'til tonight."

"Still pretty skittish, huh?"

"Well, she was getting used to us, but this will be a setback. Still, I don't see that she has many options." I was on my hands and knees, trying to blow life into the cold fire. The others stood talking in a happy ring around the smoking embers. Luke was hopping up and down, wanting to wedge his way into the conversation, but it flew by over his head. Finally he caught at Laurie's sleeve and she squatted beside him earnestly listening above the babble of voices to his disjointed version of our stay.

Twenty minutes later the plane coughed into action, and with a wave of hands thundered out of our lives. It circled once, bright wings waggling good-bye against the clouds, and was gone. Suddenly aware of the silence, the four of us gathered on the empty shore, pulled into a group hug by our isolation. The tightest arms of all were Laurie's, her eyes streaming with tears. Luke wriggled up between the bodies and clung to our necks, happy to be in the middle. I smiled at Laurie, her wet cheek close to mine. I felt that I had known her always.

"Don't mind me," she sniffed, "I cry easily."

"I like that," I said.

"Hey, I'd cry too, if I were in your shoes," Tom kidded, gaining a guffaw from Laurie who broke the hug to blow her nose loudly on a blue kerchief.

Despite the tears, she already seemed to belong here. About my height and strongly built, Laurie could have been my sister, my daughter, myself fifteen years removed. But where I was now soft and plump, she was young muscle. It was hard to tell in the practical outdoor clothes, oversized Goodwill boots, and "Smokey-the-Bear" hat, but above her broad hips and sturdy legs were a slender waist, lovely breasts, and gracefully proportioned torso. Her shoulders were broad, her hands large and competent, her feet well planted on the earth. Eve, mother of nations, should have looked like Laurie.

There was no pretense about her. She had bobbed her light brown hair for the trip and it was tied away from her face with a rolled bandanna. Her complexion seemed fair until I remembered that she lived in Seattle. She had a generous mouth and a ready grin that revealed large, even teeth. Her nose was prominent, and wide, gray eyes were framed by brows that reached their highest point somewhat early, giving them a quizzical appearance. Hers was an open face whose unique charm was its unabashed mobility, ranging from gentle smile to clown in an instant. It was a face one never grew tired of watching.

I was reminded of the last time I saw her mother, our friend Darlene, a smaller, older version of Laurie, tears glistening as she contemplated our trip. When I thanked her for the gift of her daughter, Darlene had replied, "Laurie has been a gift to me all of her life."

"You want to see Luke's Creek?" my son was asking. "We named it after me." He tugged on Laurie's hand and we all started for the delta.

"We found a good cabin site," I told them. We were talking excitedly, ambling beside the slough until we could cross onto the delta. This was but one of several fingers of the creek that joined the river over the expanse of gravel. The main channel was two hundred yards away. On the open bar a breeze kept the mosquitoes at bay, and we were treated to a view of mountains rising into the clouds. We stopped to take it in.

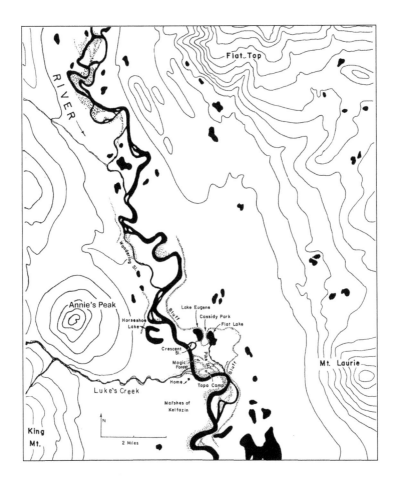

"That's Annie's Peak," Luke informed, always happy to play host. "We named it after my Aunt Annie." To the west stood a promontory shaped like a cresting wave. Tom and my sister had climbed its flank two years before, and we had christened it in memory of that adventure.

"You mean it didn't have a name?" Laurie asked studying the green peak, its details sharp through the clear air.

"None of them do," Tom answered, opening his arms to encompass the land. We had told Laurie of the isolation and size of this country, but a person doesn't readily grasp it. She was a mere two hours from newspapers and fast food, and I could see his words both intrigued and frightened her.

"Could we name one of them after me?" she asked shyly.

Tom grinned and pointed to the lone conical mountain that filled our eastern view, directly across the river. "Mount Laurie?" he asked all assembled. There was a nodding of agreement and Laurie broke into a dazzling smile.

We had reached Luke's Creek, a jade torrent of icy water rushing over gravel and small stones of many colors. There were mysterious pools where grayling hid amid tangled trees torn out by spring flood. Pink dwarf fireweed and yellow Indian paintbrush festooned the three-foot cutbanks, while circular mats of yellow dryas grew on the open sand. The creek wandered in sweeping bends, cutting west from a fold of high mountains where snow lingered. It drew us on past bright green thickets of poplar into dark spruce forest among a symphony of blue lupine. We laughed above the noise, sometimes straggling out along the creek and at others holding hands, swift water to our knees as we crossed the broad current.

Tom was ahead on the far side, out of earshot when I stopped to look about. Ahead, the creek appeared too deep to ford and our shore had deteriorated into dense willows. "Luke," I asked suddenly, "do you know how to get back to camp?"

Embarrassed to be caught unprepared, he shrugged and began making silly faces to show that it didn't matter.

Laurie was grinning as she caught up with us and halted. She looked as excited as the pup to be exploring this new world.

"Laurie," I queried, "if you got separated from us, which way would you go to find camp?"

She studied the area thoughtfully, a signature trait I would come to know well. She was not one for brash decisions or bluffing. With hesitation, she pointed north toward a large mountain with a flattened ridge showing above the trees. "That's Mount Laurie, isn't it? I guess I'd head that way."

My heart skipped a beat as I took in the implications. I had known that Luke would need careful watching, but had not realized Laurie was so vulnerable. I could have lost her on this maiden walk!

"No," I answered. "Mount Laurie is cone-shaped and we can't see it from here because of the trees. I call that one 'Flattop.' See how it looks like that long ridge was shaved off? Until you learn the landmarks and get a real sense of direction, maybe you should stay close to us. You can't depend on the sun for direction. Right now it rises in the north, circles south, and sets in the north. But that will change. Just remember that water flows downhill. Your best bet here would be to follow the creek back to the river."

The mosquitoes were thick along the creek, and now that we had stopped they settled in a moving blanket over our bodies. I pulled a small bottle of repellent, pure DEET, from my shirt pocket and offered it around. Large grizzly tracks showed clear and fresh in the mud ahead, punctuated with an impressive pile of poop. There were older prints too, showing regular usage. Upstream, Tom emerged from the bushes. I beckoned and he turned toward us.

"I think it's time we got back," I said, feeling suddenly uneasy. We had romped off without so much as our raincoats and the sky was again pulling down.

Before we reached camp, it was sprinkling. I put rain jackets on Luke and myself and then dug out my old red poncho for Laurie. Tom's jacket was still packed away, so we bunched together under a large spruce, protecting him with our bodies as the rain increased to a deluge of pelting hail. It was the kind of storm, wild and fierce, that doesn't usually last, and we crowded happily together to wait it out. Glancing around, I noticed the tent door was down and our bedding was protected only by the insect netting. Leaving the huddle, I bolted for the tent and pulled the zipper around the arc of the door. To my horror, I found myself holding a useless flap of nylon as the zipper separated.

By now the world had receded to a dim shadow of stinging hail and rain. It drove mercilessly into the opening as I squatted, trying to protect our haven with my body, the flap stretched between cold hands. Behind me I could see the laughing faces of my little family, still unaware of this calamity or the impact it might have on our lives. What would we do if I couldn't fix it? Perhaps I would sew the top zipper shut, leaving the bottom one for us to crawl through. Could one survive without a mosquito-proof tent in such a land? Early people had, but I couldn't imagine it.

Why had I forgotten my first rule: stay prepared, always look after your equipment? I had wandered off with people who couldn't tell direction, leaving our life's possessions in a heap on the shore. There was no dry tinder set aside to restart our fire after this soaking, not even a dry rock on which to strike a match. Did everyone have matches and mosquito repellent? I wasn't sure. My little family trusted and depended on my experience, and I didn't want them to learn the hard and bitter way about this unforgiving land. I was a fool to let down my guard and the Arctic does not long abide fools.

Such were my thoughts as I groped about for damp twigs along the trunks of spruce trees. The storm had swept on, leaving us chilled and sober and the ground glistening with hail. A cold wind drifted from the south, further taxing my fire-building skills. Even Luke was subdued and had nestled under Laurie's soggy poncho like a damp chick. Laurie seemed a little scared and forlorn, wondering perhaps if she had made a terrible mistake.

As a reluctant trickle of smoke began to ascend from my efforts, I looked at my three wet companions. My eyes met Tom's across the small blaze in silent understanding: It would be up to the two of us to keep our little clan safe. Quietly, he set to work on the zipper and managed to realign it (at least temporarily) while I built up the fire and put on the grill.

"First of all," I began, "let's get something hot to drink and warm up. Then while I start dinner, you guys bring up the remaining gear and stash it back here in the trees. It's not a very good system, because things are hard to get at, but at least it'll be safe."

"I can put up kind of a pavilion of tarps for the stuff we use all the time," Tom suggested. "It'll give us a place to keep rifles and camera equipment handy."

"Good idea," I agreed, "and it will give us a place to get out of the rain. The tent is too small for anything except sleeping, and we don't want to ruin our bedding."

"The less we use that zipper the better," Tom concurred. "Good thing there are two doors. With care perhaps we can make it through the summer."

"Well, let's get started." The drizzle had returned.

It took me almost an hour to catch our nameless mutt that night and drag her stiff-legged into the tent. There she cowered, ready to bolt through the cloth at the slightest movement from the two strangers. It rained all night.

❦

THE FOLLOWING DAYS DAWNED bright and hot. I awoke early each morning with a sense of purpose, freed myself from the companionable heap of bodies, adjusted my contact lenses, and sat up. After pushing the dog out, I dressed in worn jeans, leather belt with holstered knife, and cotton work shirt smelling of sweat and smoke. Before emerging, I applied mosquito repellent, twisted my tangled blond hair back and clipped it up with a barrette, then pulled on a cloth hat. Our wet boots and socks were stashed outside beneath the big spruce trees.

I would start the fire and put on the coffeepot before rousing the others with the same prophetic words, "Winter is coming." They groaned but followed me into the heat of morning, thinking my words a joke. Who could imagine winter while sweating under this constant sun? Yet, although snow still clung in crevices on Mount Laurie and the river ran high with spring melt, the Solstice had already passed and the Northern Hemisphere was imperceptibly sliding back into cold and darkness.

After breakfast, we would troop gaily up to the cabin site to begin a hard day of cutting and hauling logs for our home. We laid the area out in our minds and found that what had once been anonymous boreal forest quickly took on new dimensions. Here was the tree where we kept the tools and hung the gloves. There was the trail to the river. Before the first log was placed, our home was taking shape in our eyes. We staked out the floor and cleared a few tiny trees from its interior.

"Six feet to here," called Tom as he and Laurie triangulated the corners that first morning.

"Really? That doesn't look like six feet." She lay down next to the string to check. "Yeah, I guess it is."

"A true literalist," I laughed. "Just like me. Okay, guys. Gather 'round." I spread the plans near the fire that was already burning inside our fantasy structure.

Tom and Laurie squatted next to my drawings. Luke was tossing moss into the fire to make it smoke. He was wet to the crotch from playing in the river and a fine coat of dust covered his boots and trousers turning them a uniform chocolate. Nearby the dog had started excavation of a squirrel hole in the steep bank of the dry creek bed.

"We need a corporate decision," I went on. "We have two possibilities. There's the regular and deluxe option. The regular is fifteen-by-fifteen feet inside and has a sleeping loft, if we want it. We can decide on that later. The deluxe model has an additional eight-by-ten foot utility room off this side," I pointed, "and we need to choose on that now."

"I'm agreeable to what everybody else wants," Laurie said. "I have no experience in this."

"We just make it up as we go along," Tom told her. "You get to vote. We're all equal partners here."

"I want a vote too!" Luke chimed in. "I want to have tunnels all the way down to the river, maybe even under the river to the other side." He had the small ax and was hacking at a dead tree. "You could never build a cabin, well you could, but it would be awfully hard without me," he said over his shoulder.

"So what's it going to be, guys?"

"Let's go for the deluxe," Tom decided. "We're gonna need the extra room. Okay?"

The others nodded. I ran my finger over the drawings. "If we don't plan we'll run into problems. Our sill logs need to go this way—I indicated on the ground—so we can hang the floor from them, if Tom can rip us a floor. The outside door will be here; this indicates windows, lots of windows because I hate dark cabins. There's a large opening between the two rooms to keep the utility room from becoming an ice cave in winter."

"I think the entrance should be in the utility room," Tom stated, indicating its position on the plans.

"What about fire danger?" I asked.

"Well, it's not that large a structure. It would keep us from tracking snow in and keep the wind out. Also, let's make the room ten-by-twelve. We still have to cut all those notches and pins."

"I was hoping you'd say that. I didn't want to push my grandiose designs." Ours eyes met over the plans and we grinned knowingly. It was a balancing act when Tom and I worked together. We each brought an area of expertise to the project, and it was sometimes challenging to blend our visions. Tom was a good partner, I thought, and no more stubborn than myself. Given a shovel, he could quite literally move mountains, not by superior strength but through dogged determination. His actions were concise and well-planned.

I glanced about, studying the traffic patterns. "Where do you want to put the toilet?"

"Let's scout around," he answered, rising. "I imagine it'll be over that way."

We walked south along the spine of the bench some thirty yards to a small grove of spruce where we chose the site, then returned to the plans and settled the door issue. It would be in the utility room, as Tom had suggested.

❦

WITH QUICK DECISIONS WE outlined the coming months and set to work. We wanted to have as little effect on the country as possible, and this took thought and care. There were a number of dead standing spruce (the only trees we cut) scattered in the open forest of the bench. To minimize damage to the ground cover from hauling heavy logs, we laid out a network of routes.

Arctic spruce are generally small, twisted, and gnarled—like people who have lived long and hard lives—but the occasional one might reach fifteen inches at the butt and stand seventy feet tall. Although there are only two varieties, they seemed to take on several distinctive personalities. Their trunks range from reddish brown to almost black. The branches, seldom larger than my wrist, hold their upper needles to the sky, but gradually droop with age, bent by the snows of winter. Fine, green-gray streamers of moss hang from lower limbs like wispy beards. At a distance the trees appear too tall and thin, and when seen in a high wind the limber tops swing in great arcs.

Beyond the rocky bench, where primitive curls of caribou lichen mingled with the needle-leaves of crowberries, the terrain was often boggy or cushioned in shin-deep feathers of kelly green sphagnum moss. Treading this ground had a spongy feel, the foot never quite hitting bottom. Often there was a bramble of blueberry bushes, their small, round leaves hiding minute red flowers. These were interspersed with Lapland rosebay sporting olive leaves and magenta blossoms like azaleas, and Labrador tea, rusty edged and clustered in white blossoms smelling of spice. The moss was laced with the shiny lowbush cranberry plants of Christmas red and green, miniature gardens of kinnikinnick with tiny pink bells, alpine berry, anemone, and dozens of others. While few species attained a height of three feet, beneath us lay a wealth of beauty and variety. A rich, warm smell arose to our footfalls, as well as biting clouds of mosquitoes.

We fell into an easy routine. Together we would scout an area and decide on a plan. Then Tom dropped the dead trees with his chain-saw, cutting eighteen-foot or fifteen-foot lengths for cabin logs. Smaller or more twisted trees, and the tops of larger ones, were gathered for firewood or rafters. Laurie and I would "buck" the logs, using axes to blade away the branches and stobs, then drag or carry them to a trail. It often took both, or even all three of us, to drag the big ones using flat nylon slings. Throwing our sweating bodies into the traces like oxen, we heaved against the weight, veins protruding with the strain.

"Get up there!" I cried like a mule skinner, as we struggled for footing, banging into one another and laughing, too winded to keep our balance.

"About ready to take a break?" Tom croaked from his position ahead of the log, doing the major pulling.

"Yes . . . well, no . . . Just a bit farther," I wheezed. Laurie and I were lifting from either side of this big monster to keep it from furrowing the ground. "We're on a roll now!"

"Oh, jeeezz!" Laurie exclaimed.

"Free hernia operations for everyone," gasped Tom.

On we struggled. In a few days we had accumulated an impressive pile of logs and the pickings near home were beginning to peter out.

"Anybody seen Wonder Boy lately?" I puffed, peering about through the sweat in my eyes when we stopped for breath.

"Over there," Tom pointed through the trees.

"Why do we always leave the biggest ones for last?" Laurie wanted to know.

"For the challenge of it?" Tom suggested.

"Laziness," I asserted. "But it doesn't really work."

❦

THE DAYS BLENDED ONE into another, sultry mornings giving way to afternoon storms that blew up black and dramatic from the north, blotting out Flattop and growling with thunder. By evening they had swept over, or more often around us, leaving a fresh light upon the land. We would labor until the clouds towered aloft, then head for the delta and a quick bath in the icy river, dressing hastily by a gusting fire as the storm marched upon us.

"We've got this all wrong," Tom announced as he rubbed down with our community towel, his white, furry skin prickled with goose bumps. "An hour ago I would have killed for a cold bath."

Laurie was poised on the edge of the river trying to screw up courage to take the plunge. "I'd have killed for a cold beer," she retorted, eliciting a groan of sympathy from Tom. Mosquitoes hung in a mist downwind of her naked body, and half a dozen biting flies the size of kidney beans zoomed in, causing her to hop and swing her arms.

I had been the first one in-and-out, taking my usual "get it over with" approach. My head still ached with the cold, my shocked scalp bunched in a tight knot at the crown, but I was feeling exhilarated, clean and noble.

"I'm putting on fresh socks and underwear," Tom informed us.

"Luke, don't you think it's time you came out?" I called. "How can that kid stand it?"

Luke was diving under the muddy water, grubbing about for pretty stones, as if the bar itself wasn't a treasure of them. He hadn't cared for river bathing at first, but now it was the highlight of his day. He was angry that he'd been forbidden to swim out in the main current. Like a polliwog he kicked along, mostly submerged, with his burden of rocks. Enjoying the action and the water, the dog paddled a ring about him.

"Luke!" Tom called. "Time to get dressed, Son. A storm is coming." A sudden shift in the wind brought a drift of sand down the beach.

"Look! My dog is trying to save me!" Luke shouted back.

Tired of her battle with the bugs Laurie suddenly dove, emerging in an instant with an unnerving shriek. It was always the same, but I hadn't gotten used to it. She scrambled up the gravel to stand chattering by the fire while lathering her hair. Luke arrived as well, his torso as clammy and cold as a fish, lips blue.

"The first dive's always the hardest," I informed Laurie. "Next time it'll feel almost warm." She rewarded me with a doubtful scowl.

"How come I always get the wet towel?" Luke wanted to know.

"Because you're always the last one out."

"I'll be the last one today," Laurie told him consolingly.

"We need two towels," he said.

"One for the rest of us and one for you?" I asked. "Two towels means more wet things in camp. Just dry and dress. And stop dragging the towel in the mud."

"I'm hungry."

"How does hash made with dried potatoes, onions, and textured vegetable protein sound?" My mind was already on dinner. It was difficult to come up with interesting meals from our stock of dried food, but the appreciation of the group always made the effort worthwhile.

I had planned to share this task, but I was the best cook and had chosen all the food. It seemed natural that we gravitate to chores that suited us. While I cooked, Laurie handled dishes and Tom cut firewood. The hardest job, washing clothes, was shared by all. We were harmonious and easily supported one another, using our various strengths. Laurie proved to be an enthusiastic participant and a quick learner. She had a rare ability to take instruction without defending her knowledge, a trait foreign to the rest of us.

We returned to camp and were perched on stumps drawn up around the fire. The storm had circled east, following the ridge to Mount Laurie. The peak loomed strikingly black, but the river was bathed in brilliant sunshine and young poplars stood out in vivid green against the somber backdrop. Our camp lay in the shade of the forest; the sun to our backs, glimmered through the trees. Downstream a steady flow of swallows poured like smoke from beneath the cutbank and danced out over the calm water.

"It seems criminal to even walk around here," Laurie stated. "It's so beautiful and fragile."

"In some ways we're actually helping the forest," I told her. "When we take dead trees out it creates better conditions for the young ones."

Tom settled on a stump next to me and peeked into the pot. "I thought we were having hash," he said dismally. "I was all ready for hash."

"I lied. I couldn't find the cubed potatoes, so I made cornbread and vegetable soup instead."

"Is the canister empty again?" Laurie asked, rising.

"Relax. We'll worry about it tomorrow. Here, hold the lid a second while I try to flip this bread, will you?"

In Arizona I had mixed up several hundred pounds of oat, corn, and chocolate breads and packaged them in meal sizes. They contained a variety of flours, milk, eggs, and nuts, and would prove to be a major food throughout both summers. The bread could be mixed with water and steamed in its own plastic bag or poured into the cast-iron skillet to bake. The trick with skillet baking was to heat it slowly enough so the bread cooked inside without burning, then flip it halfway through. I held my breath and flipped. The cornbread was a perfect golden brown underneath. Laurie placed the lid over it and I stirred the soup. She had already set enamel bowls, spoons, pie tins, and margarine on top of the grub box.

"So when do you want to start building?" I asked.

"Let's get all the sills and a few more big logs," Tom answered. "I think perhaps tomorrow we should scout across the river. It's come down two feet this week and I don't think we'll have much trouble getting logs over."

"No, just getting them up the hill from here," Laurie observed dryly. We looked at one another and grinned.

"I found a spruce hen setting on a nest of eggs today," Tom told us. "It's on the ground. I'll show you, but we have to figure out a way to keep the dog . . . Isn't that a wolf?" he interrupted himself, pointing across to the sunlit shore where a gray form was melting in and out of the trees. Cautiously, the animal made its way downstream, checking each stick and stone. A chorus of ground squirrel alarm calls marked his progress.

We watched in silence.

Evening was upon us with that rare clarity of light one only sees in the high latitudes. Back in the shadowy woods my cathedral bird began his mystical chant. Tom sat comfortably gazing out on the hypnotic patterns of the river. His eyes were peaceful, meditative and quiet. Already his body was losing its soft, plump contours, the lines of waist and shoulders taking on a smooth definition. Luke was at rest, snuggled against Laurie's side while she crooned a song about a nanny, a little boy, and a pet beetle. And me? I couldn't have been happier.

Tom and Luke cut sod for the roof.

Laurie uses a drawknife to skin rafter poles.

Tom planes a log before ripping it into floorboards.

Jeanie filming.

Luke takes a break.

*Laurie hands Tom moss to cush-
ion a utility room perlin. Loft
rafters are in the background.*

Jeanie and Shylo on the delta.

CHAPTER 4

Our days fell into a pattern of intense activity. Although we had promised ourselves Sundays off, the need to utilize the brief summer kept us in harness. Sometimes we would break for lunch and sleep like the dead, sweating on top of our down bags in the midday heat, and rise in the late afternoon. In a land where the sun never sets, it seemed natural to release schedules. We kept a clock in the tent, but gradually it began to slide and time lost its meaning.

The river dropped rapidly, clearing to jade green and freeing us to walk emerging beaches as we explored our new home. Often when the workday ended we would line the canoe up the dancing current until we tired, then climb aboard and allow the river to carry us back. Downstream from camp did not interest us much, for it required a long homeward pull. More than that I believe, it represented civilization and the end of a journey we were yet beginning.

Like wild animals, much of our desire to explore was hinged on survival. We needed to know about this country: where to fish, where the timber was, where the berries or bogs or easy walking lay, where the moose traveled. All information seemed relevant, something to be stored away for future use. And like animals, in studying the land we claimed it in our own minds. It became a part of our culture, comforting in its familiarity and something we could share in our conversations around the fire. It was as natural for us to name its features as it was for the wolves to mark it after the fashion of their kind.

I was reminded of naming Luke. We had taken the month after his birth to choose, saying we wouldn't know who he was until he lived with us awhile. Friends reacted with discomfort, and I was surprised to observe my own superstitious fears as well. It was as if, without a name, our infant son was not solidly attached to the planet and might leave us. I found that the very act of naming something captures and claims it in the human mind.

Thus there soon came to be Pike Slough, Grayling Slough, Wandering Slough, Horseshoe Lake, King Mountain (this from Luke, who thought it resembled the turrets of a castle), and the Marshes of Kelfazin (from the book

Watership Down). There was Tom's Bench, Daddy's Magic Forest, and Clam Springs, bubbling mysteriously from the bank below our camp. Tom had told Laurie that the bubbles were from clams, and in willing innocence, she had dug.

It was Laurie who finally named the dog. She badly wanted to make friends with that wild creature, who for her part spurned all contact. Because of this timidity, Laurie began calling her Shylo.

If Shylo was anyone's dog, she was mine. She tolerated the others for the privilege of sleeping on down bags away from mosquitoes, but unless she was on a leash, I was the only one who could touch her outside of the tent. Our short period alone had established Luke and me as the family unit leaving Tom and Laurie forever intruders in our camp.

Bright and quick to figure out situations that did not involve her fears, Shylo was born to wilderness. She was a good swimmer and took several baths a day, often paddling out from shore for a drink. The first time we crossed the river, Shylo refused to be caught and so was left in camp. As we paddled against the broad sweep of current, she breasted the river. Her small form was swept far downstream, coming to shore in a soggy, long-legged mass. She soon rejoined us, smiling with self-congratulations. It only took a few trips, however, for her to choose the humiliation of being hefted aboard and tied to a thwart over the long, icy swim. It was a calculated decision and demonstrated there was more to her behavior than shyness. She was, and would always remain, her own dog.

WE SCRAPED ONTO THE rocks, the aluminum canoe making an unpleasant noise and leaving a trail of silver on the rounded stones. I stowed my wooden paddle and rose in one movement, stepping over the side and grabbing the bow. The rocks were slimy with mud and I lurched awkwardly as I heaved the craft further aground.

"Don't get out," I ordered Luke. "Sit down until I say so."

"Look at Shylo," he wailed. "I think she's gonna drown!"

"She won't drown," I reassured him. "And anyway, there's nothing you can do. Look, she's almost to shore."

"Can I get out now?"

"Wait for Daddy to carry you so you can keep your feet dry."

"I don't care if my feet are dry. See?" He swung his leg over to dangle a boot in the river.

"Cut it out, Luke," Tom called irritably from his place in the stern.

"I'll take you," Laurie offered. She was already standing on the slippery stones. "Wait 'til I get my life jacket off. Here, let me help you with yours."

Soon we had unloaded the canoe and carried it high into the scrubby poplar. Across the river, our camp was invisible, hidden in forest. Tom smiled indulgently as I tied the bowline around the roots of a stranded driftwood tree. Better safe than sorry, I thought. I didn't know what could happen on a lovely day like this, but I wanted to be sure our canoe was here when we returned.

The bar had recently been inundated, but already pink clusters of wild sweet peas massed along the gravel. The hot, still air was thick with their perfume. A hundred yards separated us from an island of mature spruce. It was only an island occasionally now, its ten-foot cutbank ending in gravel as if it had somehow run aground. Marginal soil intact, it hosted a rich shady world above the sand and rocks. As we climbed the bank I could see that we were not the first to discover this oasis. An extensive camp had once existed here complete with toilet, tent sites, and a cache platform nailed high between four trees. There was a stack of cut firewood and two rude benches, a small split-log table, and a couple of old gas crates. On one was stenciled, "USGS care of Bettles, Alaska."

"The Topo Camp," as we called it, probably dated from a survey conducted in the fifties. At that time the river may have been close by. From the shelter of the woods one had a view of the bar, west and south. Topo Island was dry and covered knee-high in blooming, white milk vetch. The trees were unusually tall and straight. It was a neat and well chosen camp, and the former residents had left a minimum of garbage. Someone had been handy with an ax and full of imagination. It's interesting how much we communicate about ourselves through the dailiness of our lives, especially in places like this where human thoughts may lie undisturbed for decades.

We built a fire to deter the bugs and establish a home base for Luke. It organized the area in our minds. Then we set to work culling dead trees and yarding them up on the edge of the cutbank. It would be a long pull to the river, but the timber quality made the effort worthwhile. We were used to working together and wasted little energy. The buzz of Tom's saw was broken intermittently with a yell of "Timber!" and the crashing "Whomp!" of a tree plummeting to earth. Laurie and I kept up a steady flashing of axes as we knocked the old branches off close to the trunks. Once the logs were pulled free, we cleaned the area, piling the dead branches over stumps as shelters for wildlife.

It was fun to work with Laurie. Child of the TV generation, she would often break into weird advertising jingles and snatches of old songs. She had a quick turn of phrase and nimble wit that bubbled up in one-liners faster than my brain could assimilate them. It was like playing volleyball with Tom. I would register events after they happened, while he was able to anticipate them and react. My brain, like an older computer, could get there but not at the same pace.

"Can you give me a hand?" Laurie called.

"Be right there. Just let me get the last couple of stobs off." Nearby, Luke was chopping determinedly away at a small log.

"Do you know where the slings are?" Laurie asked. She was wearing my old green paisley shirt, her khaki trousers splotched with pitch, and my floppy blue hat. We were close enough in size to exchange some clothing. In pictures of that summer it's sometimes hard to tell us apart. Sweat now darkened her back and her shoulders were festooned with twigs.

"I want a hand, too," Luke called.

Patiently, Laurie untangled his sling and helped him pull his log, still bristling with stobs, to the pile. It took diplomacy to work with Luke, for he wanted assistance in doing it alone. As Laurie joined me, I noticed Luke had become distracted and abandoned his ax. He was now sneaking toward Shylo who dozed in the shade.

Together Laurie and I strained against a log, wresting it free from a fleece of shorn limbs and other downed trees. Stumbling and grunting, we heaved it toward the bank like a matched set of mules in harness, laughing and joking.

"Why are we running?!" I gasped.

"Why are you running? I'm just trying to keep up!"

"I think we can carry the next one," I said as we headed back. We hefted it onto our shoulders and wavered off through the brush and between the trees, so overcome with mirth and exertion that we staggered and swayed perilously under the burden.

"Hey, Beef Cakes!" Laurie called as we shouldered another twisted log. It rolled and swung between us, seeking stability where there could be none.

"Moose Cakes, to you!" I corrected.

"Which way are you going?" she asked. We were threading our awkward load between the trees, through a maze of brush and downed timber. Laurie, as usual, had quietly taken the heavier end.

"To the right! You doing okay back there?"

"Just trying to do the limbo."

I glanced back to see her dancing. "Stop making me laugh, Laurie, you're a menace!"

"Whoa! Whoa! You said right!"

"Your other right."

"A little dyslexic, are we?"

"I forgot to warn you about that . . . Oh hell, does it matter? I'm going straight through here . . ."

"Wait! Wait! Back up a bit! That's it. Okay, now. Forward."

"Anybody ready for food," called Tom as he paced toward us through the dappled light. He was our lunch bell. The little chain-saw swung casually in his right hand, double bit ax in his left. His blue work shirt was stained and ripped at both elbows. A bandanna was tied pirate style around his balding head to protect it and keep the sweat from dripping into his eyes. His marbled beard was a tangle of sticks.

"Ready? One, two, heave!" Laurie and I called together as we dumped the crooked log onto the pile and jumped aside to avoid the backlash.

There were so many ways a person could be seriously injured doing this kind of work. It was another common question we had been asked: What if someone gets hurt? We had a good medical and dental kit along and would be able to sew up wounds, treat infections, and handle a variety of situations, but mostly we relied on prevention and general good health. The vast majority of humanity manages without benefit of modern medicine. Life isn't safe: you pay your ticket and you take your ride.

I built up the fire and set on a pot of leftover kidney beans. Tom joined us, drawing up one of the old benches made from a split log and poles. Laurie hauled up the rickety little table, its hewn surface stained and weathered.

"We could take these back to camp," Tom observed. "They're not much, but they're usable until I get around to making something better." His voice was soft and not much lower in pitch than mine. He looked at home straddling the bench as he removed his glasses to wipe clean. He was practically blind without them, and they were a constant annoyance, trapping mosquitoes and dirt in summer, fogging in winter.

Luke abandoned his seat on the ground and made himself comfortable in front of his dad, leaning back against the familiar chest. His clothes were dirty, silty trousers held up by orange suspenders; the frayed cuffs of his small checkered shirt always muddy.

"I think the bugs are getting less, don't you?" I said.

"You say that every day," Tom observed. "It's just hot now. Remember last night?"

We had crossed the river after dinner to explore the looping bend downstream as far as Pike Slough, carrying little except a fishing rod, a snack for Luke, and the .357 Magnum pistol Tom wore strapped to his belt during our outings. I didn't believe it necessary, but he said he felt more comfortable with it. The unspoken word, of course, was bears. We had continued up Pike Slough

J. ASPEN 94

until it became a deep and narrow channel meandering through muskeg. Here the land was a jigsaw puzzle of deep frost cracks and "heaves," overgrown with tussocks of cotton grass and small bushes. These tussocks wobble and recoil, throwing one off balance into mucky crevices that are hidden and often quite deep. Muskeg is exhausting country to travel over, for one is never able to take a measured step, but must hop and teeter, lurch and recover.

By the time we had arrived at Flat Lake where the stream emerged, Luke was very tired. Our map, the only scale available, showed about five miles to the inch and was therefore vague for a person on foot. To the east, the ground rose perhaps eighty or a hundred feet, and on the far side was a second lake. When we climbed the bluff (later named Cassidy Park) we looked down on an unusually deep and dark circular body of water, Lake Eugene, half encompassed by the promontory on which we stood. Rather than risk another slog through the dreaded muskeg with its hordes of mosquitoes, we decided to circumnavigate this lake and return to the river far upstream of where we had left our canoe.

Cassidy Park was a beautiful and wild spot. There were massive (for us) spruce trees interspersed with alders, birch, black currant, and prickly rose. Death camas lilies bloomed greenish yellow, and thatches of lowbush cranberry, yellow saxifrage, and kinnikinnick grew along the edge. Although the land descended in rolling gradations to Flat Lake, there was an abrupt drop of raw earth into Lake Eugene. Looking down, we could see the tops of trees marching into the depths where whole tracts of forest had suddenly dropped. It gave one an uneasy feeling. Bluffs along the river erode slowly allowing trees to pitch forward and slide down the bank, but here a pingo of glacial ice was probably melting beneath the land, causing the surface to collapse into a very deep hole. Looking at the forest of Cassidy Park, one couldn't help but think of stability and the continuity of life; but glancing into the lake at those drowned trees disappearing in darkness, I was reminded of how temporary and ephemeral it is.

Fascination with this lake held us on the brink. In an age where even the code of our own genetics is being methodically unraveled and manipulated, there is still a longing for mystery and quest within the human soul. We want to believe there is more to life than can be mapped on a computer. We revel in the mighty outbursts of nature, when our safe, regulated world is suddenly shaken or washed away, for it leaves us in awe of something greater than ourselves. And surprisingly, it also bestows an expanded sense of ourselves.

As we traversed the rough edge of the mysterious lake, we could hear the occasional uneasy clatter of rocks as the bluff crumbled beneath us. Whatever forces had formed it, they were still underway. The mosquitoes were terrible, even driven back by a breeze off the lake. Below us, a pair of loons and several grebes dove for fish in the deep, clear water. Arctic terns wheeled and skimmed against a backdrop of sunset and painted lake. The rim of peaks was etched into that pastel sky where high overhead a bald eagle chittered repeatedly as she circled us.

Sunset was fading to dusk before we hit the river. Luke was very brave, stumbling along through the dense brush singing "The Ants Go Marching One by One" with me to keep back the tears. Twice we had to wade murky backwaters above our waists, me going first to test the depth, followed by Tom with Luke piggyback, and then Laurie, stalwart as ever but frightened at the intensity of mosquitoes. They were so thick it was hard to breathe without choking. Luke started to cry each time he gagged on one.

That had been last night, but now at midday around our fire the bugs were tolerable. I pulled a bag of trail mix from the black knapsack that we used for lunch and handed it around. Next came some oat muffins I had baked that morning, passed with a small tub of peanut butter. The bean pot, with one spoon, went the rounds as did a jug of lemonade.

"Real silver," Laurie commented, hefting the spoon as if she had just noticed it.

"My grandmother's," I said. "I don't believe in roughing it. Life is hard enough. Say! Are you feeding the M&M's to that dog?"

Shylo was paying special attention to Laurie's back, where her hand was innocently out of sight.

"Well . . . she likes them," she replied sheepishly. "Don't you Princess Dog Nose?" Shylo flattened her ears and backed away.

"You're bribing her," Tom concluded.

"I'm making friends."

"Eeuuww, look at Laurie's teeth!" Luke interrupted.

We all stared and Laurie smiled cautiously, holding a smashed raisin in place with her upper lip. "I learned this trick when I was a counselor at church camp," she told us proudly. "Want to see me blow them out my nose?"

"Yes! Yes!" howled Luke, his eyes shining with admiration.

"She's the Nanny From Hell," I turned to Tom. "Did you get references?"

"Only from her mother. I don't think Darlene has any idea." He was shaking his head mournfully.

Laurie grinned shamelessly, losing her raisin. "All those years of charm school, wasted. It's better that she doesn't know, don't you think? It can be our little secret."

"For the next year and a half anyway," I said dryly.

"I can be a lady though, I can!" she stated in an offended cockney accent.

"Get out," laughed Tom in disbelief.

"No, really. You should 'ave seen me all dolled up for that weddin'. I was as pretty and pink as a pi'ture. And there was this guy . . ." She seemed to become more serious. "He was best man for the groom," she looked shyly down at her hands.

"Well, go on," I prompted. I hadn't seen this side of Laurie before. She had spoken warmly of her many friends, but seemed cautious about romantic involvements.

"I was a bridesmaid so they paired us up. We really hit it off. After the wedding we went out and just talked. Then the next morning I caught the plane for Alaska."

"What was he like?" I asked.

"Well, his name is John. He just got his MBA in California. He's in his late twenties and, like me, never been married but feeling ready. He's into bicycle racing. He has dark hair and is kind of tall and has wonderful blue eyes.

I listened, hearing yet another Laurie emerge, the lovely, cultured girl who could wear a pink formal and be swept off her feet by a tall, dark stranger. It all seemed so remote at the time.

"You think he might be the one?"

"Oh, who knows where we'll be in a year? I think it's necessary to respect one another's dreams. Someone might be right for you but on a different path when you meet them. People can be separated in time as well as space."

We sat in companionable silence, each with his own thoughts. It was easy to be together out here. Tom was quietly eating as he studied the surrounding woods. Shylo had given up on the candy and was digging an enormous hole, dirt flying up behind her as she descended into the earth. Nearby, a red tree squirrel scolded us, his little body jerking with each angry "chit!"

"Have you ever noticed how each area has its own personality?"Tom asked. "Its own energy? Look at these trees. There's a sense of order and peace here. Now you take down at the river bend across from Pike Slough, the trees are all tangled and falling every which way. It feels very chaotic and close."

"It's like they're a community," I put in.

"I wonder what trees think of us," Laurie said.

"I imagine we're so fast and fickle that we hardly register on them," I told her, "like mosquitoes."

"I think our energy must be very abrasive and frightening to them," Tom said, "coming into their sanctuary here with our noise and axes and fire."

We were all silent awhile, slowing ourselves to listen to the thoughts of the trees. As if they knew, a gentle whisper of wind traveled through their tops. They were certainly living beings, though vastly different from us. I thought about the old "does-it-exist-if-I-don't-perceive-it?" argument, and tried to imagine these trees growing here throughout the years. They had seen dark winters bent with snow and summers with birds in their hair. While I was yet unborn, these trees had been here, drinking the rain and dancing to the breath of the planet.

Our reverie was broken by Shylo flying past, fast and graceful as the wind. She turned her proud gaze toward us as she sped by and abruptly fell into the cavernous hole of her own construction, her forward momentum ceasing as completely as if she had been shot. How human, I thought. It was so comical that we broke into peals of laughter. Humiliated, Shylo climbed out of the pit and slunk away.

"You know what?" I started, before I caught myself.

"Chicken butt!" Both Laurie and Luke chimed together.

"Old. That's going to get very old."

"You know why? Cow pie!" Luke continued merrily.

Undeterred I began again. "We need to haul the big one next." There was a communal groan. A monster log, destined to be our main ridgepole, lay some distance down the island. "Time to get on with it," I prompted. "That log is not going to move itself."

"Go! Go!" shouted Laurie in the direction of the log. "I think it can! I think it can!"

"I think we're just procrastinating."

"This is a magic pear," she continued, pulling dried fruit from the trail mix bag and holding it up with both hands. She squeezed her eyes shut in mock concentration. "There are three wishes in this pear. I wish the log would move!"

By the time we had finished for the day, the sky had grayed and the afternoon turned flat and chilly. More than a little wind pounded through the lonely old trees. We still had another day of cutting and perhaps two of hauling our heavy treasures across the beach to the river and rafting them home, but there was a tidy pile of logs yarded at the cutbank attesting to our efforts.

We gathered up tools and set off for the canoe. Away from the protection of the forest, we met sheets of blowing sand. The canoe had been flipped by a gust but remained tethered to its log. After that, we made sure it was always tied, even when safely ashore.

❦

TWO DAYS LATER FOUND us dragging those logs across the open bar as we strained and sweated together through the heat of the day. Gradually the pile shifted from the cutbank to the water's edge. There we tied them into a raft and towed it slowly upstream, splashing over the slippery stones while Luke rode. When we reached a point above camp, Tom fastened one end of our hundred-foot rope to the raft and the other to the canoe. While Laurie and Luke waited on shore ready to shove the raft off, Tom and I paddled hard for home. Wanting to be near me but not wishing to be caught, Shylo swam after us. We could see her little head being carried way downriver, bravely arrowing for the distant bank, and hear her soft whimpers.

When we hit the end of the rope, the massive raft began to swing into the current, dragging us backward. We paddled for all we were worth, grating inexorably along the far shore, a mere tail to the action of the raft. I jumped into the shallow water and braced against the weight until Tom could join me and pull it in, hand over hand. After we grounded the raft, we dismantled it and hauled the logs up from the capricious river. Later we would drag them up the trail to where our future cabin remained a dream. I called Shylo, but she refused to come. As we returned for another round, she once more swam behind.

By the third trip we were fatigued and numb. I remember sitting stupidly in the sun on the end of a log with my partners, each unable to make a clear decision or take another step. Luke had been pulling little logs, insisting on being in front and often blocking the way. Now he was whining irritably, his face red and splotchy from the heat.

I realized we were beyond the point of thinking clearly. "Let's take a bath and cool down," I said, "then have a snack in the shade. I vote we take what we have and go home."

"I didn't want to be a whiner," Laurie commented, "but don't you think the distance is a bit excessive?" Topo Island lay perhaps two hundred yards away, across the open bar.

"We did get a little enthusiastic with this lot," I admitted. "It was a nice group, but there are other trees."

"Now she tells us."

"We left the big ones for last again," I lamented.

"Lazy?" offered Tom and raised his eyebrows at Laurie.

"Stupid?" she suggested innocently.

"Okay, everybody up. Next time we'll go for trees closer to the river, but these are ours now."

ORIGINALLY, WE THOUGHT TO gather the majority of logs before starting construction, but we needed a change of pace. We had also planned to build a meat house first, a place for food storage and a retreat should the cabin burn down, but we longed to begin our real home. Unanimously, we scrapped the plan and began happily fitting together our great Lincoln Logs. Slowly the piles fell into order as the foundation of a cabin emerged. At last Luke and Laurie could begin to visualize our home.

We alternated between the forest and home. Several days a week we headed upstream, lining the canoe with tools and lunch aboard. Tom usually preceded us and had already downed several trees by the time Laurie, Luke, and I arrived. Decked out in life preserver and paddle, Luke would ride in the canoe, jabbering questions or calling directions as I threw my weight into the rope, feeling the familiar bite of it across my shoulders. One end was attached to the bow, the other to the rear thwart. The canoe rode out from shore and slightly behind me. By playing the two ends through my hand, I controlled the angle of the craft in the current. There's an art to lining, allowing the current to ferry the canoe in or out to accommodate the ever-changing shoreline, but one invariably has wet feet. For two or three days we would fell and haul trees and then raft our prizes home, two of us riding the logs down through the rapids while the other followed with Luke in the canoe. Then for a few days we would work on our cabin.

As the days wore on, my feet began to bother me. The hard work and constant wet inflamed old tendonitis in my heels and by evening I was usually hobbling. Laurie would massage my feet and hands as we lay in the tent. The work took its toll on each of us and we nurtured one another, adjusting to keep healthy. Laurie took over most of the canoe lining so that my feet could stay dry. Tom's knees were holding up, but he was experiencing carpal tunnel symptoms in his arms at night. Even Laurie was having trouble with her hands going to sleep. For the most part, however, our bodies were doing very well. We had each taken up several notches on our belts and at bath time I noticed muscles beginning to stand out on the calves and shoulders of my fellows.

Building was far easier and more fun than hauling logs. Each log was first skinned of its bark with a "drawknife" (a blade with handles at either end) then muscled into place. The bottom logs, or "sills," were chosen for their size. These were laid upon bare ground, brought to level with flat stones, and the ends saddle-notched together. Notches were also cut in the sills for floor joists. First a log was laid in position and marked, then it was rolled and strapped in place and the notches chopped. These faced downward to prevent water from collecting in them. This process had to be repeated until the logs fit. Our logs were often twisted, and areas that touched between them needed to be cut away. We padded the notches with moss and squared them using a plumb bob made from a bullet and string. Eventually, the spaces between logs would need to be chinked with moss.

The utility room almost doubled the work involved. Although it shared a common wall with the cabin, it added three extra logs for each round, and these were doweled to the layer beneath wherever an opening would be cut. To do this, someone slowly twisted an auger down through the wall. We had two augers, one an inch and a half in diameter, the other a quarter inch larger. Augers gnawed a circle through the wood, bringing the chips back up the screw of the shaft. If the logs were tight, chips jammed between the layers, clogging the hole. Once the hole had been drilled through two logs and into a third, the auger was withdrawn and a dowel (fashioned with an ax from a small dead tree) was pounded in and sawed off flush. This secured the logs so that a section could be cut away for a window or door.

At first we left the logs whole, but as the structure rose to waist high, we cut away the lower parts of doorways, leaving the top log intact for continuity until the next level was completed. This gave us access to the interior without having to climb over.

It was hard work, but we enjoyed it. We generally found ourselves in an easy alliance and rarely disagreed. If a problem arose, it fell between Tom and me. There were times that he seemed grumpy and remote, and I began turning to the easy friendship I had with Laurie. She remained a center of quiet strength.

Willing to work at whatever needed doing, she shone on each of us, never infringing or making anyone wrong.

The work went slowly and we usually counted our progress in terms of one level a day. The cabin was our consuming passion and our major topic of conversation. Each challenge was greeted with cooperation and excitement as we talked through the possibilities. Often one or another of us could be found of an evening, sitting on the wall or staring contemplatively at the growing structure in the slanting, golden light.

"What do you think of it?" I asked Luke when he joined me on the low wall after dinner one night. "Can you imagine it as a little house?"

He studied the small corral of bare poles a moment and shook his head sadly. "No. Can you?"

"Yes, but I've built one before. Remember seeing my old cabin two years ago? Well, it started out just like this. I remember looking at it and thinking it would never be a home."

I smiled at my scruffy little boy. "Are you enjoying your life out here, or is it hard?" I asked him gently.

He snuggled into my arms and answered, "I enjoy it. And it's hard."

"Do you think we work too much?"

"Yes."

"Me too," I admitted. "But it's important."

He looked tired, and I wished I could get him to bed earlier. He needed more sleep but refused to be put in the tent alone. It didn't seem fair to him that humanity now consisted of grown-ups and him—a kind of exclusion. He wanted to be counted a full partner. Fortunately, we all needed the rest and usually retired soon after dinner.

Luke had seemed depressed lately, quiet and subdued or picking fights with those who should have been his allies. Our obsession with building left little time for him. He would quickly tire of helping and spent most of his time playing alone and lost in his fantasies. As we staggered up the hill harnessed to a mighty log, he would rush ahead and flap bushes in our faces, his "car wash." Tom in particular was sometimes short with him.

Even his imaginary playmate, "Zaza," had turned on him. Zaza had emerged years before but hadn't been around for a while. He seemed to be a little boy who looked a good deal like Luke. Only that day, Luke had come to me in tears to report that Zaza was being mean, but he had killed him. Unfortunately, Zaza kept coming back to life, hundreds of him in fact, stronger than ever. I had suggested that he retire Zaza and pretend to play with his real neighborhood friend, Troy, whom he had known since infancy.

I looked down at Luke and smiled. He was drumming his heels against the wall where we perched. "You had a run in with Daddy?" I asked.

"He doesn't love me anymore," he replied bitterly, eyes welling with tears. "Could we get a different one?"

"Well, that's not easy to do. Especially here. Maybe you need to talk to him about your feelings." I wiped his nose with the tail of my shirt. "Was it about fishing?"

He nodded. "I don't like that stupid pole he gave me. It never works. And he won't let me use his. And he doesn't even want me to come!"

Tom had his heart set on catching fish and wanted a little time to himself in the evenings. Luke's heart was set on fishing with his dad. It touched me to see the little fellow set off determinedly up the beach after his father, clutching his pole and calling "Wait up, Dad!" It annoyed Tom because Luke would soon be frightening the fish and asking for help, his reel snarled or lure caught somewhere out in the cold water. I didn't know how to tell Tom that the fish meant less to me than his relationship with his son. I wasn't even certain that it was my place.

When Laurie had caught her first fish, Luke's eyes had filled with tears, angry that she had caught one and he hadn't. She had set aside her rod and helped him cast his lure into the reeds of Pike Slough, wading out when it snagged, but they didn't get one that day.

"I'm the littlest member and I can't use all the tools," he continued sadly.

"You need to talk this over with Dad and not yell at him about it. You'll find that people listen better when you talk to them politely."

"He's just mean."

"He has a lot on his mind these days," I countered. "We all do. But I think Daddy takes it harder. He probably feels it's up to him to make sure we have a safe home before winter."

❦

IN MANY WAYS WE were far from comfortable. There was no place to get out of the bugs except lying down in the tent or balanced on stumps around the fire. We cooked or washed dishes kneeling on the ground or standing beside the tiny, rickety table. Scrubbing clothes was an all day chore: heating water on the fire then leaning over the washboard in the galvanized tub. Everybody's skin was weathered from constant exposure to sun, smoke, and repellent; our hands were chapped and bashed, our bodies creaky and sore from the heavy work.

But the country made up for it. It was an overwhelming presence in our lives. There was a deep energy about it that penetrated even the busiest mind, slowing it to an older rhythm. We became quieter and gentler as the days passed. A sense of peace prevailed in our lives. We treated one another with affection and took each moment as it came. Even Luke, who often fantasized about engines and went around sounding like one, was settling down. He seemed to sleep more deeply, with less of the flopping and grinding that had made him such a wretched bed partner. Sometimes I would hear Laurie comforting him softly as he turned in slumber.

The zipper condition worsened and we were reduced to squirming under the door flap. Because the bottom zippers were also showing signs of fatigue, we tried to exit or enter as a group, thus saving wear on them. This kept the inside mosquito population to a minimum and soon evolved into a custom known as "grown-up pee hour," for Luke was generally asleep when we made our last nocturnal dash through the bugs. The good news was that they were definitely on the wane now, thousands instead of millions. It made every aspect of life easier.

The outside world gradually receded from our minds and conversation. "The other world," as Laurie called it, was sliding away from us. Cut off from the dominant culture, we were developing our own. A deep affection was taking root between us. By day we worked and Luke played with his small toy car or Legos as the neat ring of logs we called "the cabin" grew around him. In the evening we sat about the fire and told stories. Laurie taught Luke clapping games and Tom often rocked him to sleep, standing in the smoke with the little figure draped over his shoulder.

A month had passed and the cabin was more than chest high. It was hard to measure time, for our old life had ceased so abruptly there was no bridge between our two worlds. We would find ourselves saying, "Last week I saw a movie," as if these lives existed side by side without touching. In a way, the rest of the planet had stopped. It remained for us as bright and unchanged as yesterday. Perhaps by way of compensation, we traveled there in dreams, discussing our vivid double lives upon awakening.

I hadn't felt so peaceful in years. I was happy to be away from the complexity of that world. Life here, if hard, seemed simple and straightforward. The very intensity of work brought its own joy. There was something fulfilling about building our home, a sense of solid accomplishment missing from the more esoteric forms of labor. I often heard myself singing, strangely content in the present. With ample time to think, I was empty of thoughts as I watched my weathered hands slowly twist the auger down through the layers of logs.

❧

ONE SUNDAY WE SET out to explore the creek. It was a lovely, bright day, and we ambled happily along. Luke loved walking in the water, and often forded the creek to his waist just for the fun of it. While the river temperature ranged into the fifties, the creek remained an even thirty-four degrees. Shylo thoroughly enjoyed herself, grinning broadly, ears flopping and curly tail a proud banner over her back as she splashed ahead.

The stream was shallower now, racing clear over colorful stones. The deeper pools sparkled emerald green and were shadowed by overhanging banks of horsetails, speckled with the tiny stars of grass of parnassus and stellaria. I was surprised at how much Luke remembered of our hike two years before. At six he was stronger, but long before we reached the base of Annie's peak, he was holding my hand and beginning to lag. He kept up a happy monologue as we walked, salted with bits of philosophy.

"Your pockets won't hold any more rocks," I told him at one point. "Your pants are so heavy your suspenders can hardly keep them up." Collecting special rocks had become important to each of us. It was hard to resist when there were so many.

"But just look at this one," he answered, holding up a perfectly average looking stone.

"It looks like a plain old rock to me," I said flatly.

He stared at me in astonishment. Speaking slowly as if explaining to a small child, he replied, "There is something special about every speck of dust."

By this time the creek tumbled over large boulders and the footing was difficult. When Luke slipped and fell into the icy water we stopped for lunch and built a fire. We determined that Laurie and Tom would scale the peak while Luke and I returned home. He was angry and hurt at being excluded.

"You have a big heart, but your legs aren't long enough yet," I told him as we started back. My heel tendons hurt with every step, and I too had to face my limitations. Long before we reached familiar country, the sky had turned black behind us and snow dusted the encircling peaks. Racing the storm home, I hoisted Luke onto my back and carried him the last mile.

Tom and Laurie arrived home late—tired and hounded by swarms of bugs—but they had scaled the peak. From the top, Tom had chosen a piece of white quartz for Annie, a memento of their previous try.

🦋

"WE HAD A BEAR near the tent last night," I told Laurie the next evening as I prepared dinner. I was making spaghetti and clover sprouts. The sprouts, grown in Tupperware containers, were our only fresh food besides an occasional fish.

"That must be what I heard," she answered. "I thought it was a moose." We both glanced at Luke who was lost in play along the creek. He was building canals and a city of mud and stones on its bank. The river had dropped three feet and our slough had become a small stream of clear water. I had found the big, man-like tracks in the mud when I filled the water bucket.

We could see Tom out on the delta, casting out where the two waters met. He looked happy and complete, alone against the slanting sunlight and green river. "I wish Tom would include Luke in his fishing," I said.

Laurie listened without comment, a quality I found disconcerting at first. I would search for an echo, a reflection. Did she agree or approve? She offered no opinion, just quiet attention.

"I mean, it seems so easy to be with you," I continued. "You just pick up where I leave off. We're interchangeable around here. Tom doesn't always seem to notice unless I say something." Which, I suddenly realized, was what I needed to do.

Later, as Tom sat on the bench changing into his camp shoes and Luke was watching Laurie shake out the bedding, I broached the subject.

"I don't think he's ready for it," he told me. "I let him reel in fish I've hooked, but that doesn't count to him. He doesn't have the coordination or the attention span yet."

"Couldn't you set it up for him to hook one? He doesn't work at it because he feels like a failure. It's real important to him."

Then I dropped the subject. Tom would handle it in his own way. He had placed a freshly cleaned grayling in a pie plate on the little table. I dredged it in a mixture of flour, powdered potatoes, and spices before setting the cast-iron skillet on the grill. A few mosquitoes caught in the updraft of flame rained gently into the pan. The "hot oil treatment," as Laurie called it.

Late afternoon expanded gold over the river that coiled endlessly past in its ancient quest for the sea. Swallows flitted across the surface after the diminishing insects. A drift of herringbone clouds dappled the vault of powder-blue sky. The woods were silent now. Birds, involved in raising families no longer sang about territory and love. I knew the feeling. Most of the flowers were through blooming and the land was fruiting into a mature green.

Laurie was finishing up in the tent while Luke squatted by the door watching. I could hear them talking softly together. I stood behind Tom and rubbed his shoulders a moment and he leaned his head back against me in quiet companionship.

"Luke, it's okay!" Laurie called. "I didn't know it mattered to you."

Luke rushed up to me and flung his arms about my waist. "She killed a spider!" he wailed in the tone of one who has discovered that Santa is an ax murderer.

Laurie was right behind him. "It was just a spider," she said.

"Luke," I told him softly, "most people do kill them."

"You mean you don't?" asked Laurie.

"No, my mother used to call them 'little hunters' and put them outside. They're different from us, but they're living creatures, part of God, like everything else."

"Not to me. They're spiders. They crawl on you."

"I'm not big on that part either," I admitted.

Luke was glancing from one to another of us. "I don't want you to kill them anymore," he informed Laurie.

"For you, Pumpkin, I won't. But your mother better put them out of the tent before I get to them."

"Let me help you with your wet boots, Son," Tom called. "Get your camp shoes and socks out of the tree. How about a nip, Laurie?" Tom had a small stock of bourbon and had gallantly offered to share with Laurie, hoping she'd decline. They were both relieved that I didn't drink.

"Count me in," she replied. "I'm just gonna close up the tent."

I smiled at my little family, happy with our close, familiar group about the fire. I couldn't imagine anywhere else I wanted to be, or anyone I would rather be with. These are the good old days, I thought, drinking in the smells of driftwood smoke and frying grayling. Maybe that's always true, but I felt rich in the things that really counted. Wealth, I was discovering, is more accurately measured in what you enjoy than in what you possess.

As I reached to turn the browning fish I caught the familiar sound of an airplane. We had become so accustomed to silence that it took a moment to register. We were not expecting contact until our one scheduled mail flight in November. Suddenly we were all on our feet. A second later a Cessna angled into view, low and clear in the crystal air. It made three sweeping turns about the valley, obviously mistrustful of low water, then lined up over the trees with silver floats extended to the rush of green river. We could hear the change in pitch as it dropped and flared, followed by the rapid pounding of waves on pontoons as it rushed upriver toward us.

The other world had not stopped after all. From far away it had reached out to change our lives.

CHAPTER 5

As the plane came to shore, we raced down the beach, jumping the small creek channels to keep our feet dry. I had the video camera going. The delta seemed crowded with laughing, talking men. Steve Ruff was the only one I recognized. He introduced a shy, sandy-haired young man in a Christian camp T-shirt and sunglasses as Ken Howard, the pilot that flew his 185. It took me a while to realize that the third person, a tall, dark-haired fellow in his late twenties, was John—the man Laurie had told us about. He had chartered the plane to visit her!

"We can send him back," Tom told me in an angry aside.

My head was still spinning. "You mean he's staying?"

"For two weeks. But Steve told him that if we didn't want company, he was taking him straight back to Bettles."

"What do you want to do?"

"Well, if it was up to me, I'd send him back."

"What about Laurie?" I asked. "He's her friend."

We glanced at the pair of them. Laurie was flushed as she laughed and chattered. She seemed totally at a loss. One hand unconsciously fumbled with her unruly hair where the tied ends of a kerchief stood up like two green antennas. She had changed in the month since she met him. Rumpled and splotched with pitch, she bore no resemblance to the princess in pink at the wedding. I watched her tenderly, wondering if John was disappointed. He didn't seem to be. He was beaming excitedly and talking loudly. Everyone was loud. Was that how it was out there?

"I don't want to simply reject him out of hand," I whispered. "It's only for two weeks. We didn't plan it this way, but let's make the best of it and enjoy him. He can haul logs."

"We're doing fine," Tom answered. "We've invested thousands of dollars and a great deal of time in this dream, and I'm not comfortable with having someone just drop in. But if it's important to you and Laurie, I'm willing."

"He must be pretty serious about her to come all this way."

"Or just want a vacation."

"Well, it cost him plenty. Charters aren't cheap."

I felt caught in the middle, as often happens when I am trying to please everybody. I turned and smiled a tentative welcome to the nervous young man. He swung his borrowed backpack easily onto one shoulder and the group headed up to camp.

"I've got my own tent and food," John told me. "If you don't want me, I'll understand. I'm prepared to just go off by myself."

"No, that would be foolish," I answered. "We're in this together. If you're staying, it's as one of us."

"I've been staying with the Warteses. They weren't gonna let me come at first. They said to bring food and be prepared to work."

I followed the excited group, wondering how I was going to stretch dinner for three extra. I needn't have worried, for arctic pilots rarely perch long. Like the summer birds, a sense of hurry propels them, as if they smell the approach of winter.

I left the others talking and hurriedly packed up videotapes for our producer. Then I penned a brief note to Denise Wartes asking for tent zippers and extra mosquito repellent. We had run through much of our supply and still had a summer to go. The feeling of urgency pulled my stomach into the old, familiar knots. Did I have to live alone, I wondered, to keep inner peace and balance?

"What are we going to do?" Laurie asked, catching me as I emerged from the pavilion. "I had no idea he would follow me up here!" She looked excited, flattered, overwhelmed.

I put my hand on her shoulder and grinned. "Laurie, my dear. The female luna moth can attract a mate from ten miles away. I think you may have set a new record. But Laurie," I intoned with mock seriousness, "he does look like a Yuppie."

"Anything you want us to bring you?" Steve asked as we headed back to the plane.

"Beer!" Tom and Laurie sang out together.

"Beer?" I sniffed. "What about vegetables?" For some reason I have never felt mature enough to either drink or wear makeup. It looked as if I would pass from youth into old age without reaching that illusive state of "grown-up."

Soon the men from the sky cast off and drifted into the current. They promised to return in two weeks. The water was much lower now and shallow in places. Our pilots had cautiously studied the diminished river, pleased that John and his gear would not be aboard. For several minutes they idled out in midstream, warming the engine as they worked their way up to the rapids. Then tight turn and full-throttle downstream, swinging with the curve of the shore, they thundered passed and lifted into the air in time to clear the trees at the bend. As the throb of propeller vanished in the big sky, we found ourselves staring at one another and our new companion.

John was a pleasant-looking young man with a full head of short, dark hair. He had large, widely spaced blue eyes under heavy brows and a strong chin beneath the shadow of a dense, two-day beard. Standing almost a head taller than the rest of us, he had the angular look of a groomed athlete. His ready, nervous smile revealed perfect white teeth. Outfitted in rugged Eddie Bauer style, he looked like the all-American boy in a sporting goods catalogue as he settled onto a bench before our fire, trying to make small talk. For openers he presented us with a bag of fresh fruit and a gift of frozen halibut and ground moose meat from Mark and Denise.

"Sorry, I'm kind of dirty," he started to apologize, spreading his large, manicured hands. "I've been in transit for two days." I believe he was serious, but we hooted him down. Wait until he spends two weeks with the logs, I thought.

"I want to honestly be able to say that we built the cabin ourselves," Tom informed him that first evening. "You can help with hauling and skinning logs, and I'll be glad to let you try all the aspects of building, but we want to do the majority of the work."

"That's fine. Just show me what to do," he answered.

He erected his small tent near the pavilion of tarps where our supplies were stored and eagerly joined us for a spaghetti dinner.

The next morning we tackled the large pile of stranded logs below camp, hauling them one by one to the cabin site. This was one of our hardest and least rewarding tasks, and even with the extra help it took all day to move about eighty logs up the bank. Laurie and John paired off for the smaller ones, laughing and talking as they wrestled trees onto their shoulders, their young bodies a study of strength and grace. They looked good together and it was easy to understand what they saw in one another. I was impressed how rapidly Laurie had regained her composure, choosing to be herself despite this abrupt and unexpected courtship.

It was a hot day and by late afternoon we were dusty and soaked with sweat. When we stopped for a bath, there was a moment of embarrassment. I lit a fire on the beach while Tom laid a tarp over the gravel and set out the bath supplies. Then I shrugged and peeled out of my clothes. I didn't intend to go dirty for two weeks. Bathing together by the fire made sense and there wasn't a place on the beach that was hidden from camp. To Luke and Tom, the extra person didn't matter except that John was more willing to frolic with Luke in the icy water than the rest of us.

Laurie and John smiled shyly at one another. "I'm not gonna be the only dirty camper," she declared.

"When in Rome," he agreed and began to strip, laying his clothes in a neat pile on the tarp.

"Look at how white his underwear is!" I couldn't help but exclaim. John grinned and politely refrained from a similar comparison. "Better hurry, the bugs'll get you," I warned.

Our ablutions were necessarily brief, but they were becoming an important ritual. Watching Luke cavort in the river, I could see naked brown children of ten thousand years ago. Our ancestors must have lived much like this, I thought. Despite hardships, I was sure there had been laughter. I imagined members of those little, wandering bands as people who loved their children, respected their elders, and felt a connection with the web of life. It wasn't possessions that made life worthwhile, I concluded as we dressed by the fire. Poverty like wealth was, at least in part, a state of mind.

❦

THE FOLLOWING DAY WAS wet and cold, and nobody suggested bathing. The temperature never rose above forty-six degrees and thoughts of autumn came soberingly to each of us. Already the light was failing, the sun setting behind the peaks at night as dusk came over the land. Soon there would be stars at night and then frost.

The smoke from my morning fire billowed sluggishly, dropping down over the slaty river as I roused the others with my usual call, "Winter is coming." Clouds obscured the top of nearby peaks and the wet smell of bark and leaves hung on the air. There wasn't a mosquito to be seen.

"Look at my breath," Luke said, huffing out a little cloud of steam as he joined me in his bare feet, soggy boots in hand.

I seated him near the fire and reached into the branches for his woolen socks, still wet from the day before. "You might want to try to keep your feet dry," I suggested. "It isn't always going to be hot."

Crawling forth, the others ringed the blaze, no one wanting to sit on the wet stumps. I handed around blue enamel mugs of scalding coffee. "It took a lot to evict Shylo this morning," I commented. Our dog had gone wild again with John's arrival, but nothing could keep her from sleeping in the tent.

"She does like her comforts," Laurie acknowledged. "And snore! Can that dog snore!"

"You're one to talk," I laughed, turning to John. "Did she tell you that her nickname is 'Snorie?'" He was wearing an expensive red-and-blue Gore-Tex raincoat and a baseball cap. His arm was looped about Laurie's shoulders and she nestled comfortably against his chest, looking almost petite beside him.

"No, she didn't."

"Now don't go spilling everything at once!" Laurie defended.

Tom squatted by the fire and replenished his cup. Then he straddled a wet bench with the chain-saw propped between his thighs and began to methodically sharpen it with a file. Luke was still trying to pull on the wet socks. "I hate this old job," he said to nobody in particular.

"What do you want to do today?" I asked the assembly. "You think maybe cut trees? At least there's no wind." Felling in wind is dangerous work.

"Shylo has my sticks!" Luke wailed suddenly. We turned to see her dragging them from his "fort." But they proved awkward for a fast getaway and John managed to rescue them. Anything of Luke's interested her greatly. Having overcome her fear of him, she liked to play by grabbing his arm with her teeth or knocking him over with a body slam. He was happy to have her attention and they spent much of the day chasing one another, but there was a competitiveness to their interactions that I did not altogether like. It remained to be seen what would happen as the dog grew larger.

After a breakfast of pancakes with syrup made from dried apricots, we started upstream to cut trees. Laurie lined the canoe, icy water rushing around her knees as she worked it up beyond the rapids. Then we boarded and paddled for the far shore where the cutbank supported a long strip of old forest. Here we fell to, Tom dropping the dead trees and the rest of us limbing and hauling them out to the river.

Luke was cranky and tired from the excitement. When he cut himself on a stob I tied the injured finger with a strip from my bandanna and settled him by the fire with a little bag of trail mix. The thick moss was damp beneath the trees, and I pulled up a log for him to sit on. There he stayed, feeding twigs into the blaze and dreaming of a magic land where he and Troy had marvelous adventures. I knew Tom wanted to keep working when I suggested we call it a day. Shortly after lunch, we piled into the canoe and drifted home beneath a lowering sky.

Soon a cold rain drove us into the pavilion where we hunched together on boxes and I read aloud from the original *Pinocchio*. I had brought along a number of the children's classics that my mother had read to me. Luke wedged his way between Laurie and John, his small, dirty face peeping out from the crush of their jackets. Tom was working on a broken microphone mount, carving a replacement from a piece of willow as rain drummed monotonously on the tarps above. A few desolate mosquitoes drifted about. The smell of wet wool suffused the shelter and from outside came Shylo's insistent whines. She wouldn't come in with John there, but she wanted us to know her feeling about the situation.

"I think it's going to be a poor berry year," I said, looking up from the book. A blue light filtered through the fiberglass tarps turning our complexions a dismal color. "I've seen very few, and they should be getting ripe by now."

"Well," Tom replied, "I doubt we'd have time to pick many."

"It'll be hard on the animals," I continued. "It was a late spring. The moose may be lean and certainly the bears will have problems. I'd prefer fat, happy bears."

"I hope it's not an early fall," Tom said, peering out at the dripping woods. "I think the rain is letting up. Why don't we try to make some dinner?"

The sky relented long enough for me to fix scalloped potatoes and the last of the moose burgers followed by chocolate pudding made with lumpy powdered milk. The taste of fresh food had been a welcome change, and I blessed those who had thought to send it. By the time we had eaten, it was drizzling again. John had no padding under his sleeping bag so I gave him some from our tent. There seemed no point in standing in the rain so we went to bed early. The ground beneath us was cold and bumpy as we huddled in for a long night. It made me appreciate how cozy our nest usually was.

❦

JOHN PROVED A LIKABLE, outgoing, and enthusiastic companion. In many ways he was perfect for the country and for our group. He joined in, cheerfully doing whatever was asked. His long legs carried him easily over the rough terrain and on the end of a log he was worth any two of us. He had arrived with a present for Luke and they were soon flying balsa wood airplanes out on the delta. Luke followed him about, asking endless questions and trying to lure him into wrestling matches. Here was someone young, full of energy, and willing to play with a small boy. John was just what Luke needed.

True to his word, Tom tried to make the best of things. He was pleased to learn that John had bought a fishing license in Fairbanks. They spent evenings casting out over the river together or exploring the nearby ponds and sloughs. With little skill or knowledge, John was surprisingly successful. The first fish he hooked flopped free into an icy finger of the creek. Without hesitation, he threw himself across the stream, damming it with his body. He grabbed the wriggling fish and bonked it thoroughly. We killed fish with a blow to the head rather than allow them to suffocate on a stringer, but in his eagerness, John tended to overdo it. It became a family joke that one could always tell by the broken bones which fish were his.

However, having an extra person changed the dynamics of our lives. Fresh from civilization, John carried the louder energy of that other world back into our midst. In addition, daily interactions with one another were geometrically expanded, and there was a tendency to fragment into couples. Although he and Laurie were unfailingly cheerful and willing, Tom and I became shorter with one another and with them. It was a relief to everyone when at the end of a week they decided to take a two-day hike up Annie's Peak.

They set off Sunday morning after a late breakfast of powdered eggs, hash browns, and catsup made from dried tomato sauce. We loaded them up with packs, tent, maps, pistol, and food, and watched as they disappeared happily up the creek bed: two young people off on an adventure.

The day was warm so the three of us decided to take a leisurely bath, enjoying the breeze and sun on our skins as we stretched out on the dry gravel of the delta. It felt good to just relax for a change. The water was beautiful, emerald in color and clear as glass. As we dressed, Tom spotted a grayling dodging in and out of the shoal. Sunlight rippled over its body in shifting colors.

"What do you say we go fishing?" he turned to Luke. "See that fish? He's gonna stay there until we get back."

I was washing breakfast dishes when Luke came proudly up the bank. His face radiated joy as he trudged into camp, a fine grayling clutched tightly with both hands, wet trousers dragging at the cuff. Reverently he laid it on a plate, lifting the large, turquoise dorsal fin for me to admire.

"There was a fish out there . . . he showed it to me, and he let me do the whole thing! I got to use his pole . . . and everything!" He was stuttering with excitement and his hands whirled as if still cranking a reel, "and, and I just caught the fish, on my first throw out!"

"Oh, Luke! Your first fish," I said with admiration.

"In my whole world!" he said seriously.

I helped him clean it in the river. He wanted to do it all, carefully working the silver scales off with the Swiss Army knife he carried in a pocket secured to his belt loop with string. We covered the fish and put it in the shade for dinner.

That evening a high overcast drifted in from the south, and by the time we were sharing Luke's first fish a cold mist prickled our skins. Dinner seemed very quiet with just the three of us around the fire. I gazed often toward Annie's

Peak, wondering how John and Laurie were doing. I hoped they would camp near the creek and not attempt to sleep on the mountain. It could be very unpleasant in a storm up there with no water or protection and little firewood. Did John know any more than Laurie about the outdoors?

"What do we really know about him, anyway?" I wondered aloud after Luke had been put to bed. "I hope he takes good care of our girl."

"Well, he has to come back here," Tom assured me. "There's no place else to go."

"What if he loses her? Do you think he knows what he's doing?" We both glanced toward the peak, now buried in cloud. My eyes met Tom's across the fire. "It is difficult to have someone else here," I acknowledged softly. "So much more talking. Instead of feeling that I'm cooking for my family, it's like being the hash slinger. I get resentful thinking my time isn't appreciated."

Tom was silent and we both listened to the somber ticking of rain on miles of dark spruce. The river looked flat where the tiny drops broke the surface, and the far shore was smudged in mist. A family of gray jays chortled nearby, back in the forest. Smoke from our fire rose in a gray, sluggish pillar.

"Thanks for taking Luke fishing. He was so proud. You should have seen him." I took a deep breath of the cool, moist air and faced the issue I'd been avoiding. "I've been mad at you lately," I said at last.

"So I've noticed."

"You seem so testy. I feel like I'm walking around on eggshells all the time, afraid I'll offend you. You're often sharp with Luke, and he needs you. I need you too. I've been thinking that I don't want to live this way for a whole year. We only have each other out here and if that isn't working, we have nothing."

Tom waited until I finished. It was our agreement and he kept it better than I did. "It seems like you expect me to read your mind," he stated. "You ask my opinion when you don't want it. If you have something to tell me, just say it. Don't ask how I feel and then expect me to guess what you want."

"You experience that as manipulative?"

"We've been through this before. You know exactly how you want things done, but instead of saying so, you ask what I think. If I don't give the right answer, you'll return to the attack from another direction until I do."

I sighed, trying to piece it together. I had the knowledge but lacked the self-confidence to be a good leader. Why was it so difficult for me to just tell Tom what I wanted? It was easy to direct Laurie, but then she was always cheerful and willing to do what I asked. With Tom, I sometimes didn't know where I stood.

"I'm just trying to be tactful," I said, feeling like I'd been here before. "When you're grumpy I'm afraid to express my opinion. So I try not to give orders."

"My 'grumpiness' is my own business. You needn't take it personally."

"Well, I do. You don't have to be grumpy, you know. It's a choice." I thought for a while about what he'd said. "It's true," I admitted presently. "I know what I want, but I try to say it in a way that will avoid conflict."

"Your communications are patronizing and confusing," he responded bluntly. "I wish you'd cut it out."

"It isn't easy trying to lead indirectly," I acknowledged.

"I imagine not. Like trying to push a rope. Why don't you give it up and say what you mean? We'll all be a lot happier."

I glanced up and smiled. "Okay. Hey, you know I love you?" His eyes softened and he looked vulnerable and a little sad.

"I miss having time alone with you," he said gently. "It's a hard way to live with no privacy. And I admit I'm feeling intruded upon with John here."

I looked at him, perhaps for the first time in weeks, and saw my husband—a man who needed my attention and support and was getting very little of either. I reached across the gulf between us and stroked his cheek. "Well, it's not forever," I said, "and it means a lot to Laurie."

Laurie did seem to be blooming. She and John were both at a stage in life where finding a mate becomes important. Discussion of marriage and children that would have taken months of careful probing in another setting had followed an easy progression. Half-seriously we joked about building a second cabin for the new family. I thought of the simplicity of relationships out here, how easy it would be for all of us to drop away from the other world and forget it. Then I remembered the conversation I had just had with Tom, and wondered if relationships were ever simple.

❦

THE WEATHER REMAINED COOL, sprinkling off and on throughout the following day. Low fog clung in tatters to trees across the valley and the mountains seemed to float like islands in the sky. We worked quietly on the cabin. Progress had slowed since we reached the level of the windows. The walls were higher than my head and now required sixteen dowels for each layer. In addition, one needed to climb the logs to work, and this became progressively more difficult as they rose. My hands were giving out and I found scaling the walls almost more than I could do at times. Tom had finished a ladder but it was heavy and awkward and we didn't readily move it from place to place.

Luke was out of sorts, perhaps missing John and Laurie. He climbed onto his "airplane," (the end of a log that jutted out behind the cabin) and pushed imaginary buttons as he made quiet engine noises to himself. When he slipped and fell, Tom gathered him up and sat propped against the wet logs, singing and telling little jokes to comfort him as rain splattered into their faces.

We stayed up after dinner, listening for our returning family. Still they did not come. Tom wanted to search up the creek, but I dissuaded him. "You're tired and we don't even know which way they'll come," I told him. "They have enough food and a tent. If they're not back by morning, then we'll search."

I left a warm supper for them banked over coals and crawled into our tent out of the drizzle. Perhaps an hour later we heard them return, escorted by clouds of mosquitoes. Tom got up to join them, relieved to have them safely home.

❧

"YOU'RE GETTING GOOD AT climbing," Laurie said to Luke. He was straddling a wall, tenaciously sawing off the end of the top log, while she and I sat twisting augers.

"I've been practicing," he told her, stopping to wipe the pitch from his hands onto his wool vest. He lived on the walls, clambering up and down the big jungle gym or working his way around, often lost in a fantasy world.

The sky was washed blue, and a cold wind rocked the trees that sheltered us from most of it. Nearby, our squirrel was busy cutting cones from the tops of the spruce, flinging them in a noisy spray. He worked his way down from the crown of the trees while Shylo followed the activity, her eyes and hopes high.

Tom was ready to notch the front "plate" log that would cap the windows and support the bottom of the roof. Together we had hoisted it into position, one end at a time, and cinched it down for him to chop the notches. Because of the loft, the back wall would be much higher. He wedged the double bit into a crack and mounted the logs. "I'm teaching Luke how to use the different tools," he told us.

"Want to learn how to use this auger?" Laurie teased. "You get sixteen tries per level."

"It's too boring," Luke replied candidly.

"Sixteen pins and what do you get?" Laurie sang out. "My shoulders rotate all night," she demonstrated. "And my bum! Mother Mary, I don't think God intended me to sit like this." High places were the one thing that frightened her, and I knew she felt vulnerable perched eight feet in the air, nevertheless, she laughed about it.

"Hey you should try the ax work," Tom commented, settling himself for the first swing. He was straddling a log, gripping it with his thighs.

"John," I called. "How are you coming with that next log?"

"About done," came the cheerful reply. "Want me to start on that other pile?"

"Nah. We'll stop for lunch. Don't anybody steal my place."

"You wish," Laurie snorted.

Stiffly, I swung my leg over and dropped to the ground. The T-handle of the auger remained sticking out the top of the wall.

"You about finished with that hole?" I asked her. "Want a stake?"

"Yeah, medium rare. Hold the 'tater."

I selected a dowel from a pile of small, dead trees and shaved it to size with the ax. Then I handed it up and started for the door. The ground was littered with bark and wood chips. Shylo lay in the sun gnawing a stick. Her adult teeth were coming in and she had hauled off much of our firewood in pursuit of the perfect chew. Greeting me, she fell into step. She was maturing into a lovely animal with snowy paws and shiny black guard hairs over a toffee undercoat. Her large, dark ears stood erect except for the tip of the right "dorky" one. Deep through the chest, supple and amazingly fast, she loved to show off and toy with us, confident in her superior speed.

I emerged from the doorway. A homey smoke issued from our roofless structure where Laurie and Luke were singing about the old woman who swallowed a fly. I heard Luke say, "It was the fly that killed her," and Laurie answer, "Yeah, but mosquitoes won't hurt you at all."

John was standing astride a heavy pole using the drawknife. One end of the log was propped over our "sawbuck," a short log with four sturdy legs doweled into the bottom at angles and pegs driven into the top. A vanilla smell rose from the old tree as its dry skin was bladed away in strips. Beneath the bark, the yellowed wood was decorated with the twisting patterns of larva. The bark beetle infestation caused by warming climate had killed this elder and was desiccating forests across North America. Skinning was a dirty, hard job and John's hair was peppered with dust. His beard was growing and his clothes were beginning to fray. I noticed that he had given up wearing a watch.

I put my hand on his shoulder and said, "Thanks. You're doing a fine job."

"I'm having a good time," he answered, pushing his sunglasses up and sticking the drawknife into the end of the log. "You're all really nice to have me here. Tell you the truth, if you were to say the word, I'd go back to California, tie up my affairs, and return."

I hesitated a moment, one foot on either path. "That's quite an offer," I said at last. "If things were different, I'd say yes. But we're making this video and Tom has his mind set on having our adventure a certain way. Maybe I do, too. I just don't think it would work right now."

"I understand."

I turned down the trail for camp, Shylo and Luke following at my heels. At the river, the south wind was much stronger, gusting over the sparkling water and blasting the flames as I built up the fire and heated the coffeepot, cold beans, and skillet. Smooth, lenticular clouds eddied off the leeward side of mountains—visible standing waves in a river of air. Across the water I noticed the first yellowing poplar leaves.

"I wish I was a dog," Luke said. He was sitting on a bench watching Shylo. She was gazing out over the river, ears attentive, fur rippling like a field of grain in the wind.

"Why?" I asked as I mixed an oat bread and poured it into the hot skillet.

"Dogs are so beautiful and strong. They run fast and they never get tired. If I was a dog, Shylo and I would play together and chase each other."

"You do that now," I said reasonably.

He gave me a withering look. "You know it's not the same."

I had to admit it wasn't. Being flattened several times a day could hardly be compared with running like the wind. Shylo's idea of fun was to hit you unexpectedly from behind at thirty miles an hour.

I sat down near Luke and put my arm about his shoulders. "Has anyone ever told you that these are the best years of your life?"

"No. I don't think so."

"Well, if they do, don't believe them. When I was about your age, someone told me that. But it wasn't true. There are wonders and beauty waiting for you that you can't even imagine. I enjoy life more now than I ever did. My body is a bit rusty, but I like myself more every day. Wait and see. It just gets better."

We watched Shylo. She had wandered onto the delta following her nose. She seemed beautiful, wild, and complete. Luke looked unconvinced.

"I thought you wanted to be a wizard," I said.

"Well, yes. A wizard would be my first choice."

"What would you do if you were a wizard?"

"I'd do things faster."

"Like what?"

"I'd make the cabin go up faster. Fast-forward it, like a video."

"Don't you like building the cabin?"

"We could still build it. We'd just do it at super speed." He waved his arms violently and made a thrumming noise through his teeth.

"You'd fast-forward your life. This is it, you know. Life is just made up of details. Without them there wouldn't be anything."

"Don't you want the cabin up faster?" he asked, his expression puzzled.

"Well, I don't think it would be as satisfying, do you? I mean every time we get one of those big logs in place I feel very proud. I think we'd miss a lot if it was just done. The trick in life is to look for the good in each situation. Sometimes you don't recognize the gifts that life has for you because you want chocolate and it hands you strawberry. Enjoy the strawberry."

"Boy, I'd take either one right now," he said and we both laughed.

I pried the lid off my little black pot and stirred the beans. The pot was an unlovely relic of earlier years. Like a hope chest, I had stored my treasures against the day I might return to the Arctic. Here I was with my ancient backpack, the rifles my mother had taken with us down the Mackenzie River, and my sleeping bag—revamped but worn to a soft rag. I had kept Phil's big Case knife and now carried it in a holster on my belt. I had the same old camera, veteran of capsizing and a thousand miles on foot.

There's something exciting about camping gear. Shabby and stained, it nevertheless evokes a lifestyle and a season when it's pulled—reeking of campfires and wet earth—from the back of the closet. It endures the rugged life and with it I endure as well. Through the years I've abandoned many a beautiful dress but kept my wool jacket.

I glanced fondly about our camp making sure that all was in order. Tom had fashioned a kitchen, mounting the old Topo gas crates as cupboards in a tree. I liked having a shipshape outfit. It put my mind at ease to know that our belongings were safe and that we were ready for the changing moods of the country.

"Did I hear someone say lunch?" Tom asked, as he rounded the trail into view.

"Are the others coming?"

"Right behind me."

"Hot water in the coffeepot. Get yourself some instant coffee or cocoa. Luke, don't eat candy right now. I want you to have a good lunch." He had the trail mix out and was sorting through the container for M&M's.

Tom straddled the bench behind Luke and peered hungrily over his shoulder at the little pile of chocolate he had accumulated. "Oh, thank you," he said, helping himself.

"Hey! Those are mine!"

Tom pretended to eat a candy and then slipped it into Luke's protesting mouth just as Laurie and John came laughing into camp. Tom opened the peanut butter, dipped his knife into it, and thrust it into the trail mix—eating from the point. Laurie joined him with banana chips, scooping up the peanut butter like a dip.

"Don't tell my mother I do this," she whispered.

"Start the beans around, I'm about to turn the bread." Carefully I ran the spatula under it, lifted and flipped. It disintegrated into a steaming mass.

"Omelet cake," Laurie observed. "Just like Mom used to make."

"This stuff's kind of gooey," Tom said, poking suspiciously at the plate I handed him.

"I've got some that's burned and some that's raw," I offered.

"Give it to Laurie," Luke piped. "She'll eat anything."

Laurie had already started on the black beans. Suddenly she spat in disgust. "There's a spider in the beans!" she shrieked in horror.

"Let me see," I asked.

"Oh, I can't look! It's a huge, fat, bloated one. It looks just like the beans!"

"Humm . . . you're right." I extracted the soggy intruder and flung it into the bushes. "Laurie, you really need to make peace with spiders. Nobody else has these problems."

"I'll never eat another bean!"

"The beans aren't the problem, my dear. Does anyone else think we ought to toss these perfectly lovely beans?"

There was a chorus of "Yes!"

"My stomach isn't so great anyway," I admitted, setting aside the contaminated pot. "This dried food just doesn't wear well." It was true. We had all been suffering from stomach problems and seemed to lack energy. Dried food may contain calories, minerals, and vitamins, but lacks something. It has no sunlight in it, no Life. We were all looking forward to hunting season.

THE SATURDAY BEFORE JOHN left we had a grown-up's slumber party. We started the evening with a sing-along around the fire. I began it with our usual rendition of "Another Saturday Night and I Ain't Got Nobody," and Laurie picked it up with "Love Me Tender," crooning into her toothbrush. There was a general grabbing of silverware as Laurie, Luke, and I took the stage for an Elvis binge. John refused to sing and Tom would not be caught singing into a fork.

"I've got a Mr. Microphone and I love it!" Laurie said brightly for the make-believe audience. "Oh, I do hope my dentist isn't watching." She held out her toothbrush for me to speak.

"Laurie has a challenge with over-flossing," I said into the proffered mike. "Not a current problem."

After dinner, I tucked Luke into John's tent with Oliver and his blue blanket. Although he didn't really want to, he had agreed to spend the night alone a few feet away. He requested Shylo, but she refused to be lured into the alien structure and I was afraid she might rip a hole in it trying to exit.

"Don't unzip!" we all yelled when John stooped to enter our tent. "You have to snakey-snake under the door." Three of our four zippers were now defunct, and we were understandably protective of the remaining one.

"Is anybody going to tell him about grown-up pee hour?"

"Nah. We have to maintain some dignity with guests."

"Hey, I want to be treated like a real person," John protested, echoing Luke's earlier argument.

We stayed awake while the light faded, playing poker for M&M's. Laurie kept eating her chips and had to borrow from the bank. Tom, a serious poker player, disapproved of such frivolity. Shylo was horrified that her tent had been invaded by the stranger but stayed on when she discovered the chocolate stakes of the game.

With four adults and a dog inside, the tent was indeed crowded. John did his best to fold up, but there was no denying his size. We played cards and laughed and ate candy until we felt sick. I could hear the morning song of golden-crowned sparrows in the willows along the creek when we curled up beneath the covers of our open down bags.

❦

WE AWOKE TO A cold north wind and scattered clouds. The men set off upstream to fell dead trees. Dressed in wool jacket and cap, I took a turn at lining Luke and the canoe into the wind a mile or more. My feet were numb and I was clumsy and cold before I arrived, stumbling over the slippery stones. There a mat of downed timber had been left by a big ice jam, and we cut and hauled the logs free from the tangle of dead trees. After we built the raft, the men continued upstream to fish at Wandering Slough while Laurie, Luke, and I boarded the raft for home.

"Are you sure you're up for this," Tom asked before we shoved off. Sitting in the middle of the raft, Luke was wearing his yellow life jacket over a heavy wool shirt. I had carried him out to keep his feet dry, but had slipped and fallen, wetting us both. Laurie and I each took a pole and climbed on either end of the awkward craft. It was only a collection of twisted logs bound together with our intertwined slings and stabilized with two sticks lashed across the bottom. A length of rope was tied to one end.

"Yeah, I think we can handle it," I assured him. "You guys have a good time and bring us back some fish for dinner."

"Remember, if you get into trouble, let the raft go. It's just logs and rope," he told me.

"Our logs and our rope," I said stubbornly.

It was exhilarating to scoot over the gray expanse. The logs rode low and water splashed up between the uneven cracks. We could see the bottom sliding by below as the current carried us over riffles and shoals. The wind was still blowing cold from the north, puckering the river and making it hard to read. We did well until we rounded the bend at the rapids above camp. We could not set the heavy raft over, for the current pushed us out and the deep channel gave little purchase for our poles. It became apparent that we would be carried past camp and into the downstream rapids where the river swirled against a cutbank.

Holding one end of the rope, I shucked my wool jacket and jumped into the river. I wished I had brought my life preserver. The water was over my head and I kicked for shore in my clothes and boots. As I hit the end of the forty-foot rope and the weight of the raft, my strength began to wane. I'd been certain I would soon touch bottom. Now I wasn't so sure.

I could see Laurie pushing hard with her pole. Luke was shouting "Go, Mom! Go!" I kicked and kicked, feeling at last the sloping ground beneath my exhausted feet. I staggered out of the river and gallons of water drained from my clothes. That was stupid, I thought. But I made it. Panting for breath, I braced against the rope and watched the raft swing slowly toward shore. Together, Laurie and I walked it up to camp. We worked quickly, untying the logs and hauling them onto the beach while Luke stood chest deep in the river holding the disintegrating raft.

♦♦

IT WAS RAINING THE morning John left. The swallows were gone now, and out on the gray river a pair of loons drifted south, calling to one another in wild, free voices. Slowly, John pulled up stakes and folded away the small tent. In a drizzle he loaded his backpack and set it ready under a tree. As if preparing for the other world, he had put on his watch. I could see him saying good-bye to Laurie down on the beach. They were talking in low tones, their heads close together. He stood in the falling rain in his shirt sleeves and placed his Gore-Tex jacket about her shoulders.

Watching them I felt sad. How often, I wondered, do we limit ourselves by what we are willing to experience? What if we'd been flexible enough to consider John's offer? But we walk only one path at a time, and this was the one we chose.

Around midmorning a small plane appeared out of the low sky. It banked steeply and disappeared through the trees to the south. Ten minutes later we heard him take off. He circled, eyeing our makeshift wind sock of pink ribbons fluttering from a pole, and landed upstream, cutting alarmingly close to the bank as he crabbed into a crosswind. I felt a wave of gratitude to these brave and skillful pilots who risked their lives and planes for us.

Ken was alone. He had put down on a nearby lake to off-load fuel and lighten his takeoff from our short stretch of river. He was obviously uncomfortable with the conditions. Denise had sent mail, mosquito repellent, and an assortment of zippers for the tent.

John hugged each of us good-bye, thanking us for his visit to our world. Luke handed him a long letter to Troy, painfully composed and the first thing of any consequence he had ever written. Laurie had helped him. After Ken stowed the duffel bag aboard, the two men cast off. Working to gain a bit more runway, Ken idled the Cessna into the downstream rapids. We saw him run aground at the bend and could hear the bellow of the engine as he tried to work his way off the stones. Tom raced down the bank to lend a hand, but the plane rocked free.

He angled into the current and we heard him pour on the power. Slowly the little ship gained momentum, blasting past us as it bounced into the windy sky.

Laurie stood in John's red jacket with Luke in her arms. Both of them were waving, their eyes swimming with tears as the plane circled south with a waggle of wings and was gone.

The rest of the day was quiet and thoughtful. Laurie was melancholy and Luke was sad. I too felt the loss. No one spoke much as we worked on the cabin. We seemed suddenly a smaller and more vulnerable group. A gentle rain fell the rest of the day.

CHAPTER 6

The fifth of August and already the air smelled of fall. We had arrived near the solstice, six weeks before, and it was now too dark to read at night. It's hard to grasp how brief the arctic summer really is. Ice is king of these northern latitudes, winter the true temperament of the land.

Hunting season opened in less than three weeks, and then we would need to shift our attention from building to getting in our winter meat. Once they start rutting, bull moose run off most of their summer fat in the ancient rituals of procreation. Domestic animals are never devoid of fat, but wild ones can be. Because truly lean meat has very few calories, it was critical that we hunt once the weather was cool enough for meat to keep.

There were signs that it was going to be an early autumn. It remained cool, though mostly sunny. Blueberries were ripe (what we could find of them), their turning leaves like sprays of tiny rose petals to our knees. More gold showed in the alders across the river. The high peaks were russet ("sunburned" as Luke put it) and birds were flocking up. We often heard their groups rushing like wind through the trees, talking excitedly of the coming migration. The moose too were restless with the advancing season, and we would see them from time to time striding on long legs across the river bars. The trees seemed alive with busy squirrels, claiming territory and storing cones.

A sense of change vibrated the air, building like inaudible music. The land itself was aware, with a consciousness older than thought, dancing in interlocking patterns of perfect symmetry as it celebrated and released the harvest of summer. With the wisdom of millennia, each species embraced autumn and prepared in its own way for the coming cold and dark.

With John's departure the dynamics of our clan shifted again. Perhaps we, like the symphony of life around us, sensed in some dim way that it was time to release our summer roles, for we seemed less jocular and became more tender with one another. We had been brushed by that other world but were no longer a part of it. The contact had only emphasized our isolation. Whatever became of our little band would be entirely up to us. If we were to survive the coming winter, we would need to set aside modern thinking and listen to the deeper wisdom of our beings, learning to harmonize with the cycles of the planet. We could not confront this land with the arrogance of our species, for it was vast and powerful beyond our imagination and cared nothing for our opinions.

The morning after John left, Tom fell ill with a severe migraine. I tucked him into the tent with a cold washcloth over his eyes and he stayed there most of the day. It was sobering to work with Laurie on the unfinished cabin, worrying about Tom.

"When I'm sick I like to be fussed over," I told her as we sat twisting the augers, "but Tom hates it. So I've learned to leave him alone. Still, I'd rather keep an eye on him." Below us, Luke and the invisible Zaza were engrossed in a debate as they swung on the hammock. Shylo was sacked out in the sunlight, snoring loudly.

"You think it's more than a headache?" she asked, raising her gray eyes to mine.

"Mmmm . . . probably not. I keep thinking that his father died of a stroke at fifty and he's only four years short of that. His blood pressure and cholesterol are fine. I'm sure it's nothing."

"Would you use the Emergency Transmitter?"

I sighed. "He wouldn't want me to. I don't know. I try to respect his wishes about his body. We've given one another permission to die and neither of us is afraid of it. More afraid of medical bills than death."

Laurie listened and said nothing. She was willing to express her thoughts but never added anything to mine. It was a freedom that took some getting used to.

"There wouldn't be any point in using it if he died," I went on. We had all agreed on this in principle, but I found it disquieting to consider.

"I guess it depends on how we feel about going on alone," she said thoughtfully. "I think we'd be fine."

"We might have to settle on a smaller cabin. I don't know if the two of us could get those huge ridgepoles up. You and Tom maybe, but not me." It was hard to admit my limitations, but it was true.

"So forget the loft," she shrugged. "We could do it. The main thing I'm concerned about is the chain-saw. Can you run it?"

"Yes . . . but it's been a long time, and I don't know the maintenance. Truthfully, I'm afraid of the damn thing. How about you?"

"I think I could learn," she answered.

It's good to specialize, I thought, but everyone should be competent. My aunt and uncle had told me how they started exchanging skills as they got older, preparing one another for life alone. He showed her how to manage investments and she taught him to cook. It made sense.

I glanced fondly at Laurie. She was thriving, her face open and happy, body tough and limber. A strong walker, she was daily more at home in the woods. I wondered if she was becoming me and I was becoming my mother. Perhaps that was as it should be: that we give away what we have learned and relinquish our roles. Certainly, I was no longer the wild arctic girl I fancied myself. It was painful to watch part of me die, but necessary to the birth of something new. It's unnatural (and in the end fruitless) to deny the next step.

There's always a gift in releasing the past, but it's sometimes hard to recognize. When I became a mother I thought I would expand, superwoman-like, to this new challenge, but pregnancy was hard on me; my body let me down. I discovered my weakness and my great strength. For the first time in my life, I had to ask for help. I had to be vulnerable. Not the lesson I wanted, but the one I needed to become a deeper, more compassionate person.

My thoughts were interrupted by Luke. He was standing below us, blackened coffeepot gripped in both dirty hands.

"May I have grown-up coffee?" he asked.

"No, it wouldn't be good for you and there's none made."

"I already made it," he told me, holding out the pot of cold water to which he had added grounds.

"That's just a waste of coffee," I blurted before I thought.

His face fell. "I made it for everyone," he said.

How quickly we forget our moments of inspiration when confronted with wasted coffee, I thought, shaking my head. "Come on," I said to Laurie. "Maybe it's time we did take a little break. Let's heat up Luke's coffee and have a snack."

To our great relief, Tom was his old self the next day.

❦

THREE DAYS LATER WE set off for more logs. We had cut and yarded the day before and hoped to finish up and raft them home. There was a strong south wind and the temperature hovered in the forties as we climbed the river bluff east of Lake Eugene across from John's Stone. It was a mile from camp, but we had cleaned the snags from the shoreline closer to home. The area looked promising from below but had proved a disappointment, for many of the larger trees were punky or riddled with ant colonies and the smaller ones were very twisted.

An expanse of brilliant autumn colors stretched below us as we topped the bluff and looked back: scarlet alpine berry, blueberry bushes ranging from pink-gold to purple festooned with smoky-blue droplets, scrubby arctic birch of salmon and flame orange, bright yellow poplar, and willow leaves of pale gold edged in red. The river ran turquoise, muskegs were tawny expanses delineated with the somber olive of spruce forests, and the peaks glowed burgundy. Close at hand, lime green moss and pale lichens were laced with bright red-and-green cranberry plants, their berries like enameled jewelry. The sky was clear, but a high, gray smudge stretched along the southern horizon, creeping toward us even as we watched.

"I should be able to drop these downhill," Tom said. "It won't be much fun working on this slope, but they ought to pull easy—if they don't run over us." His eyes were squinted into the wind and his hair and beard whipped about his shoulders.

"I don't like cutting in this wind," I stated.

"Well, I think it'll be okay. It's the river I'm not looking forward to. Where's Luke?"

"Sliding down the cutbank. Laurie is down there."

We stepped near the edge and could see eighty feet down to the water. Luke had climbed the steep hill and onto the loose cut. "Luke, that's dangerous!" I bawled into the wind. And hard on your pants, I thought. "Don't climb so high!"

"It is not!" he yelled and launched himself on his bottom in a cascade of dirt and stones.

Tom shook his head and turned away, angry at Luke's defiance. I felt a wave of sadness. I could love my family, but I couldn't direct their lives. Not even Luke's.

"There are ducks on Horseshoe Lake," Tom said, pointing east across the river. "Want me to try to get a couple for dinner?" He was observant and often the first to spot wildlife. He seemed at home in this country, looking wild and somewhat aloof, as if he had traveled a step beyond the need for companionship.

I shook my head. "It's a shame to kill them for such a small amount of food."

"You're probably right, but I'm sure tired of beans."

"It won't be long before we have moose." Somehow it was easier to justify killing something big that would feed us a long time. I grinned at him sheepishly. "I'm an old softy, aren't I?"

Tom smiled gently at me and nodded.

That set me to wondering about how we measure life. Why would a moose be more important than a duck or rabbit? They have the same components, only one is obviously larger. If size factors in worth, do we value an adult over a child? A corporation over a human?

I turned away from the view and set off to scout for dead trees. Soon the whine of Tom's saw marked his progress along the bluff. I followed, balancing on the steep slope as I limbed the felled trees. The butts of several were riddled with ant colonies. Tom had cut the nest sections free and carefully replaced them on top of their stumps, capping each with a little hat of sod.

Earlier in the summer I had pulled one of these honeycombed logs over to the cabin site. When Tom sawed it into sitting stumps, giant carpenter ants boiled out. Thinking they would infest our home, we set the stumps over the fire. Several quarts of pearly eggs fell while the frantic ants tried to rescue their brood and the smell of burning flesh soiled the air. Since then we had honored ant trees. The fate of an ant isn't the issue, I decided, but what it does to us when we approach the miracle of life without respect. If we carelessly wipe out another being, dismissing it as unimportant, we spiritually impoverish ourselves.

By the time we took our lunch break the sky was gray overhead and our patch of blue was being pushed north up the valley. A cold wind kicked spray off the river, blasting our cheerless fire and blowing sand into our eyes. After a hasty lunch we decided to take what we had and go home. I gathered up tools and loaded the canoe while Tom and Laurie hefted logs over the slippery rocks and into the icy river, allowing me to keep my feet dry. I wasn't looking forward to paddling the empty canoe into the wind, and I knew they would be miserable on the raft.

"I'll try to get down through the rapids first in case you need help getting to shore," I said as they shoved the raft into the gray current and stepped aboard, poles in hand.

"Don't worry about us," Tom answered. "You'll have all you can manage with the canoe."

"Come on, Luke," I called. "I'm gonna need your help paddling. Shylo! It's a long swim home girl. Better join us." I tied Shylo behind the first thwart and put Luke in the bow with his short paddle.

"How come I never get to steer?" he asked.

It was a rough trip home. Like a giant leaf, the canoe spun in the wind, carried this way and that by the blasting air. It took all my strength to control it. Fortunately, the wind didn't affect the heavy raft, and Tom and Laurie arrived home safely long before us. We were all cold by the time we had the logs pulled up on the bank beside our camp. It was to be our last trip.

❦

THE NEXT DAY TOM and I were examining a stockpile of logs near the cabin. "Okay, so what about these two?" I said, pointing out a modest pair as roof supports for the utility room. The ones I indicated were smaller than I wanted for purlins, but an acceptable compromise. "They need to be strong enough to hold up the snow."

"They will be. Look, it's only a ten-foot span."

"Okay," I nodded. "I'll skin them." It had been the same over the loft, me insisting that the supports be large and higher than our heads, Tom wanting to just get them up. I had a tendency to overbuild, but I was sure the effort would pay off.

It was late afternoon and had been overcast much of the day, but now the sun slanted toward the mountains and streaked brightly beneath the layer of dove gray, illuminating the autumn colors in an almost unnatural radiance. Across the river, Mount Laurie stood forth in black silhouette, but the foreground was a blaze of yellow, green, and red. From the forest below I could hear Luke and Laurie as they collected sphagnum moss for chinking. Large cracks showed between the logs of our new home, and one might justifiably call it a "moss cabin," the logs forming only a framework. Moss was plentiful and with careful gathering would not be harmed by our harvest.

"Okay," I heard Laurie say reasonably as they climbed the bench toward me, "do you want me to help you carry it?" Up the trail they trudged, each with a large duffel bag of moss. Laurie had hers on one shoulder. Luke seemed upset and was yanking his along the ground. Perhaps the strain of our long efforts and lack of a home was telling on him, but he had been volatile of late, angry and demanding even with Laurie.

"No! I want to do it myself!" he snapped. As she turned again he kicked the bag and yelled, "You're just stupid!"

Generally I allowed them their own relationship, but Laurie was so gentle there were times I felt obliged to step in. "That's enough, Luke," I informed him, reaching for the bag. He began to hop with rage, yanking the strap from my hand. "Stop!" I commanded. "You are very close to a smack!" Furiously he kicked the bag. In one gesture I pulled him forward and delivered several whacks to the dusty seat of his pants.

"You have no right to hit me!" he glared. "It's my body and no one has a right to touch it without my permission!"

"That's true, but sometimes I don't know what else to do. I can't allow one little kid to terrorize three adults. Are you going to settle down?"

"No!"

I gathered up my furious, kicking son and sat on a log while he struggled in my arms. His eyes filled with hurt and he whispered violently, "Don't make me cry in front of her! She's not part of the family!"

"Yes, she is," I informed him. "For the next year, this is the only family we've got. You better start taking better care of your Laurie. You need her. We all do."

I held him until his enraged struggles ceased. Laurie had seated herself cross-legged on the ground and was chinking between the bottom logs, tongue sticking out the corner of her mouth in concentration as she packed the damp moss with a wedge-shaped tool Tom had fashioned from wood.

"You have a right to your feelings," I told Luke, "and you have a right to express them. But you don't get to abuse anyone. You don't get to scream at people or hit them. Can I release you now?"

"Uh-huh."

Luke walked away with as much dignity as he could muster and took refuge in the hammock with his imaginary friends. Then he moved to where Shylo was napping on the sawdust pile and began covering her with wood shavings until she got up and left. After awhile I saw him laughing with Laurie, teasing her to blow on his tummy as he rolled in the moss beside her.

My eyes swept the clearing and the mahogany hills. Everywhere, alpine berries were arrayed in scarlet, and blueberry bushes were layered in shades of pink and purple. This was the day Phil and I had stopped walking upriver and started work on a cabin twenty years before. How glad I was that ours was now nearing completion! By next August, I thought, I will have spent six summers watching this river go by and nine (that I could remember) in northern wilderness. That was a significant part of my life. For Luke it would be four of his seven, an even bigger percentage.

It was getting late and we soon called it a day, stacking our tools in a corner of the cabin and trudging down the familiar trail to camp for a dinner of applesauce and bean burritos spiced with powdered cheese. We found comfort in our simple, familiar routines. A certain blue plastic cup was always used to mix the powdered milk, and an old margarine container held leftover oatmeal from the morning. Each person had favorite branches for socks and a place in the pavilion for rain gear or jacket.

"It's important to know where things are as the season advances," I told my crew as we gathered about our evening fire. "It's getting dark nights, and one of these mornings we'll wake to snow on the ground. If we mislay a tool we may not find it until spring."

Soon conversation turned (as it often did now) to hunting. Dredging up my mother's advice and my own experiences, I shared what I knew of shooting, animal habits, and butchering. Tom had hunted squirrels and rabbits as a youth, but Laurie had never fired a gun until she arrived in the Arctic. Tom had set up a target and taught her the basics of each gun in camp, and she proved to be a decent, though hesitant, shot.

"A moose looks big," I told them, "but your actual target isn't. The head is mostly sinus cavities, muscle, and bone with a brain the size of an orange. If you aim for the spinal cord in neck or back, you must hit a relatively small area. The middle is all guts. Your best shot is six inches up from the belly just behind the point of the elbow—where the heart and lungs are. Even so, don't expect him to drop right away. It takes awhile for an animal that size to die.

"Look for a big, fat bull," I went on. "A good animal will give us twice the meat of a poor one. It's surprising how much we'll eat in a year. We may have to take two, but we can decide that after we get the first one. They'll be traveling soon, and if we're out, we'll run into them."

"Do you think we'll get any caribou?" Laurie asked.

"It's hard to say. We may see the edge of the migration around November, but we can't count on it. We'll need to get our moose in September. I wish we had a meat house up."

"Are you worried about bears?" she asked me.

I hesitated. "I'd sure hate to have to shoot one," I answered truthfully. "Grizzlies are rare—not here perhaps, but in general. We'll hang the meat high in the trees and hope the bears will be denning soon. I've never had a problem with them, though many people have."

"What about wolves?" Laurie wanted to know.

"No problem unless they find the moose before we get it all home. They're big eaters, but they're shy. The main trick will be to kill our animal upstream and near enough to retrieve easily. Moose are really heavy. And as my mother told me, never shoot one in the water or you'll have to stand there and butcher; you're not going to move it. They tend to run toward water, and I have butchered two in this river. I never want to again."

"I was just thinking of what it'll be like to eat solid food again," Laurie said. "On our gums."

"Haven't you eaten meat before?" Luke asked.

"Oh, sure. Not moose meat, but I've eaten lots of meat."

"That really gets stuck in your gums," he informed her.

Tom and Laurie were seated together on a bench sharing a bowl of rehydrated applesauce while I sat near the fire cooking tortillas in the cast-iron skillet. Luke was quietly removing "special" pieces of firewood from the pile and stashing them in his "fort." Those streaked with rose, he said, were too beautiful to burn. Shylo watched with keen interest, and when his back was turned, I saw her making off with the prized sticks.

"I miscalculated on the nails," Tom informed us. "I'm going to run short before I finish the floor."

"I suppose you could dowel it," I suggested.

"I may have to, but that's a lot of work."

"There are a few nails over at the Topo Camp," Laurie offered.

"I was thinking of that. Want to head over after dinner and maybe do a little fishing down at Pike Slough?" he asked her.

"But we're going to play poker tonight!" Luke interjected. He was becoming a fairly good player, though unwilling to bet with candies, so we had switched to pumpkin seeds. Shylo liked poker because she thought there would be M&M's, but quickly lost interest with the new stakes.

"We did say that," I agreed.

"Shhh! Shhh!" Tom suddenly froze and we all followed his gaze onto the delta. A large grizzly was rolling toward us, wind ruffling his coppery coat. He had appeared as if by magic within forty yards of where we sat. We held our breaths, delighted and perhaps a bit apprehensive to see this beautiful apparition. Within moments he sensed us, and with remarkable speed, turned and vanished into the willows.

"You see, Luke. There are bears here," I told him as if solidifying my point. However, it wasn't long before I saw him start for the bar to investigate.

After dinner we set large kettles of water over the grill to heat for baths. It was too cold now to brave the river, and we took turns in the galvanized washtub. We had a lovely view, and bathing tended to be a more prolonged and enjoyable time. There were still mosquitoes and we helped one another by pouring water over the head and back to keep the bather warm and protected from bites. Tom usually went first, for he valued clean water. Laurie and I weren't as fussy, preferring the fuller tub as new water was added. Luke was always last, remaining immersed with his toys until the bath nearly iced over.

"I think you can stop losing weight now," I told Tom as I washed his back. He was proud to have taken up five notches on his belt, but he was beginning to look as thin and sinewy as Gandhi, the muscles in his arms and legs standing out in ropes. It hardly seemed fair that I was still buxom while my companions had changed dramatically. Laurie belonged on the cover of a bodybuilding magazine, but I thought Tom looked a bit gaunt and wild. His long hair and beard were stringy, and without clothes his sun-weathered head seemed a bit large for his white body.

"Look! Geese!" said Laurie softly.

Tom reached for his glasses and we all turned to watch. Into view drifted a small family, rafting quietly downriver. The young were almost the size of their parents and all of them were molting and unable to fly. When they spotted us they pulled back, paddling like tiny kayaks into an eddy to confer. It thrilled me to see their brave little expedition, so much like our own, but without possessions or home. I couldn't view them as flying drumsticks. Geese mate for life and may live thirty years. They travel in families and rely on the wisdom of elders during their migrations. I silently wished them well on their long journey.

Luke stood watching, one hand unconsciously working a loose tooth. "It came out!" he said in dismay. He thrust the tiny pearl at Tom and beamed, showing a new gap in his lower jaw. "Can I put it under my pillow for the Tooth Fairy?"

Tom held out his hand and examined the worn incisor. "Why that's wonderful, Luke! Let's see the hole." Gently he wiggled the neighboring tooth. "Wow, looks like there's another one loose. Want me to try and pull it?"

"No!" Luke answered, backing hastily. "I'm saving it. There's steam coming off your head, Dad. Can you see it? Let me pour more water over you."

I put the tooth in a film can and Luke carefully tucked it under his pillow that evening as he settled in for the night.

"Do you think she'll bring me a quarter?" he asked.

"It's hard to say about fairies," I warned. "They're very capricious. That means unpredictable. And if she brought a quarter, you wouldn't be able to spend it. We'll just have to wait and see. Maybe you'll get moose dropping or something."

He looked appalled. "You really think so?"

"No. I was just kidding. I'm sure it'll be something nice."

"Mama, I am lonely out here," he confided.

"I know." I smoothed the hair back from his eyes.

"I've been making puzzles," he told me. "I smash rocks until they break into pieces, then I try to put them back together again."

"I think it's neat the way you invent things," I said. Life out here was hard for him, I knew, but there was a gift too. I thought of his little friends who were already miniature Yuppies. They didn't dig holes or nail sticks together. It seemed to me that there was a kind of childhood poverty amid the opulence.

"And I have my dog," he went on. "She's so playful and I really love her. She's like a sister to me. She bites me and hurts me, but she loves me anyway. Don't you Shylo?" He sat up and threw his arms around her furry neck. She endured his embrace as the price exacted for her spot in the tent, but there was no affection in her eyes.

That night we saw the full moon for the first time. It rose late in the evening, pale as winter butter and big in a southern sky that spread mint green behind black clouds. In the Arctic, the moon is up for two weeks and gone for two. During the summer there's only a sliver that one rarely notices in the bright sky. Winters are the time of full moons, and the soft light is most welcome when the sun has gone from the land.

We had arisen for a nocturnal visit and stood a long moment watching. A touch of ice was in the wind and about us the darkening wilderness loomed vast, silent, and suddenly unfamiliar. I thought of bears as I shivered in my bare feet and night clothes, and of how dependent I was on vision. I'd grown used to the constant light and now felt vulnerable in this strange, new world.

LUKE WOKE US EARLY with excited cries. The good fairy had left a small toy under his pillow.

We erected the stove in our roofless cabin that day. It was a makeshift system, but out of the wind, and it now served us better than the fire. Tom was hard at work on the floor. He had fashioned a simple jig for holding short logs while he ripped them using the hand-eye coordination gained through years of cutting glass. Unaware that our little chain-saw was designed for pruning small branches, and could not (according to the manufacturer) be used for such a purpose, he slowly chewed logs into lumber. We hoped it would hold up, for we needed 450 square feet of floor and loft, plus boards for furniture.

Tom was on his knees, planing and fitting his hard-won floor "boards" onto the joists. Luke was busy with his new toy under the shelter of our unfinished loft. It would be seven feet wide extending the length of the cabin. We had set the first planks as scaffolding for work on the west wall. Laurie and I were setting the gable logs. Each level was won with great effort now. It had turned colder, and a gray drizzle made the icy logs slippery and treacherous. Perched high on the exposed walls, Laurie looked frightened and grim as she drilled the endless holes that would pin the gable logs in place. These stood alone above the sides, so the twelve-foot-high gables seemed fragile and rocked somewhat with our movements.

"I have to remember to breathe," I said as I balanced to drive in a dowel with the back of my ax. "I think that's why I get so tired."

Laurie managed a weak smile.

"One more pin, Kiddo, and we set the last purlin and then the ridgepole."

Tom and I had placed the first purlin the day before, each rolling an end

J. Aspen 94

of the huge log slowly up the gables. Although I was unable to lift it with my arms, I could brace my knees under the log and use my leg muscles. It was very tricky with nothing to hang on to. Despite her fear of heights, Laurie had climbed ahead of us to film the process.

"I don't think I can lift the ridgepole," I confessed.

"The ominous log," Laurie intoned, looking down at it.

"Hey, I almost had Jeanie talked into letting me make it into lumber," Tom called up from his work. He paused to remove his glasses and wipe sweat from his eyes.

"What talked her out of it?"

By afternoon heavy rain forced us to retreat to the tent. There we sat amid damp folds of down and played poker as evening fell. The temperature was in the thirties and the tent felt clammy in the wet air. Outside, a double rainbow spanned our valley arching into the gold of balsam poplars across the river.

The following day we hauled both the final purlin and the massive ridgepole onto the gables and notched them in place. It was a long awaited milestone, much talked about and feared, and it completed the main structure of the cabin. I brought up the purlin with Tom, but Laurie did the big one. It was all she could do to manage it, and I could see her strain to the limit of her strength as she slowly worked her end up the swaying gable logs. I held my breath watching her lift, her muscles quivering and knees shaking as she fought for balance on the high, slippery wall. When she was safely on the ground again, she burst into tears and threw her arms around us. We each have our demons, and I believe putting up that ridgepole was the bravest thing Laurie did all year.

❧

"It's going to freeze tonight," I said as I crawled from the tent the next morning and sniffed the air. There was an autumn clarity about the day that spoke of dropping temperatures.

Gathering my boots and socks, I left the trees for the sunlit kitchen area and sat down on a stump. Thoughtfully, I rubbed my stiff hands together and worked the fingers. Like Tom's, my hands had deteriorated. He now wore a wrist brace during the day and a splint at night. Even Laurie complained of nerve problems in her arms and hands. It was difficult for me to perform small movements like writing in my journal. My legs were strong and my balance good on the walls, but it was painful to climb them and it often took all my strength to pull myself up.

Most of our summer birds were suddenly gone. I had felt the emptiness of the forest the last few days. It was time, I knew, but their going left a void in my heart. The winter birds were still here—the ravens, chickadees, crossbills, and gray jays—but the gay crowd had departed. As I laid the fire, a great wedge of migrating geese spread the autumn sky, coming low and fast down the valley. They swept over me with a haunting cry of wild voices, and I felt a tightness in my throat. I could imagine our camp pass swiftly beneath my outspread wings and hear my own call, ringing back through the ages.

That evening, Laurie was French braiding my hair as we sat before the fire. We had just finished a dinner of curried rice and were watching a storm play over Flattop, beautiful and grand in the evening light. Cradling Luke in his arms, Tom was telling a story from his childhood.

"This is why we decided not to bring a tape deck," I told Laurie after Tom finished. "I wanted to make our own music, play games, and tell stories. It's a lost family art."

"At first I missed home," she admitted. "It's strange not to be able to pick up a phone and call someone. But our family here, and this country . . ." She let the sentence trail off.

I nodded. "You can't get out, you know," I said, half-seriously. "You'll go back, but you'll never be the same."

"It's too bad more people couldn't experience this," she said.

"Most wouldn't want to," I told her.

Tom was nodding. "People will say, 'Wasn't it cold?' or 'Tell me about Alaska,' and there's nothing you can answer. It's like meeting God. You can't communicate about that. It teaches on some level beyond language."

"Maybe each of us seeks meaning in a different way," I said. "People can share an experience and yet come to totally different conclusions. The key for me is to see life as a spiritual quest. You choose, step forward, and let go."

"Choosing makes a big difference," Tom agreed. "What's the difference between the guy who's lost everything and the man who gives his possessions to the poor? Nothing outwardly. Just choice."

"I'm glad John had a chance to see it, just a little while," Laurie said wistfully. "I feel like he knows me in a way he couldn't have otherwise."

"That's one reason I wanted to share it with Tom and Luke," I told her. I glanced at Tom and he smiled.

We were silent, listening to the fire. I noticed a sudden shift in the air. The storm seemed to be approaching rapidly from the north, burying Flattop as it came. There was an unusual aggressiveness about it, and I stepped down to the river for a better look. Just then, the first wind struck. We hurried to secure camp and get into the tent as the air filled with flying crystals. Darkness drew on and the wind passed, but the temperature continued to drop. All through the night I could hear the faint tick of snowflakes against the tarp. It was August 17.

❦

LUKE WAS DELIGHTED WITH the white world that greeted us next morning. Shylo seemed subdued. Although she had yet to see a winter, she recognized it from the core of her being. I knew this first snow wouldn't last, but it was a warning and I was up before the sun.

The day was clear and still, the land obscured and transformed under sparkling white. It was well that we had counted our tools each night: three axes, the maul, two augers, three large slings, three small, two drawknives, and bow saw. I dusted off the grill and grubbed about in the cold fluff for the coffeepot and skillet, then started our morning fire.

We were all in great spirits. Luke worked splitting wood with the eight-pound maul while Laurie and I skinned poles for the roof. Tom was busy with the floor. There was still a great deal to do and it was difficult to know which way to divide our energy. We needed a couple hundred poles for the roof, and formed expeditions into the wetlands southeast of the cabin to gather small dead trees. Luke was eager to help and managed to chop through a number of them unassisted.

That evening Tom and Laurie visited Pike Slough by way of the Topo Camp, returning with six grayling and a can of nails. I helped them clean the fish, but the water was so cold it made my hands burn. Laurie was as happy as a kid on Christmas morning with the windfall of nails she had pulled, and settled onto a bench before the fire to straighten them.

❦

THOUGH THE PEAKS REMAINED white, snow soon disappeared from the low country and our world reverted to a patchwork of autumn colors. We celebrated the entire week that Laurie turned twenty-nine, cooking special treats and doing small kindnesses to make her feel loved. We sang "Happy Birthday" and ate poppyseed cake with hard sauce and shared the last of the apricots on pancakes for breakfast. She cried when she opened the surprise present from her mother.

Laurie was doing most of the rafter skinning while I hauled the poles home. My hands were too painful and weak to use the drawknife for very long. Tom was deep into the floor, needing to permanently set the stove before we put on the main roof. Once Laurie had enough rafters skinned, it only took a few hours to place them over the utility room. The next day we covered them with a plastic tarp and laid a roof of sod. Not wanting to disturb the ground, we cut sod some distance away, from a bank that was collapsing into the river. Tom fashioned a stretcher of poles and we carried the turves between us.

"Isn't it beautiful!" we said to one another as we stood outside the front door in the blue shadows of evening looking at the new sod roof over our utility room. Crowberry and kinnikinnick sprouted in a colorful quilt—a bit of the ground transported above our heads. A small, solid-looking room had emerged from our log corral. It seemed dark, damp, and very quiet, like entering a cave, and I secretly wondered if I would enjoy being so closed in. I found that it depressed as well as exhilarated me to step inside, the first "inside" we had known in two months.

"Now we have a place to get out of the rain," I said aloud. "If we had to, we could live here."

"I don't want to move in until we have most of the interior work done," Tom told us. "We'll just be in our own way. Tomorrow I'll cut the gables to the correct pitch and we can get started on the main cabin roof."

"It's a real work of art," Laurie said, as if she didn't quite believe it.

"It is," Tom agreed.

"Every log is so beautiful, so different," she went on. "And I love what you're doing with the door between the rooms. Who'd have thought to cut it into an arch?"

Tom grinned. "I'm happy we didn't just slap something up, but I'll be glad to get inside. You know, we've only taken three days off since we started? And we spent those walking."

"I want to acknowledge that this hasn't been easy for Luke," I said, drawing him close. "You're a brave kid. We're going to have a real home soon. Can you imagine it now?"

"Sort of," he answered doubtfully. "Walls and door. But it doesn't look very cozy." Slits of light showed between the upper logs and open holes gaped black where the windows and door would be. I had to agree that it looked far from inviting.

"Not yet, but it will," I reassured him. "Wait 'til we finish chinking and Daddy gets the floor in. That'll make it seem a lot lighter inside. Are you happy to be here?"

"Well, I'm glad to be away from Billy, that big, mean kid at my school."

I laughed. "It'll be more fun once we can take some time off."

"I'm going down to the beach to start taking my time off right now," Luke decided.

"Please don't go out of sight. We'll be working up here a little longer. Maybe you could pick some berries nearby. I'll make a blueberry bread."

"Ohhh, that sounds good," Laurie added. "Let me put my tools up and I'll go picking with you."

❦

Tom took time from crafting the floor to chisel windowsills and make frames for the two south windows in the utility room. Most of our windows would be eighteen by thirty-six inches. Eventually they would be double glazed, but for now keeping rain out was the main concern.

I worked chinking the utility room and hauling rafter poles home. Laurie was still skinning them and, uncomplaining workhorse that she was, had started to look discouraged. The long grind was beginning to wear us all down. We were weary and seemed to move slowly and ineffectually. Luke whined and was out of sorts, often hurting himself by falling over logs or egging the dog on until she bit him. We were in need of a rest but feeling too pressed for time to take one.

"Getting burned out?" I asked Laurie. It was drizzling again. She had on my black-and-white wool jacket, her hat pulled low, leather gloves cold and soggy.

"Skinners burnout," she joked. "Nasty stuff."

"You can trade places with me if you like."

"What are you up to?"

"I've been digging the toilet."

"Ah! You really know how to tempt a girl," she said, moving her hands as if weighing two exciting propositions.

"What about lunch then?"

"Better all the time."

We gathered about the stove in the roofless cabin, holding our fingers to the faint heat. The damper was merely laid on top of the pipe and the stove didn't draw well. Laurie and Luke were singing "Froggy Went a Courtin'." I lifted the lid from the skillet and carefully worked the spatula under the blueberry bread and flipped. "I turned it! Did you see?" I said, triumphantly.

"No, can you do it again?" Laurie asked.

"Yes. Tomorrow."

"Boy, is that crust black," Luke commented.

"I like it that way," I answered. Just then, sunlight pierced the clouds and the falling rain became a million diamonds. Laurie burst out singing "Here Comes the Sun," while Luke and I smiled up at the spreading sky.

"We need a ladder for the loft," Tom observed as I passed around the tin plates. "Once we chink these walls, we won't be able to climb them."

"I hadn't thought of that," I admitted.

A few minutes later the clouds ripped open. Hard rain pelted steadily and there was nothing to do but retreat to the tent. We remained there for two days while the forest became soggy and the thick moss soaked up water like a sponge. The steady drum of rain on the tarp was accented by the deep growl of the river and creek as they rose and rose in a wild, muddy torrent.

At first we slept a good deal, recovering from our days of labor. We were packed like cordwood within the cold, damp tent, needing to turn over practically in tandem. Tom usually slept on his back, sometimes with a head on each shoulder. He suffered with his arms and a wrist injury so that his hands were often asleep at night. I had back and arm problems and lay on my side, usually with my knees in Tom's ribs. Luke sprawled, arms and legs flopped out and body often turned sideways. Shylo took up the foot space. Only Laurie was a gentle and reasonable bed partner. She fit into a depression known as "Laurie's Hollow," and because of the contours of the ground, was not able to roll far.

As the downpour continued I made quick forays to bring in cold oatmeal, yesterday's applesauce, and leftover cornbread with peanut butter. It was soggy and unpleasant fare and we swallowed it without ceremony, crouched in our small sanctuary. When these ran out, we lived on trail mix and powdered milk. And still the rain fell. I read aloud to Luke from Kipling's *Jungle Books* while the others napped. Then Laurie entertained him from a large volume of *Calvin and Hobbes*.

It was fairly sophisticated humor, but Luke was captivated. Calvin was destined to become a major hero and Luke learned to recite every line. Soon he was reading it to himself and telling us endless Calvin jokes. It's alarming to have a six-year-old enamored with a role model of this caliber, but I was pleased at his new interest in reading.

The storm lifted just enough the second evening for me to get a fire started and fix a hot supper. It drizzled while we ate, but I managed to cook extra in case we should need it later. We returned to the damp tent as black night and more rain descended.

CHAPTER 7

It's better to get up and face the weather than lie here another day," I said as I shoved the reluctant dog under the tent flap and crawled after her into a quiet rain. "I'm going up to the cabin. I'll call you when the stove is lit." One becomes lethargic and depressed imprisoned in a cold tent eating trail mix. Even if we couldn't work, I knew we'd be better off outside.

The river was at our door, higher than I had ever seen it here. An icy flood of roiling, muddy water buried the whole delta. Big trees hurried past, ripped from banks upstream, and I clearly heard the roar of Luke's Creek; it would be days before we could cross it. So much for moose hunting, I thought. Three of the four quadrants were now closed to us, and in the remaining direction lay dense thickets. We may as well put all our efforts into getting a roof on, I decided. Besides, we needed to handle our lives here before we undertook anything else.

The view from camp was grand and awesome in its power. To the north, Flattop emerged white and clear above the pearl-gray clouds that massed along the lower ridges. I stood transfixed, watching the tendrils of fog curl down the slopes and dissolve. Above me, clouds scudded, a gray-and-gold river of sky glistening with shafts of sunlight as they melted into one another. Winter was rushing down from the pole to reclaim its land. Across the valley the country lay wet and somber, painted in tones of yellow, brown, and olive green.

The stove was full of water and charred wood; the cabin was a dismal mess. After I got a fire going, we stood about the smoldering stove, holding stiff fingers to the lukewarm metal in the rain. We breakfasted on cold oatmeal and powdered milk, and then Tom and I climbed the slippery logs to nail a tarp over the ridgepole for shelter. Gradually, we picked up our work, shaping wet boards and skinning soggy logs. The river was still rising. I kept checking on it and finally pulled our canoe higher into the woods. Luke expressed concern that our camp might be washed away, but I assured him we were safe. As the afternoon wore on, the clouds began to lift and ragged blue holes appeared in the sky. By evening it was freezing and almost clear.

J. ASPEN 94

For the next few days we worked in a fever, skinning and placing the rafters—butting them against a retainer log doweled in place outside of the plate log, then nailing and tying them down with wire. Tom and I balanced on the slanted roof while Laurie handed up poles and bags of moss. I chinked where the rafters crossed the gables and plate logs, making as tight a seal as possible before we covered them with plastic. The roof was high, and the steep front pitch made for difficult work. I was afraid the sods would slide off, so I cut two long poles and Tom secured them horizontally over the slippery rafters.

For two days we laid the sod. It drizzled as we cut the muddy squares of turf from the riverbank, carried them to the cabin, relayed them up the ladder, and carefully placed them on the plastic tarp over the rafter poles. Luke was amazingly strong and persistent as he helped. It was a heroic group effort, and finally the main roof was safely covered.

Tom returned to his work on the floor and finished enough to permanently position the stove. Centrally located, it stood on cast-iron legs over the smooth, yellow bit of floor, a foot above the icy ground. From its top emerged a short piece of stovepipe and then the lovely sheet metal oven that my sister's fiancé had built. Shaped like a flattened donut set on edge, the oven captured heat from the smoke. The back was covered, and on the front was a hinged door and thermometer. Above it, the pipe with damper rose to pierce the roof.

"It's fun to make do with what you have," Tom said as he nailed flashing made from an old gas can over the purlin to shield it from the heat of the stovepipe. He was perched on a log wedged between my new ladder and the half-finished loft. He whistled as he happily banged away. He was a good whistler and I enjoyed listening to him. Nearby, Laurie was using the jack plane, smoothing the ripped logs into boards with a rhythmic scraping sound. It was cold inside and Luke was dressed in his wool coat and cap. Crouched on the small section of completed floor, he was building a helicopter from Legos. From the doorway Shylo watched him for a chance to make off with the toys, but he kept a close eye on her.

I was balanced on a crate, packing moss between the upper logs. I felt weary from the long push. The cabin seemed far from inviting with its dark, muddy floor transected with shin-high joists. I was tired of the rain and of cold, wet feet. It seemed weeks since I had taken a bath or put on clean clothes.

"I'm gonna quit early and go hunting," Tom stated, driving home the last nail and swinging to the ground. Meat was still the great unknown in our welfare and we were apprehensive. Now that we could again cross the creek, we went forth day after day.

"It's kind of late," I told him. "If you get one we'll have to stay up all night butchering."

"But at least we'd have it."

"Can I light a fire in the stove now?" I asked. "Maybe dry the place out a bit?" We had discontinued using it to lay the roof.

"Not until tomorrow. I want the putty to set up first."

"I was hoping to take a hot bath. It seems like forever since my feet have been warm. I'm just feeling all in."

"Miss Jeanie," Laurie said kindly, "I'll be happy to build a fire outside and bring up the water for you to have a bath."

"Would you? Oh, that would mean a lot. I'm kind of down right now. I think a bath would do me good, even if I put on the same clothes. My hair is full of dirt from placing the sods."

"Let's all have one," Tom suggested. "It is late for hunting. I'll get the water, Laurie, if you start the fire out front. It's too nasty down on the beach."

"It's gonna be inconvenient hauling water up here," I said.

"Oh, we'll get used to that," Tom told me. "It's seeing the river that I'm gonna miss."

We were all silent, thinking of the living river that had flowed through our lives for a summer, as much a part of us as breathing.

"Well," I sighed, "we can always move down in the spring." Here we were, I thought, anxious to inhabit our new cabin and already planning to abandon it for a tent.

❧

TOM AND LAURIE SET out hunting at first light the next morning. I could hear the squirrel alarms across the river, marking their progress toward Pike Slough. Laurie was unsure of herself and they traveled together along the dry river channels between the gold avenues of poplar and dark strips of spruce forest. Shylo always stayed close to me so I was not concerned that she would follow them.

Luke and I crawled from the tent after they had gone. The day was still, the sky clear. Cold sunlight streamed bright across the gliding river. There was heavy frost on the beach and yesterday's tracks were frozen. As I made breakfast, Luke played near the water, prying up thin slabs of sandy ice with red fingers and tasting them.

"Yuck," he intoned as he bit into the gritty ice. He handed it to the dog and tried another. "I can hardly wait for it to snow," he told me. "I hope it gets really deep so I can make tunnels."

Arriving at the cabin, I lit the stove, delighted to discover that the oven doubled the usable heat. Despite the gaping door and window holes, and dearth of chinking in the upper walls, our home began to warm and dry. I took off my coat for the first time in days. An amber, woody light suffused our new shelter and I looked around contentedly. It had changed dramatically with the addition of a roof. Even Luke could see the potential. The floor was growing daily and four unusually large and straight-grained boards leaned against the wall, destined to be our kitchen counter. However, there was still a great deal to do before we could really move in. It was no longer pleasant down by the river. Despite Tom's protests, we had almost abandoned our old kitchen, so life was now complicated with possessions underfoot. Gradually the damp, awkward spaces between the joists had filled with wooden crates, buckets of food, camera equipment, and garbage cans of clothing. Not wishing to leave our things unattended, we were slowly transferring the tonnage inside. We still slept in the cold, cramped tent, but with the loft nearing completion, I couldn't imagine doing it much longer.

Humming to myself, I mixed bread and let it rise in a bucket hung from the ridgepole, a surprise lunch for my two hunters who had breakfasted on cold leftovers. I was pleased at the way my new ladder had turned out. Building it had been hard on my wrists, but left me with a feeling of competence. I was reminded of something Laurie had said about the joy of appreciating things. What profit a man if he should gain the whole world and not value it? In part, it was this very austerity that I wanted for my son, and through it, the ability to cherish life.

THE FOLLOWING MORNING, TOM and I set out early. We paddled upstream above the creek mouth where he let me out before crossing the river to walk the far shore. He wanted to hunt together, feeling perhaps protective of me; I preferred being alone, my attention on the country. So we compromised, taking separate routes but keeping in touch.

I buttoned my wool jacket, glad to have dry feet for the moment. It had been drizzling at dawn, but the rain seemed to be lifting. Glowing like embers with sunrise, buttermilk clouds rode the long ridge to the east. Above me the sky was mottled pink and blue like handblown glass. I caught a glimpse of Tom as I entered the willows.

Fall colors were fading after the hard frost, and spruce cones cut by the squirrels had opened. The scarlet of bearberries had turned to rust, and arctic birch had gone from flame to brown. Everywhere leaves were withering and dropping in a quiet rain of gold. The sharp smell of autumn brought back memories older than thought as I quietly followed the curve of the beach. Moose were on the move, and I could see their deep tracks crisscrossing the damp mud. It was time to hunt: the smells told me so. Before my conscious memory began, my father had carried me on his shoulders through the falling leaves to butcher moose. It was the way of life in this land, the celebration of bounty that secured a family through the coming winter.

The world was so beautiful and different now. Quietly I wandered through the bushes, dark spruce to the left, the open river on my right, fading leaves like yesterdays flowers spilling about my waist. Soon my legs were soaked from the dripping foliage. I carried my mother's old .30-06 comfortably on a leather strap over one shoulder, Phil's knife on my belt, matches and repellent in my pocket. In one hand I held a chunk of cold muffin, which I chewed as I stepped along. The rifle had open sites, easier to keep in alignment than a scope, and I had walked hundreds of miles with it. It felt somehow like an old friend in this benign position.

I was thinking about the hunting ceremonies of people who lived on the land that affirmed their place in the cycle. "The wolves and the caribou are one," the Eskimos had said. It seemed important that I, too, purify myself in some way before partaking in this great mystery of life and death. For me to intrude in the ageless dance of moose, wolf, and forest, I needed to approach it with humility. Inwardly I blessed the great moose and thanked him for the gift of his life as I prepared myself for a violence I dislike.

I wondered at my place in Creation. As a girl on the Mackenzie River, I had wished to become a part of Nature, yet humans can no longer live a totally "natural" existence. The earth cannot support our great numbers and our bodies are embarrassingly fragile. Nearly devoid of protective fur, we are subject to cold, sunburn, and abrasions, and we have neither the teeth nor digestive systems to live on food in its native state.

Somehow, in raising our celebrated cerebral powers, we have become separated from the rest of life—shut off, as it were, from the Garden perhaps as much by our judgments as our physiques. Certainly, man has reached a stage of moral responsibility. We cannot go back; the only path is forward, through wisdom. Thus do we stumble about in the dark, seeking a return to the Garden, not as innocent children, but as Gardeners.

The river bar ended in a cutbank at the bend and the going soon became more difficult. Tom kept pace with me on the far shore and I lifted a hand to him whenever he appeared, small and dark between the trees. Near John's Stone I surprised a large animal and it made off rapidly through the brush. I didn't get a good look but thought it was a bear. The evidence of fresh digging in the area seemed to confirm this. Tom had scaled the high bluff and I waved at him before cutting inland to check Horseshoe Lake. Such ponds are common in the north, remnants left behind by the river's changing moods.

As I emerged from the trees into open marshland, I could see a large cow moose, water to her belly, feeding in the middle of the long, shallow lake. The reeds around the edge had turned gold and a faint mist clung to the water. I stalked her, keeping two dwarf spruce between us as I worked my way over the boggy ground and through the brush. Every time she put her head under, I hurried forward. When she raised it—water dripping from the bell under her chin—I froze. The ground was wet and very cold as I crawled the last few feet.

She was a beautiful animal. Bereft of a calf, she had used her summer to pack away a thick pad of fat. I lay there in the wet sedges for most of an hour, listening to the voices in my head: My mother's, "Never shoot a moose in the water," Tom's voice, "It's too far to haul a moose from that lake when the river is low," and in the background my concern, "What if we don't get another chance?"

The cow was a picture of health and serenity as she browsed undeterred by the freezing water, and I cringed at the thought of piercing her sleek body with my bullet. She was broadside to me and so close I could hear her breathing.

Her big ears remained above the surface, scanning the exposed shore like radar as she listened for danger, while about her milled half a dozen ducks. They didn't appear to be feeding but to simply enjoy her company.

My joints were beginning to ache and I was starting to shiver. With a smile at the moose, I rose. She jumped and started across the lake, taking great, splashing strides directly away from me. Within moments, she was gone and the marsh was empty. We think of the moose as "awkward" and "clumsy," and may fail to see the animal through our opinion of it. A giant member of the deer family, moose are perfectly adapted to the moods of this difficult land and amazingly graceful in crossing it. Like timid ghosts, they melt into the forest and disappear before your eyes. I defy anyone to follow a moose over this boggy, pitted ground and not come to respect them.

My clothes were wet and I was cold, but I felt suddenly happy as I turned for home. My life had been brushed by magic. Just as I reached the river, I heard Tom's shot, clear and far away. I held my breath and counted shots. One, two, three. God, I hope he got it! He was using his old .30-30 carbine with open sites. My worst fear is to wound an animal and have it escape.

It was a long walk home and I arrived tired and hungry. Tom was waiting by the canoe, impatient to get back to his moose. I checked the load for pack frames, rope, buckets, skillet, and lunch items before we paddled across the river. Tom led the way about seven hundred yards inland through stands of yellow poplar. There a modest bull lay, shot through the head and neck. It was a good location, for the ground was dry and fairly level. I was deeply grateful that I had resisted shooting the cow. Better a hundred shots not taken than a single wrong one placed.

"I'm so excited," Luke said, extracting his little, red pocket knife. "I can hardly wait to start skinning."

"Let's take a moment to thank the moose," Tom told him. Kneeling beside the animal he put his arm around his son's shoulders. "This is not like ordering a hamburger. Somebody else had to kill that animal. We had to kill this one."

For a few moments we gathered quietly around the big, dead creature, patting his smooth, brown fur and silently acknowledging his life. "Thank you moose," we each said in turn and smiled shyly at one another, knowing that something great had been given to us and something beautiful had also been taken away.

The day had turned warm and the host of insects that traveled with the moose now alighted upon us. I built a fire and Tom fastened his tag around the antler, though no one would ever see it. It took all of us to maneuver the heavy carcass onto its back, a position it could not maintain—chest high as my hips.

We pulled the antlers back and planted them under the great head and I tied his front leg to them with a piece of parachute cord. With Phil's old Case knife, I cut the first incision. The skin was tough and my technique less than perfect as I slowly worked up the belly.

"We need to peel the hide back before I slit the abdomen," I told them. I was the only one who had butchered anything larger than a rabbit, but the others were eager to help, each whittling away at some part of the great animal. Already the guts were beginning to bloat, distending the abdominal wall so that care was needed as I ran my blade through the sheaths of connective tissue and released the hot billows of intestines.

"Let's roll him sideways and try to paw the guts out." I wiped strands of hair from my eyes with a bloody hand. "They're fastened along the spine and you have to get in there and cut them free without puncturing anything or we'll have a mess."

"Nothin' up my sleeves," Laurie retorted, as she felt around, shoulder-deep in entrails. She grinned at me and wiggled her eyebrows. "I can cook too!"

Luke was tugging away at the thick hide, working his knife ineffectually but with determination. "Don't try this at home, kids!" he chimed in for an invisible audience.

"This makes me feel like I'm part of a clan," Laurie told us. "There's something very ancient about all of us butchering together. We'll have meat tonight and the drums will play. Something like that."

Butchering a moose is hard, gory work and I had forgotten much in twenty years. The appendages and organs are well fastened and not intended for easy dismantling. As I leaned into the cavernous chest, my back ached and my hands were fatigued from pulling against the heavy hide. Luke soon tired of skinning and wandered about while we called him back repeatedly. A strong, meaty smell hung on the air and I kept an eye out for bears. Strangely, one had recently died here and we could see the bones, still pink, scattered in the brush. It hadn't been killed or even scavenged by larger animals, for the skeleton was mostly intact, and we speculated on the cause of death.

The Arctic is a hard place to live. It's a land of great contrast where plant growth, which feeds all life, is almost tropical for a few weeks then falls to nothing. Migratory and seasonally dormant animals exploit this brief abundance, but the rest must have strategies to survive the other nine months. Niches are limited and the number of resident species is small. Life often exists here at the edge of its requirements. This creates a natural instability, and when one species crashes it may pull several others with it.

It was late afternoon when I stopped to fry up a meal of liver, kidney fat, and pieces of meat haggled from the pelvis. There was no water for washing and our hands were crusted with blood. It was the first fresh meat we had eaten all summer and it tasted wonderful.

"Doesn't Shylo look wild?" I commented as we squatted around the fire eating with our knives. She had been gobbling morsels snatched from the gut pile and her face was streaked with blood. She now circled us warily, wolfish eyes alert.

"Shylo?" Laurie laughed. "You ought to see yourself!"

I grinned. "Tom, ya done good. Shall I cook up some more?"

"Not for me," he answered. "It's almost too rich." He wiped his hunting knife on the leaves and reached into a bucket for the stone to sharpen it. "Laurie, did I tell you the history of this knife?"

Most of our knives had a story, but the strangest was this one. My cousin Ralph had longed to win the Congressional Medal of Honor and volunteered for one tour after another in Vietnam. It was secret work, deep behind the enemy lines, and through all those years he'd carried a folding Buck knife and this hunting knife. He had been wounded physically and psychologically by the brutality of those years, but had never won the metal. Once he came close, but all his men were killed and there were no American witnesses.

When Ralph heard we were going to the Arctic, he called to ask if we'd take his knives. "They mean a lot to me," he told us. "I once cut my way out of a downed helicopter with the Buck. Took me forever to get a good edge on it again. And the hunting knife . . . well, all I want to say is that it's time I let it go. It needs to skin a moose."

I looked over at the knife. Several ominous notches were cut in the handle. I wasn't sure I wanted to know about them. "Here's to cousin Ralph," I said, raising my mug of tea. "And to releasing that which no longer serves us."

I thought of the people and situations that had molded me. My mother's pack frame leaned in the bushes, carrying patches from Australia and Tasmania. After she died, I had cleaned the mud from it and unraveled the odd array of knotted strings. My mother, the helpless explorer, had still been doggedly hiking the Pacific Crest Trail, one section a summer from Canada to Mexico, in her sixties. Yet her gear was held together with old shoelaces and rusted safety pins. In half an hour I had refurbished the pack, smiling as I set it right. Phil had taught me this. From him I learned that one can repair and even design equipment. He, who had never built a log cabin or butchered a moose before we came to the Arctic, had taught me how and I was now passing this gift along.

Evening approached as we worked and storms ranged across the valley. It seemed inevitable that we would be caught in one. Black clouds rolled down the peaks leaving them dusted with snow while sunbeams played like great searchlights over the foothills and river. We were all exhausted by the time the woodland giant had been reduced to a slippery pile of cold meat. He had become merely a head with antlers, a neck, a pelvis, two sets of ribs (one with spine attached), four legs (cut off at the knee), a hundred pounds of hide, and several buckets of organs and gut fat.

Strapping awkward, hundred-pound quarters of meat to our pack frames, we slogged back to the canoe. I dropped onto the cold rocks, staying with Luke while Tom and Laurie returned for another load.

"It'll be dark soon," I told Luke, "and I'm afraid it's going to storm. How would you feel about staying alone in the tent? We have to get this meat home, but it probably won't take too long."

"I don't want to be alone," he answered, seating himself on my knee as if I were a chair. Our clothes were stiff with gore.

"I don't like it either," I agreed, "but at least you'd be under shelter."

"Well, okay . . ." he said bravely, "but can Shylo stay with me?"

"That's a good idea. It'll keep her out of mischief. But you can't control her in the tent. I'm afraid she'd just tear right through. So I'll tie her nearby."

When the others appeared out of the twilight, we splashed over the rocks with the heavy pieces and muscled them into the canoe. The four of us set off across the darkening river. When we reached shore I tied Shylo to a tree. Hurriedly, I settled Luke in the tent with Oliver and the beloved Calvin book while Tom and Laurie grappled the meat ashore onto a tarp. Within minutes we were skimming back across the river in a race with the fading light and the weather. As we grounded on the far side, Shylo began to wail loudly.

"She's calling every bear within miles," I muttered angrily. Stumbling with fatigue, I made one fast trip for meat and then asked Tom to paddle me back across. Moose or no moose, I could not leave my child alone. I was almost useless anyway. I would make a warm dinner for the family, I decided. The supportive role was important too, and if I was no longer a prime mover, there were other things I could do.

Laurie and Tom finished the job, bringing out the meat and paddling back in growing darkness. Together they hauled it up the bank and put it into the pavilion. The stars were out, cold and bright in a clearing sky as we washed the blood from our arms and crawled into the tent for the night.

๑

I AWOKE LATE, FEELING tired and sore. It had turned unseasonably warm. A few blowflies were buzzing around the meat. Bright sunlight bathed our camp and it seemed far from winter, but I knew it wouldn't last. I rose quietly, compelled by a feeling of urgency at the passing days, and left the others asleep.

I have always enjoyed mornings alone. It's my special time and from it I gain the balance for the rest of my day. I lit a fire and started cutting up the fat we had salvaged from around the guts and organs, slicing it on a split log held over my knees and rendering the tallow in a big kettle over the fire. I would save the cracklings for dog food. In this land it was never wise to waste anything.

"A moose comes with a lot of spare parts," I said as Tom emerged from the tent about an hour later. "We'll have to handle them right away or they'll spoil. Hope you're in the mood for more liver."

"We carried off most of the animal," he agreed as he put on his wet boots and tied the laces. His fingers were cracked and mangled from the hard life. He had packed most of the meat, but had less blood on his clothes than I did. "Still, something is lost in the killing," he continued thoughtfully. "It's a relief to have the food, but you can't equate a living moose with a pile of meat."

"Well, yes," I nodded. "But all animals feed off living things. In some ways, taking life forces you to acknowledge that communion." I paused a moment, then sighed. "We should probably get another one."

He nodded. "I was thinking that too."

"He's not as big I had hoped for . . . and a good deal leaner than he might be. Perhaps we can shoot an old fellow who has lived a good life. Anyway, no hunting until we handle this."

"Shall I put on my bloody clothes?" Laurie called from the tent.

"Yeah. No point cleaning up. We're gonna hang the meat today. It'll keep back in the shade, but it's too warm in the pavilion. Besides, we don't want to attract bears into camp."

"So what happened to winter?" she asked.

"It'll be here within two weeks," I predicted. "Get up, lazy bones. Half the day is gone." We had agreed on a day of rest, but things needed to be done.

"Coffee?" Tom asked, raising his eyebrows plaintively toward the pot on the grill.

I smiled. "Yes, it's coffee and it's hot. Go ahead and pour yourself a cup while I finish cutting up this fat."

"I hope someone sends me a real coffee cup in our November flight," he grumbled. "It just doesn't taste the same out of these enamel things."

We were listless and grouchy with fatigue. Only Laurie seemed her usual steady self. Making use of the warm weather, she hauled buckets of water and washed the accumulated laundry, while Tom and I built a high meat rack back in the woods out of reach of bears. We constructed it of two strong poles roped to either side of a pair of trees, about fourteen feet in the air. Tom climbed onto them and balanced as he slowly pulled the hide up, nailing it on the south side to protect the meat from sun. Using a rope over the other log, Laurie and I struggled to raise the quarters, while Tom tied them by short pieces of parachute cord.

Tom and Laurie hauled the remaining meat up to the cabin and hung it from a rack on the north wall under the roof. Not wanting to leave it unguarded, we moved our bedding up for our first night inside. As darkness came on, Tom filled and lit the kerosene lamp. Its unaccustomed glow drove back the shadows and lent a cozy ambience to our log walls against which the open door and window holes stood out black and ominous, filled with night.

Luke and I put on night clothes and ascended the ladder to the new bed. It felt good to remove my contact lenses, sleeping without them for the first time since we arrived. The bed was well padded and covered with blankets. Our sleeping bags were spread open as quilts. The loft stretched the length of the cabin and was high enough to sit comfortably at its lowest point near the outside wall. The bed was nine feet wide, ending at a break where a ladder descended. A further section of the loft (yet to be completed) would be used for storage.

After the cold, lumpy ground, our bed felt very flat and warm. I lay contentedly on my back with Luke, watching the lamp light dance over the rafters above my head. Below us Tom centered an empty crate over the joists and dealt Laurie a hand of cribbage. She was his only worthy opponent in cards and we could hear their happy banter as the plays fell out.

When they came to bed, dark filled the cabin. It was strange sleeping within the close blackness. Accustomed to hearing the wind and river, I felt cut off from my senses. The extra space was strange as well, and although I enjoyed the freedom of curling up without sticking my knees in Tom's ribs, I found myself reaching out to make sure everyone was okay. Close physical contact had come to feel natural, communicating safety and affection. I was afraid Luke would scoot forward and fall over the edge, and at one point I remember waking everyone as I groped about in some confused dream, calling for him.

There was no longer any concern about tent zipper or bugs, but since we needed to crawl over the sleeping group to get to the ladder, we continued our custom of nightly forays. There was also comfort in facing the dark together. We felt our way across the pitted clutter of our unfinished floor and out into the starry night to the designated spot. The woods about us loomed mysterious and alien, black silhouettes against the sky. Overhead, a curtain of green fire waved across the heavens, dwarfing us with its majesty. In sweat suits and slippers we bunched together, faces raised in awed silence, watching the aurora borealis ripple and curl in great streamers through the vastness of starry night.

Our third night in the cabin, I woke before dawn to the sound of wind in the stovepipe. It was very quiet inside, but the gentle tremble of logs beneath me spoke of the storm that thundered down the exposed river. I could imagine the flapping of our lonely tent and feel, more than hear, the vast tide of arctic winter rolling indomitably southward over the sleeping land. I lay awake and watched the slow, gray birth of a new day. Snow was still falling, quietly erasing the last of summer, when I roused the others. It was only September 9. Winter had come early.

Our attention turned to consolidating belongings so that we wouldn't lose them under the snow. Laurie, Luke, and I spent the day dismantling camp and finding space for it within the crowded cabin. We took down the old pavilion, folding it into tarps as we said good-bye to a way of life that was no longer friendly. Tom wanted to store the majority of our supplies outside until he finished the floor, but I was anxious about their safety and so piled them in the cabin.

I tacked a piece of plastic over the open door hole to keep in the warmth. I was still grappling with odd moose parts, cooking meals of tongue, steak-and-kidney pie, and jellied nose as I tried to organize and move our supplies. I felt discouraged at the amount of work still ahead of us. The cabin seemed dreary and cluttered as I thought of the coming winter and the effort it took to handle life at cold temperatures: hauling water, cutting frozen meat, gathering firewood in deep snow, washing clothes.

Our world had changed overnight. It had only snowed a couple of inches and would have melted off if the temperature had risen, but it hovered in the teens. Withered grass protruded through the crystals giving the land a faded, drab appearance. The autumn colors were gone and a clean, cold wind rocked the spruce, causing them to creak and moan. Back in the thickets, bare willows rattled like so many cold bones where the occasional dry leaf tapped. We dug out felt-lined shoepac boots and put away our summer footgear. Muskegs froze, making travel easier, and snow crunched and squealed underfoot. Our creek was still flowing strongly, the same thirty-four degrees it held all summer, and presented a challenge for crossing. Across the delta it built cascading layers of slippery ice honeycombed with rushing water.

Hunting again consumed a good portion of our efforts and day after day we tramped the thickets and bars. Some days were clear, but many were ghostly and unreal, seen through the whisper of falling snow. It was easy to lose one's sense of direction in the obscure light and often the peaks were hidden from view. The moose were still moving, as the great activity of tracks attested, but harder to approach in the noisy snow. Tom did bag four spruce chickens which we cached away for Thanksgiving dinner. Our local birds had become quite tame, often strutting through the yard like hens, and these we left alone. Tom always accompanied us hunting, quietly supportive while Laurie or I combed the land. He became even thinner and more wiry as miles stretched out behind him, his ragged, bearded face looking like an old prospector's. My feet were very sore and tired from trying to keep up with him, but they were warm inside my shoepacs.

The river was beautifully clear now, a deep blue ribbon laced between the growing shelves of shore-fast ice. Large pans of slush moved in a stately procession down the narrowing center, scraping over shoals with a hissing sound. It was difficult to cross, for one needed to propel the canoe over several yards of ice, paddle through the relentless rafts of slush, then heave out like a walrus onto the far shelf and slide to shore. No longer a sunny stream, its temperament changed by the hour and we were afraid of being stranded on the other side. Nevertheless, we did cross, scouting the willow thickets day after day.

"If we get a moose now we'd have to pack it home," I reminded Tom as we stood gazing from the bluff above Lake Eugene. Although Horseshoe Lake was frozen hard enough to walk on, Eugene was still open, windy, and blue-black. To my surprise a few fish eating ducks dove in its uninviting depths.

"We need to go wherever they are," he answered. "Perhaps we could cache the meat and haul it home, a little at a time."

"Yes. I suppose miles of packing beats not getting it, and every day they get thinner. But just remember how heavy a moose is."

"I enjoy seeing this country," he answered. His head was high and his eyes far away. "It seemed like all we did last summer was work on the cabin and it's good to get out."

❧

GRADUALLY, THE MOSSING WAS completed and the cabin began to look enclosed. Tom slowly chiseled out sills and installed our windows. He built a kitchen counter along the front wall and fashioned shelves for our treasured library. Laurie kept planing floorboards. I finished digging the toilet hole and built a sturdy seat over it, then erected another meat rack in preparation for a second moose.

I was learning to cook with the stove, and meat added greatly to our diet and the enjoyment of meals. The morning that Tom hung the door was a turning point for me. Light and fragile as it was, it somehow closed out winter and turned our cabin into a home. I celebrated by making sourdough donuts dipped in lemon icing for breakfast, while Tom cleaned the guns and Laurie taught Luke the fine points of chess.

After breakfast, Tom and Laurie set out hunting. It had been two weeks since we killed the first moose and the season was quickly passing. I was tired and needed time to recover from the long miles I had put in with Tom the day before, but he covered the same country again while I worked in the cabin. I wondered if he wasn't running himself too hard. They were gone most of the day, arriving home around sunset, their faces windburned and tired. I had a meal of baked ribs and fresh rye bread waiting.

"I'm taking a spin around the block," I said, indicating the loop up Luke's Trail and back down the creek.

I picked up my rifle and stepped through the new door, leaving the family warmth for a different world. It was stark and beautiful out, but no longer friendly. One sensed that foolish mistakes would not be easily forgiven.

Quietly, I followed the trail Luke and I had cleared so long ago, curving along the bench west to the creek. The snowy woods were already in deep shadow and a pastel sky of tangerine bled into yellow over the jagged peaks of King Mountain. The temperature would drop below zero tonight and there was little moon. The creek was a fairyland of ice—water rushing black through layers of white lace, but open and swift in the middle. My boots were waterproof halfway to the knee, but I took my time crossing the slippery stones, then turned downstream into the wind.

The fading light was to my back, setting the country before me aglow with sunset. The shore rose in a sandy, four-foot cutbank clothed in the short, bare stems of bushes. I could easily skirt the creek on this side and arrive at the delta to cross again. From my raised position I had a clear view of the stream in both directions, and with the light behind me it seemed I stood before a stage on which a play was about to begin. Somehow I knew the moose would be waiting. It came as no surprise when the big antlers emerged from a tall thicket across the creek about ninety yards ahead. The moose backed and drove into the willows, shaking his antlers in challenge before stepping into the open.

My heart was pounding with what I had to do. I knelt, then finally sat, in the snow to steady my rifle over one knee. It was hard to see through the open site in the failing light, but the moose stood forth as if painted. I allowed myself a moment of compassion, acknowledging the splendor of the great animal, then took a deep breath and pulled the trigger. At the first shot the bull leapt forward, splashing across the creek toward me, unaware of where his peril lay. The second round struck his neck, and as he turned sideways, I caught him a third time through the shoulder and upper ribs, taking him down. He lay panting on the frozen gravel perhaps fifty yards from me, steam rising into the cold evening.

I froze, awaiting his death, afraid he would get up and run if I moved. His throat and legs were toward me and I could see his eyes rolling. Every now and then he would raise his head. I hated to witness his fear and pain, and prayed for a quick death. I blinked away the tears and fired a fourth shot, trying for the brain from this odd angle. He jerked mightily but still did not die. Unwilling to prolong this macabre play, I stood and walked along the bank. The moose watched as I steadied my rifle and placed the final shot through his brain.

It was over. I felt numb and sad as I approached to make my peace with him. When I was sure that he was dead, I pulled driftwood free from the frozen sand and built a fire. The blaze climbed, rosy and cheerful in the purple light, gusting in the breeze that flowed up the creek. It would be dark soon and there was not a minute to waste. As I started for home, Tom appeared from the twilight, rifle in hand, and crossed the creek. We returned to the moose and together worked him onto his back. He was a bit larger than the other but just as thin. His legs were wet from the stream. His stomach was shrunken (for bulls do not eat at this season) and a strong smell of rut clung to him.

"I'm sorry to make you work when you're so tired," I said. "I think if we just skin his quarters and get the guts out we can do the rest in the morning. I'll head back for the tent and butchering equipment."

"I'll get started," Tom answered. His face looked gray in the fading light. "Don't tarry."

The trail was already indistinct as I hurried along. The cabin seemed dark as a cave inside despite the feeble kerosene lamp.

"We heard your shots. Did you get one?!" Laurie squealed as I opened the door.

"Another bull!"

"Luke, we've got lots to eat this winter!" She grabbed his hands and danced him around.

"Tom and I are staying out tonight," I told her. "I need to pack. Can you carry the butchering equipment? It's just downstream from the crossing."

"You bet. Is there anything else I can do?" she asked.

"Just take care of the boy and have a hot breakfast for us tomorrow. You'll be okay by yourselves?"

"Oh, we'll have a fine night. But I don't envy you out there. It's already eight below."

"I want to help, too," Luke interjected.

"You can help Laurie with the buckets," I told him. "Hurry or you'll have a hard time finding your way back home in the dark. You take good care of her tonight."

"I will," he promised.

They set off ahead of me and had cleared the sand of snow and put up my little yellow tent by the time I arrived. I had bought the tent after my divorce, and although worn and leaky, it had finally made it to Alaska.

Hugging us good-bye, they scurried for home. I could hear their happy chatter as Laurie piggybacked Luke across the icy stream and into the black woods. On the open bar Tom and I stood beneath a hemisphere of velvet blue sky that faded to orange at the horizon. The first bright stars were out and the northern lights played coldly overhead, illuminating snowy peaks and reflecting off the black water. A chill breeze drifted up the little valley carrying the song of the stream.

We butchered by firelight late into the night. Luckily, there was a good supply of driftwood frozen into the gravel and we didn't need to search far. The waxing moon rose late, dancing with the aurora in the creek. Blood froze to our clothes and we stopped often to warm our hands. By midnight the moose legs were mostly skinned and severed at the knees. I was proud that I had managed to get the digestive track disconnected at both ends and the organs removed without breaking the bladder or bowels as I groped around in the dark. Tom propped open the great rib cage with a stick. We cleaned our hands by rubbing them with snow as dry as sandpaper and melting them over the embers. Then we crawled into our sleeping bags and curled together in a tight knot for the remainder of the night.

We awoke in the gray dawn to the task of butchering the partly frozen moose and carrying the awkward pieces home. By lunch I had given out. I packed up the camp gear and retreated to our cabin with Luke, who was miserable and whining in the cold, leaving Tom and Laurie to complete the dreary task. The sun had set by the time they hauled the last pieces safely into our yard. Over the next few days we would need to hang the meat, handle the organs, and wash the blood from our clothes, but after three months of constant effort we were finally safe from winter.

CHAPTER 8

Peace settled upon us. For the first time we could relax. Much finishing work remained before the cabin would be complete, but the real push was over. Our task now was to gear down and discover satisfaction in daily living. Life revolved around home. The sun rose later each morning and we allowed ourselves to sleep in and linger over breakfast. In the evenings we played games by lantern light or told stories. Often we read aloud to one another as we worked inside, and each bit of progress was celebrated and enjoyed. Maybe that's the key to a good life, I thought, appreciating the details.

I spent much time preparing elaborate meals. The moose quarters were frozen hard as rock, so Tom rigged a pulley in the utility room and hung them to thaw over the washtub. These I cut into steaks, roasts, stew meat, hamburger, and sausage, then refroze in plastic bags that were stored outside. To my surprise, Shylo never bothered them, preferring her meals warm.

Tom constructed a nest for her in one corner and filled it with shavings, but she chose to sleep out as long as the weather remained reasonable. Maybe she sensed that her fur would come in thicker, but I believe she just liked to keep an eye on things. She had grown into a beautiful, wild creature and there was no way to control her short of keeping her tied, which I would not do. We found her tracks miles from home. It annoyed me that I couldn't train her, for I took pride in having well-mannered pets, but Shylo was no pet. I was reminded that you can't direct another being by force. Unless someone values your esteem, they will find a way around you.

Days were often gray and indistinct. The snow was scanty, and wind whistled thinly down the valley, powdering the frozen mud of the delta and blowing it away. Our old camp looked bleak and uninviting. From the bank there was little evidence that anyone had ever lived there. It was strange to see it, so familiar yet stripped of all human sign. Daily the river narrowed as shore-fast ice grew toward the center. We could hear the ice singing under the tension, especially at night when the temperature fell to twenty below. It made an eerie,

haunting sound, something between a lion and a harp, and could ring like a Tibetan bell or moan in deep, musical tones. Sometimes the sound was high and clear like an Andean flute, at others it was the low thrumming of a didgeridoo or a deep boom that vibrated one's chest.

Our small channel of the creek held an unexpected blessing. Fed by springs, it continued to run long after the river had frozen, providing us with open water. It worried me too, for the whole delta seeped onto the river ice and I wondered if there would be a safe runway by November. We used about fifteen gallons of water a day, carrying it up in plastic buckets that were kept by the stove. Twice a week we had family baths in the big tub, washing one another's backs and hair. We did laundry too, hanging it outside to freeze, then completing the drying on a line strung high inside the cabin.

Laurie still handled dishes and helped Tom with the floor. They straddled the ripped logs and shaved them into boards with plane or drawknife, then Tom notched and doweled them into place over the joists. Laurie seemed to grow stronger as the days progressed, but Tom continued to experience more nerve problems in his arms, causing him discomfort at night.

❧

"How'd it go?" Tom asked as he met the three of us at the door. We had taken the day to hike up Annie's Peak. Evening shadows darkened the cabin where bright sections of new floor reflected the fading light. I noticed that he had also put up kitchen shelves and varnished the counter in our absence.

"We made it." I was shaking snow off my jacket and hanging it on a peg. "Luke did really well. He's a different boy than he was three months ago."

"Yeah, Mom could hardly keep up," Luke bragged. He had wanted to climb the peak ever since early summer when he'd been forced to turn back.

"I think next summer you'll be ready for all those hikes we plan," I told him.

"Mom said we walked five miles," he informed Tom.

It had been a gray day but with good visibility. Avoiding the icy loops of the stream, we had tackled the expanse of muskeg and brushy slope that led to the peak. The tussocks were easier to travel over now that they were frozen, but it was still difficult walking. At last, we had reached the final ascent. Curving into a crevice where hardy spruce endured, we had climbed through a notch at the north end of the domed peak and up the steep slope to the treeless summit. A bleak and beautiful panorama of frozen ponds and wild valleys stretched below on every side, while mountains without name capped the horizons. There was little color in the landscape now. It was a scene of white, mustard, and olive drab.

We hadn't stayed long. It was cold and I felt uneasy at the fickle mercy of the wind. Soon we descended the notch and built a fire in the shelter of friendly old trees, eating a lunch of cold sourdough pancakes with peanut butter while we warmed our fingers and gazed at the scene falling away beneath us. Soon we kicked snow over the fire and started the long trek home.

I had left a roast in the stovepipe oven and the warm smell of it welcomed us. "You've been busy," I smiled at Tom as I set dinner on a crate covered with the Warteses' old towel.

He twinkled with pride. "I'm halfway done with the main floor."

We seated ourselves around the crate and Tom lit the lamp. A gray light filtered through our many windows, mingling with the yellow glow that radiated from the burning wick. The crackle of fire was joined by the whisper of water heating in a big kettle kept on the back of the stove. We sat on the new bit of floor with our feet resting on the bare ground below the joists and held hands.

"I give thanks for a safe trip today," I said and smiled at each of my family in turn.

"I give thanks for just living here," Luke added, "and for having the peace." His dark eyes were serious, glossy brown hair falling long around his face.

"I give thanks for the love we share," Laurie put in. "And kitchen shelves. And our roof. And easy water." Her cheeks were still pink from the cold and her eyes soft.

Tom just smiled at each of us and squeezed our hands. The elegant simplicity of our lives was spoken in gentle ceremony.

"I want to make an emergency cache tomorrow," I told them as we began eating. "I'll stash spare clothes for everyone with a tent, matches, food, cooking pot, and the ELT. That way if the cabin burns down, at least we'll have a chance to call for help. We must all be very careful with fire. Luke, if you ever need to use the ELT in the winter, you have to keep the battery warm. Put it under your coat and stand out in the open."

"I'm still hoping to get the meat house up," Tom said. "That would give us an emergency home. But the cabin is first on my list, and we need to spend a few days cutting trees before the snow gets too deep."

Laurie rose and opened the door to hand Shylo a bone. "Anybody want something hot to drink?"

"Would you make me a cup of tea?" I asked.

"Poof. You're a cup of tea!" she declared, placing the mug before me.

"Can we play cribbage after dinner?" Luke asked as he helped himself to more bread. He had eagerly taken to a number of complex card games and quickly learned to add to thirty-one. It was embarrassing, but when we played in teams only Luke and I needed to count on our fingers and he was faster.

"Not me," Tom replied. "I figure if I write a letter a night, I'll be ready for the mail flight.

"I'll play you a hand," Laurie offered. "Unless you have other work." She raised her eyebrows at me.

"Let's forget school today," I told them as I cleared the dishes, "but I want to see a boy dressed for bed and teeth brushed first."

Even before Tom finished the real table, Luke had started first grade. He was bright and quick to learn, but resistant to skills for which he saw no immediate value. It looked like he would finish first grade math and reading before Christmas. Luckily, I had brought along second and even third grade materials. When neither his private school nor Arizona public schools had been willing to guide me in teaching him, friends of friends offered advice and books. I had supplemented these with workbooks from a school supply store.

"Are you looking forward to the plane coming?" I asked the general company.

"Not really," Tom answered. "Our life is so perfect, I'm almost afraid to disrupt it." We had scheduled the flight to send out videotape and reassure our families. It would bring mail, but we had everything we needed.

"I wanna see it," Luke declared, eyes shining. He was sitting on the floor near the stove, trying to take his pants off over his boots.

"It'll be fun having company, won't it?" I grinned. Steve Ruff didn't fly in the winter so we had arranged for an old friend of mine to come from Fort Yukon. I met Joe Firmin there in 1973 when Phil and I emerged penniless from the bush. I remembered him as a friendly kid doing volunteer work with the church. He had settled in Fort Yukon and now had a family and a business called Porcupine Air.

"You're going to like Joe," I told them. "He's spent years in the woods and he's very knowledgeable. More than that, he's a man of his word, the kind of guy who will go out of his way to help you." I thought of Joe. It would be good to see him again. I wondered if he would be able to stay awhile and talk. Maybe I was beginning to miss people.

❦

IT WAS EARLY OCTOBER when Tom fell ill. He awoke one morning with a high fever and cough. It worried and mystified me. There were no viruses away from people, but bacteria can cause problems if you get run down. It crossed my mind that he could have a recurrence of tuberculosis caught in the Navy. His thinness bothered me. I pushed the thought away and started him on a course of antibiotics. He spent the day resting.

We had awakened that morning to our first serious snow. The weather was warm, and composite flakes the size of my thumb fell silently, flocking the spruce and softening the contours of the land into something mysterious and new. I put snowshoes on for the first time and tramped paths around the cabin and down to the river. The far shore looked ghostly and unreal, a smudge of trees against the falling snow. Laurie, Luke, and I sallied forth to play, building elaborate snow sculptures in the yard. I remember humming "Winter Wonderland" as I rolled the new snow into big balls. It was a perfect day, with only a hint of shadow on the horizon of my mind.

After dinner I took a walk across the delta and up the creek. It was twilight, the dramatic sky satin yellow and peach along the rim of mountains, a blanket of gray cloud overhead. There was perhaps a foot of fluffy snow and I slipped over unseen stones, listening to the gurgle of water hidden by the innocent veil of white. The land seemed strange under the creamy folds. I stood entranced by a silent music that was somehow more powerful than the busy songs of summer.

Winter is a season of quiet and spiritual renewal, a period of drawing in, when all of Nature rests. It's natural that we too should experience times of quiescence and not expect ourselves to always be productive. We pay a price when we forget the natural cycles and fail to acknowledge the deeper currents of our beings.

It was getting dark and the route home was hard to make out as I turned back, ascending our once familiar bank the way I had come. Suddenly, a snug cabin appeared through the trees, kerosene lamp burning in the window. My heart smiled and I paused to appreciate the moment. Seeing it always surprised me, and I could never quite remember how it had come about. I could picture days of toil and even the history of particular logs, but the whole eluded me. Entering the cabin, I saw my family playing cards and smelled the warm aroma of popcorn. It seemed magical to have created this haven for ourselves, that we were comfortable and safe in a vast land, watching the approach of winter with pleasure and serenity.

GRIZZLIES WERE NOT ON my mind the next morning. Snow was again falling and we were spending a pleasant day inside. Tom had coughed much of the night but seemed better. He was still resting in his night clothes and slippers. I was dressed but had on my inside shoes. Luke and I lay upstairs, light from the window falling over our shoulders as we read together. Tom and Laurie sat on the floor below us, writing letters on our crate table.

The words "Bear!" and "At the meat rack!" penetrated my thoughts. It took me a moment to understand.

"You mean now?" I asked, incredulously. We hadn't seen tracks for some time and I had hoped they were going into hibernation.

"Yeah! He's right out there!" Laurie said urgently. "Hanging on the ribs!"

I scrambled down the ladder and rushed to the utility room window, where sure enough I could see a large grizzly swinging, all four feet off the ground, teeth hooked into the bottom of the frozen moose ribs.

"Think that cord will hold?" Laurie whispered. The bear had dropped to the ground and now had his front paws on the ladder that still leaned against the rack. He reached up and took a swipe at the ribs, which swung crazily.

"Let me see! Let me see!" Luke insisted.

"Luke, I want you upstairs," I told him. "You can watch from the window up there. I'm gonna run him off." I started for the door. Saving our meat was the only thing on my mind.

"I'll go with you," Tom said.

"You're sick and in your slippers."

"I'll go with you," he repeated.

"Laurie, you stay with Luke," I ordered. "Keep Shylo inside. You know where the ELT is if you need it."

Tom and I stepped into the white world beyond our door. "Here, don't you want to take your gun?" he asked politely, reaching it down from the pegs under the eaves. Our rifles were kept outside to prevent them from icing with the abrupt change in temperature.

I grinned. "Yeah, might as well."

He handed me the .30-06 and took down his little .30-30 carbine. I heard him crank a shell into the chamber and thought, "Gee, I suppose I should cock mine too—just in case." He was right of course, but it never occurred to me that the bear wouldn't run.

We stepped around the edge of the cabin, automatically separating a few paces to give each other room to maneuver. The bear was perhaps twenty-five yards away, still intent on the meat. His coat was chocolate in color and he looked very large and dark in the falling snow.

It was like a dream when the grizzly dropped to all fours and came. There was no hesitation, no pause to consider—simply that awesome charge. It happened too fast to frighten me and yet seemed to occur in slow motion. A great silence filled my head as if all the internal dialogue had been shut off and I had suddenly entered a new dimension. I was vaguely aware that Tom was shouting, but it was somewhere far away.

Halfway to us, the bear hesitated for just a moment, bouncing to a stiff-legged halt with waves of snow billowing about his feet. There was a smooth power in his movements, an unconscious speed and grace that held me spellbound. His large, dished face was riveted upon us with fierce intensity. Then he dropped his head and went straight for Tom. I watched him come through my sites, my finger tense on the trigger, hoping to the last that he would turn. Tom must have been thinking the same, for we held our ground together and didn't fire, the grizzly looking huge as a runaway train. As he passed me, I remember thinking with regret, "That's too close," and pulling the trigger. Tom's shot echoed mine and the bear fell, plowing into the snow at Tom's feet, close enough to touch. Yet even as he tumbled forward, he regained his footing.

As he fired, Tom swung to the right attempting to sidestep the brunt of that terrible charge, but the grizzly now wanted only to escape. Already dead, his brain and neck shattered by the close impact of Tom's bullet, he turned and ran for the trees. Knowing that we could not let him get away wounded, we both fired again, bringing him down in a dark heap beneath the meat rack.

My knees were shaking and my heart was heavy with grief at the loss of this life. Even now, I fail to see an alternative. Sometimes there are no right answers. I suddenly noticed that my feet felt wet and cold. Cautiously, Tom approached the fallen bear, making sure that he was really dead before returning to the cabin to dress and put on boots.

Laurie's face was pale but it flooded with relief when we opened the door. "You're okay!" she breathed. She and Luke were huddled in the loft, eyes wide with concern. We stepped inside and stood trembling together in a long family hug.

"I was afraid he had you," she said shakily. "We couldn't see around the utility room once he got close to the cabin."

By the time we dressed, the grizzly was already disappearing under falling snow. I felt repelled, almost sick to my stomach as we set about skinning and gutting him. He was an old man bear, his molars ground to the gum line (though the canines were still formidable). The black pads of his big feet were cracked and worn. His paws and head seemed large, but beneath his scanty fur the body was starving.

"Maybe we did him a service," I said as we squatted in the bloody snow, working on the carcass. We were all feeling subdued and depressed. "This time of year he should have four inches of fat across his back. There's nothing."

"He was desperate," Tom agreed.

"It was his big chance to survive the winter," I murmured.

Tom nodded. "There's no way he would have relinquished that meat."

"It was too close," I admitted. "We waited too long. He could just as easily have gone for you as run."

"I figured he was going to. I was damned lucky. If I'd hit him any other place than exactly where I did, it would have never stopped him."

We worked for a time in silence. Shylo circled us, licking up bloody snow, her golden eyes canny and alert. As the thin hide came off, the bear began to resemble a heavyset man and the sweet smell reminded me nauseatingly of autopsies I had seen while working in medical research. Murder would be rare, I thought, if our culture abhorred killing people as much as we do the idea of eating them. There's no glamour in this torn muscle and shattered bone, be it bear or human.

"I've been thinking about the great appreciation I've gained here for living things," Laurie told us. "It's also made me realize how important it is to not take more than you need."

"It's disrespectful," I agreed.

"What do you want to do with the hide?" Tom asked me.

Because the bear had been shot in self-defense, we were supposed to give it to Fish and Game within two weeks. "Let's hang it over the canoe for now. Maybe we can send it out with Joe," I decided. I looked at the pitiful carcass. "He's awful thin. It's been a poor year."

"Well, he's old too," Tom said, "and you have to remember this has been going on for millions of years."

"I suppose so. It just makes me sad to think of hungry bears out there starting hibernation with empty tummies."

"It makes me scared to think about it," Luke inserted in a practical note.

It worried me too, but I didn't say so. Fall was not our only concern, for the bears would emerge hungry next spring. They have been known to kill people for food during hard years, and it's advisable to be cautious until their food is again plentiful.

"Were you frightened when Mom and Dad went out to face the bear?" I asked Luke.

"No . . . but I was scared when I watched from the bedroom window up there and saw him come charging up toward the house. I thought he was gonna tear the door off and come inside."

I smiled to myself. How like a child. He hadn't perceived any danger to his parents. Parents were invincible. Once you started to doubt that, there was no safety in life.

I glanced about through the falling snow. Our happy sculptures of yesterday were transforming into shapeless mounds. The yard was suddenly strange and menacing, a place where bears could appear without warning and destroy a picture-book day. No amount of planning or work can control the circumstances of life, I thought. It frightened and angered me that my world could be turned upside down so easily.

I looked over at Tom, sick but still working. A mantle of snow plastered his balding head, shoulders, and the dark straggles of his beard. His face looked pale and vulnerable, and I shuddered to think how close I had come to losing him. Right now I could be sewing up gaping lacerations instead of skinning this bear. And there was Laurie, up to her elbows in the pelvis, cutting free the rectum with never a complaint.

She saw me watching her and wiggled her eyebrows suggestively. "I feel like the Galloping Gourmet," she whispered loudly.

I had to smile. Good old Laurie. Could a person have better companions than these? My eyes traveled to Luke. His cheeks were pink from the cold and his face was intent as he worked away at the hide with his little knife. I felt an affection beyond words for each of them.

This was life, I thought. Despite all my efforts, I could not control it. I suddenly realized that its beauty emerged from the very challenges I resented, born of this fragile dance beyond my preferences: Creation and Destruction. It was the act of facing fears and limitations with courage that built the strength I admire in human beings. The inner sense of quest that drives us to explore, contribute, and achieve in the face of hardship is the element that makes life worth the effort. If I wanted my life to be flawless before I started enjoying it, I would miss the point of the whole adventure.

FOR SEVERAL DAYS I found myself feeling depressed, sullied from our reluctant slaughter of the grizzly. We were all in a quiet period of grief. Perhaps it wasn't the bear alone we mourned, but lost innocence in ourselves. Try as I might, I could not recover the sense of security I had experienced before, the feeling that all would be well if I only worked hard and stayed prepared. The forest seemed to harbor danger. Again and again I replayed the charge, seeing the awful speed and power of the bear. He had brought fear into my life, a realization that things might not turn out as I planned. I suddenly felt that I was a stranger here and knew nothing about this wilderness.

Tom asked me to take the .357 Magnum pistol on my walks. I had never carried a gun for protection before, feeling the very act acknowledged the presence of fear in my world, but I acquiesced and strapped it to my belt whenever I went out. I resented that gun and I resented the bear for making me afraid. Once the seeds of fear are planted, they are very difficult to uproot. Another disquieting factor was Tom's continued illness. Although he improved on antibiotics, he was not well.

The afternoon he finished our real table, I went out to cut braces for the legs. The table was a work of art, five feet long and nearly three feet wide. Snow had been falling for days and lay deep and heavy on the branches, making the thickets hard to traverse and dumping their soft, wet burdens on me as I sawed the tall willows. I was tired of the falling flakes and the gray cast to the sky. Floundering through the knee-high snow, I tried not to imagine how fast bears can move. Holding the bow saw in one mittened hand and a selection of sticks in the other, I backed and turned on my snowshoes, thrashing my way clear of the brush and onto the beach. It was a relief to be in the open again.

Laurie was standing in the old camp, an empty water bucket in each hand as she gazed over the silent river. It was stilled under ice, but downstream a dark flow emerged at the rapids. Below her, our little spring poured sluggishly onto the river and disappeared under the insulating blanket of snow. It would be some time before the river was really safe.

"Hi," I said gently, coming up beside her.

"It's very special isn't it?" she answered. Her eyes glistened with tears and I felt my stomach drop as I suddenly knew why. She was saying good-bye!

"Yes," I nodded. We stood together in quiet companionship. "You can't get out, you know," I said softly, repeating my words of a month before.

She turned to face me. "You knew?"

"Well, yes, I guess so. Nothing is ever really hidden in the Universe. Especially from people who love each other." I tried to keep my voice steady. I remembered now how she stared out the window while writing letters to friends and the catch in her voice when she spoke of her mother. Yes, it all made sense, but I hadn't wanted to see it.

"It's just that I'm going to miss it, and us." She blinked and tears splashed down her cheeks. I pulled out a kerchief and wiped them.

"That's not your pee-pee rag is it?" she joked, and then she started to cry. Her nose was red and the scarf around her head was coated with snow.

"No, it's a clean one. Have you decided to go then?"

She took a deep breath. "No . . . I don't know."

"If you do, I'll understand. I won't like it, but I'll support whatever choice you make."

"You'd do that for me?"

"Uh-huh. Freedom is the gift of love. Besides, those who seek it must grant it to others. I only ask that you tell Luke. You mean a lot to him."

"I know." She was silent. "How will I know? I thought I'd stay for everything, but now with this flight coming . . . and well . . . maybe I'll just go out for a while and then return."

"Listen to your heart. We should honor our feelings. No one has the answers for another." A great sadness welled within me as I said these words and I realized that it was for me. "It's just that I'll be very lonesome," I said, and burst into tears. Laurie laughed at the sight of us and got out her kerchief.

"Is that your pee-pee rag?" I asked suspiciously as she reached to wipe my eyes, tripping over my snowshoes.

"No, it's my snot rag."

"I'll use my own, thanks." We both laughed and cried and blew our noses. "Somehow it's different with you than with Tom," I admitted. "It's always so easy. I don't know what I'll do without you. And how are we ever going to eat all the damn bear meat?!"

"Now Miss Jeanie, remember how you always tell me about 'Divine Right Action,' that all things work out for the best?"

"I hate it when people quote me."

She was right. If I really believed that life has purpose, I would look for the gift in her leaving. Our power comes not from changing the world, but in recognizing its beauty. The same circumstances could produce entirely different experiences depending on one's focus.

"How will I know the right decision?" she asked again.

"You won't," I answered bluntly. "There are no guarantees. You're responsible for creating value in whatever choice you make. There aren't any right answers anyway. They change throughout life. Important questions will reappear and you must find new answers because you have outgrown the old ones."

There was nothing more to say. We stood together and looked at the frozen river and our little creek, watching the falling snow. Shylo whined impatiently, wanting me to get back to the cabin. Finally, Laurie filled her buckets, dipping up the clear water with a yellow margarine container, and then we headed up the bank together.

❧

THE NEXT DAY DAWNED clear and twenty below zero, a welcome change from the constant snow. We hadn't seen the sun in many days and found that it now traversed a low arc, twinkling golden through the trees along the southern horizon. Laurie took Luke up the river to John's Stone for a talk, giving Tom and I some needed time alone.

I saw them off at the delta, red-cheeked and happy, heading north into their long, blue shadows—Laurie stalwart as a German peasant girl, breaking trail on snowshoes with Luke shuffling behind on his new skis. Shylo circled them in great snowy leaps, enraptured with the joy of her speed and agility. I never saw an animal that loved to run more. She was poetry in motion, a celebration of strength and beauty, until she hurtled into Luke's back, flattening him in the snow. Laughing, she danced in close, ripping at his boots and clothing, and jumped easily away from his angry fists. I drove her off then helped Luke to his feet. He was hurt and crying, his face streaming with tears, mouth open loudly.

"She almost broke my neck!" he sobbed as I dusted him off and helped him organize his ski poles.

"I'm sorry," I sympathized, wiping his nose.

"She doesn't even like me. She hates me!" and he burst into new tears.

I held Shylo by the collar as they started off again. I could hear Luke's excited chatter and Laurie's patient answers as they wended across the delta. I knew Shylo wouldn't follow them far when I released her.

Things had certainly not turned out as I planned, I thought as I trudged up the familiar path to the cabin. Far from considering herself Luke's dog, Shylo thought of him as a rival for my attention. When I held him on my lap and sang, she would often try to crowd him out, and she lay in ambush for him when he played alone. It was true that he compounded the problem by trying to control her, but the relationship worried me.

Tom greeted me as I entered the cabin. "I'm going to miss Laurie terribly if she goes," I admitted.

He nodded. "We all will."

"Life here doesn't look as safe or fun without her. I like the way we gravitate into different combinations."

"We'll never have time alone together," he pointed out.

"Yes, that's true." I stood gazing out a window at the long, violet shadows across the sparkling snow. "I'm going to miss acting silly and laughing with her. It's a side I've never felt comfortable sharing with you. You're never silly."

"I enjoy watching you together." He encircled me with his arms and dropped his chin onto my shoulder. "I just don't know how to be silly. I don't even know where to start."

This surprised me. I had taken his silence as judgment and had resented him for it. "But you like to play jokes on people," I countered.

"Yeah, but that's different from acting silly. I'm going to miss Laurie's silliness, too," he admitted sadly.

❦

THERE FOLLOWED A SPELL of clear, cold weather, sunlight marching rosy-gold across the undulating snow igniting a million diamonds, the sky a faraway blue. Although Tom didn't feel up to helping much, Laurie and I spent many days outside hauling firewood. Besides our need for wood, it kept us from feeling closed in. We were as excited as if we had found gold when we discovered a wealth of fairly sizable dead trees to the south. We put in a network of skid trails, companionably pulling together like a silly old team of draft horses.

Luke trailed with us, his little motor running. He spent hours outside each day, whacking trees with sticks to see the snow fall or burrowing about the yard like a weasel. We could track his whereabouts by the constant noise.

"Don't hurt my little trees," I would tell him. "They get brittle in the cold." He had learned it from watching me give them a nudge to release the deforming weight of snow.

"Who says they're yours?" he countered.

"They're mine because I love them," I answered. "I don't 'own' them. You can't own anything, even your body, but you become a part of everything you love."

Tom had started coughing up blood, a sign I didn't like at all. He joined us only long enough to fell dead trees that I flagged and then retreated to the cabin in a pale sweat. He had trouble with cold feet and now wore my home-made mukluks, which helped. It seemed strange, for he had always been warmer than me. One night I suggested that he leave on the mail flight, assuring him that Luke and I would be okay until his return.

"Well, it may be a moot point," he answered, "depending on which plane Joe brings. And if he comes." It was getting late in the year and still no sign of the plane.

I sewed a harness for Shylo of red nylon webbing and started to work her. She was skittish and hard to catch, but I felt the discipline would do her good. With cold weather she had moved inside, curling next to my feet of an evening and snoring loudly enough to disturb conversation. She didn't care for serious cold, and the thermometer was an accurate measure of her humility. She became meek and fawning as the temperature dropped, and would put up with being fondled by anyone for the privilege of remaining inside. Still, she was fickle and would revert to independence when it warmed up. Outside, she could not be touched unless she deemed it to her advantage.

Her one loyal gesture was to accompany me to the toilet at night. For no one else did she perform this chore. It gave me a sense of security and I appreciated it. On particularly cold nights she would wait impatiently by the door for my return, but she always came out. I was fairly certain that the bears were in hibernation, but I enjoyed her company nevertheless.

Her relationship with Luke had not improved. One day I caught the faint sound of someone calling. Stepping outside, I could clearly hear Luke's screams from the river. I raced down and found him curled barefooted in the snow, trying to protect his naked feet from her attack, tears of fear streaking his flushed cheeks. She had knocked him over and ripped his boots off leaving him helpless. It was twenty below zero and had I failed to hear him, he might have suffered serious frostbite.

Angrily kicking off the dog, I gathered the boots and sobbing child into my arms and carried him back to the cabin.

"What were you doing down here alone?" I demanded as I stalked up the trail. "You know you're not supposed to leave the yard!"

"I . . . I . . . I . . . wa . . . wa . . . wanted . . . to chisel . . . ice . . ." he hiccuped. I didn't know . . . she . . . wo . . . wo . . . would . . . do that!"

He buried his face in my neck and cried.

"That damned dog!" I flared. "If she keeps this up, I'm gonna shoot her!"

"No! No!" he wailed. "You can't shoot my dog! I love her!"

"Yes, Luke. I love her too, but I won't have her hurting you!" I would grieve for Shylo, yes, but I knew where my priorities lay. I just hoped it wouldn't come to that.

❦

BECAUSE LAURIE MIGHT BE departing, we decided to celebrate Thanksgiving at the end of October, for she was a big part of all that we had to be thankful for. I sewed a tablecloth and made tallow candles for the event. We wanted it to be a joyful day and planned a special meal of apple pie, stuffed spruce chickens, cranberry sauce, bread, mashed potatoes and gravy, corn, peas, and tenderloin.

The day before our Thanksgiving, Laurie set out alone on a long hike. I believe it represented a sort of graduation to her, a rite of passage. It was something she needed to do. The temperature had warmed and snow was falling again, transforming the world into an indistinct and confusing place—hiding the landmarks and even the sun. She hugged us each good-bye, then strapped on her snowshoes and pistol, shouldered her pack, and disappeared into the fuzzy day.

When she arrived home that evening, her face beamed with triumph.

"So where'd you go?" Tom asked as he handed her a cup of cocoa. She was pulling ice out of her hair and wiping her face.

"The loop you took me on hunting," she answered proudly. "Down to Pike Slough, along the bluff, way over behind Flat Lake, then to Lake Eugene and home along the river. Shaking little trees all the way," she laughed. "I even made a lunch fire in the snow. You'd have been proud of me. I never lost my way."

"That's not easy when it's snowing," I smiled. "We were thinking about you all day."

"You know, sometimes out there I feel like I can hear trees talking together." She had a faraway look in her eyes.

Luke climbed into her lap and made the hand sign for "I love you." She had been teaching him sign language. Laurie put her arms about him and kissed his soft cheek.

"Want to see some maps I made while you were gone? They're on the table." He reached for the colorful abstracts. "There's Texas and Hawaii and the North Pole. Let's see, where do you think Disneyland is?" His brow furrowed.

Laurie bent over the pictures and took a guess.

"How about some dinner?" I asked. "Tom brought up bath water so we can be clean for tomorrow." I set bear meatloaf, mashed potatoes, and gravy on the table, putting the pots on wooden trivets Tom had made to protect the surface from the blackened bottoms.

"When this snow stops, I want to tramp a runway," I said. I took a seat near Laurie.

"Joe told me just to indicate where we wanted him to set down," Tom informed me. "He wasn't concerned about the snow."

"I'm worried there may be overflow under the snow."

"It's been twenty below zero for weeks," he countered.

I shook my head. "It doesn't matter. Snow is a great insulator."

"How come you're eating rice and milk again?" Luke wanted to know.

"Oh, I'm just in the mood for it," I shrugged. The bear meat looked and smelled fine, but I still couldn't bring myself to swallow it.

After dinner, we dealt a game of poker, playing for almonds and pumpkin seeds. Candy was getting scarce and a bowl of banana chips served as munchies.

"Come to Papa," Tom said, raking in the first pot. Laurie had already started to eat her almonds.

"Laurie, you can't eat the money," Tom admonished. She slapped her cheek and opened her eyes wide in surprise.

"But Dad's feeding all the banana chips to Shylo," Luke tattled. I could see yellow eyes shining in the darkness behind him.

Luke called seven card stud and won it with two pair. "Come to Boy," he intoned solemnly, gathering the seeds. Then he dimpled.

"Tom pulls his whiskers when he concentrates," Laurie confided in a stage whisper to me. "Do you think it means anything?"

It was my turn to deal. Tom shuffled and handed me the deck. "I'm envious of the neat way you do that," I said.

"It pains me to watch you try."

❦

OUR DAY OF GIVING thanks dawned clear and twenty-six below. The cabin seemed very cozy as I lit the stove for coffee water. The others were asleep above me. We still used our sleeping bags only as covers. I heard the creak of the ladder as Luke's stocking feet and blanket came into view. He joined me on the bench, curling into my arms with his shabby blanket.

"Sing to Oliver," he said, holding up the myopic little bear. I thought a moment and began "Mocking Bird Hill." Shylo rose from her corner and stretched, poking her nose under my arm. Luke and I petted her, and she smiled benignly then tried to push into my lap.

"I feel hurt that Shylo doesn't listen to me," Luke confided sadly. "She was supposed to be my dog. I want her to love me, but she doesn't."

"I don't think she's anybody's dog."

"Yes, she's your dog."

"Not really. She won't come unless it suits her. In the end, Shylo belongs only to Shylo."

Is that coffee I smell?" came Tom's sleepy voice.

"It is indeed," I answered. "And this is our big day. Somebody come read to me and I'll start the spruce chickens roasting." We had completed the Merlin series by Mary Stewart and were now into James Herriot's wonderful books.

There was a general stirring and Laurie's feet appeared. "Say, there's a spider outside the window," she said incredulously.

"You're kidding. It's probably fifteen below out."

"Well, come see for yourself."

Luke and I climbed the ladder, and sure enough a large spider was slowly ascending the pane. Spruce beetle larva often hatched from logs inside the cabin and we had seen several insects and spiders moving across the snow, but it was hard to believe one could be active at this temperature.

We watched the laborious progression. "He should be under the moss," I said. "Don't you feel sorry for him? Maybe we should rescue him."

"I'm leaving him to Divine Right Action," Laurie stated. Then she looked at me seriously, "But I have given up killing them."

❧

NOVEMBER WAS A MONTH of clear skies and rapidly failing light. Days often started in the minus twenties or thirties, warming slightly toward noon. We spent much of the daylight hours outside, using our snowshoes to stamp wide trails into the virgin snow and dragging home firewood. Tom was slowly recovering and usually went along.

Laurie had decided to leave on the mail flight, but return. She planned to be gone a week, and we gave her a list of items to buy. Our mail was ready, and I had marked a landing strip on the river. It still worried me, for the pattern of overflow changed daily and it was impossible to gauge the extent of water pooled out of sight under the snow. I secretly hoped the world had forgotten us. Like Tom, I felt that our life was complete and I could foresee nothing but disruption from contact. Standing in the perfect silence of the velvet dawn, it was not hard to imagine that the rest of the world had ceased. We never heard small planes and only rarely saw the contrails of transpolar jets, orange against the sky.

It was a different land now and the animals had changed too. The weasel, hare, and ptarmigan had turned white. Dainty tracks printed the thickets, punctuated with plunges into secret hiding places. The snow was an ally here, providing cover, warmth, and access to higher browse. Prints of martin and ermine daisy-chained over the surface or dove into tunnels. The caribou were coming through now, and we often crossed tracks of their little wandering bands as we hiked up the creek.

Remembering the hum of summer, when the land was so full of movement and life you could almost hear the plants growing, I stood and breathed in the winter solitude, feeling myself swell and expand to the horizon. Here, surely was God—vast, grand, and beautiful beyond words. It filled me with quiet joy, a rapture at being alive. The wilderness was our sanctuary, a living cathedral that drew us deeper into harmony as the days progressed. Introspective and thoughtful, we lived almost like cloistered monks. To speak loudly in such a world seemed sacrilegious. How could I carry this part of me back to that other world? Was it possible to "be in that world and not of it?"

Late in November the sun had nearly gone for the year. Only a fiery rim sliding along the horizon at midday and a few hours of twilight remained. As the sun departed, the full moon rose, twinkling like a golden streetlight through the black trees south of our cabin. It climbed, etching shadows into the snow and turning the heavens a milky, silver-blue. The flocked trees stood like pictures on a Christmas card. Under that great moon our little cabin with its lacy trail of smoke looked like something from a dream—which of course it was.

We had given up on the mail flight, thinking it too late in the season, when the silence was split one afternoon by the brave hum of an engine. The sound surprised me, for it was forty-five below zero (our coldest day yet) and little planes don't do well at those temperatures. In a burst of freezing steam, we rushed from the cabin and stared up as a Cessna 185 appeared, running lights twinkling, in the fading sky.

CHAPTER 9

With the engine droning in our ears, we scrambled into mukluks and down parkas before heading for the river. As we left the cabin, the air hit me like a wall. It was deadly cold out, a temperature that would quickly frost exposed skin. I could feel it penetrating my long underwear and wool trousers. Snow squealed underfoot as we hurried along the slippery trail and into the open, waving happily. Shylo was racing up and down the runway, but knowing her general caution, I wasn't concerned. Luke hugged Laurie tightly, so excited that his feet were dancing. His rosy face shone with delight, peeping from his homemade red hood like a flower between the frosted fur petals of his parka ruff.

The Cessna circled, lights twinkling in the orange southern sky. The pilot was obviously hesitant about the shadowy stretch of river marked with sticks. Clouds condensed behind his wings as he passed low over the strip gauging the distance and conditions. At last he swung north, dwindling toward Flattop, which stood out white against the slate blue sky. Banking, the plane swung back and lined up with the frozen river. He cleared the spruce then dropped suddenly, flaring over the violet dunes. Skis outstretched, the plane barreled toward us in a rush of noise and spraying snow, slowing, slowing as it sank into the surface.

Tom ran out to greet him, plunging through the knee-deep snow. I was close behind with the video camera. The lens was rapidly icing, and I popped the case open, wary of breaking the plastic in the extreme cold. Laurie hung back to be with Luke. Just as I reached the plane, I heard Luke's hysterical screams. Looking back, I saw that he had taken a different route and fallen into deep overflow along the bank—wetting himself to the crotch. He stood frozen there in panic, just screaming.

"Go back to the bank!" I yelled at him above the sound of the engine. "Laurie can't come out to you!" Behind him she was coaxing quietly, and I saw him turn and struggle toward her. She pulled him up the bank and rushed to the cabin to peel away his freezing clothes, and so missed her mother's arrival.

I swung my attention back to the plane as the propeller clattered to a stop. The passenger door opened and Darlene emerged, grinning. She was encased in a dark green jacket and enormous black rubber boots, lent to her by the pilot. Her graying, blond hair was covered with a dainty cap and on her hands were thin gloves. She seemed scantily clad for such cold weather, but then it's hard to envision forty-five below when you come from Arizona. She was smaller than Laurie, more delicately built, but had the same open expression in her large gray eyes and the same willingness to laugh or cry.

Tom grabbed her up in a hug. "I told Laurie that the plane was late because you were coming to visit and couldn't get off work until Thanksgiving!" he greeted her.

"Oh, Tom! Tom! It's so good to see you! And Jeanie!" she breathed, reaching her hand out to me, our names a benediction. Her eyes sparkled with emotion and she looked around happily. "Is this heaven or what?"

"You like it, huh?" I asked, surprised. "Sorry it's so cold. Are you going to stay awhile?"

"Oh, it's wonderful! No, I have to be back to work on Monday. He's making another trip tomorrow, so I can stay over tonight. Where are Laurie and Luke?" she glanced about anxiously.

"Luke got into some overflow and Laurie rushed him up to the cabin," I reassured. "Wait 'til you see our cabin!" I was trying not to breathe and fog the camera.

"Then she doesn't know I'm here yet?"

"Won't she be surprised!" What a gutsy mother, I thought. "Hello Joe," I called to the pilot. "Excuse the video, we're making a documentary."

The pilot had swung out the far door and seemed to be examining the skis. He was dressed in heavy down parka of international orange and a Russian fur cap. He wore dark wool trousers, rubber-soled shoepacs, fleece-lined leather gloves, and a woolen muffler that covered the bottom of his bearded face. Frost sheathed our parkas, gluing our eyelashes and making us all into strangers.

"I'm not Joe," he answered uncomfortably. "I'm sorry to tell you, Joe was killed last week."

Darlene turned to me, voice unsteady. "That's why we're late," she said softly. "We had it all planned for weeks. I really felt like I knew Joe. We talked on the phone so many times . . ."

I felt stunned. Plane crash, of course. No one needed to say it. "I'm Jeanie," I said reaching out a mittened hand as the pilot came around the front of the plane.

"Steve Porter. Glad to meet you," he replied, grasping it firmly. "It seems pretty cold here."

"Forty-five below," I answered. "I didn't think these little planes could fly at this temperature."

"They don't do well. When we left Fairbanks it was minus fifteen. It's only zero a hundred feet up, right here." That surprised me. I suddenly imagined the cold air—not as a vast front—but like an invisible river that pooled in low spots and flowed down valleys.

Just at that moment, the plane shuddered and settled—six inches of slush oozing over the metal wheel-skis. "Hey, I'm getting wet!" Tom said. Around us, the snow was suddenly turning dark, our recent tracks looking like dotted lines across the white surface.

"We've got to off-load quick, or I'll never get out of here!" Steve said urgently. "I may need more room, so let's get the stuff away from the plane," he motioned toward the bank. "Can you tie the dog up? He really had me worried."

"Oh, she'll stay out of the way," I assured him. Shylo was circling the action, fifty yards downriver.

"They all love to chase planes," he replied.

"I can't catch her," I admitted.

"Well, I'd like you to try. Offer a roast or something. If I hit him, it'll destroy me, not to mention what it'd do to your dog. Do you have any boards? We gotta jack these skis up or I'll be here 'til spring."

"Jeanie, can you get some ripped logs from the utility room?" Tom asked. He began pulling cardboard boxes from the small cabin of the plane and piling them on the wet snow. Exposed to the air, the slush was rapidly freezing.

Laurie appeared on the bank and Darlene rushed into her arms with a cry of joy. "Oh, I've missed you so much," Laurie breathed, her cold cheeks suddenly wet with tears.

"We've got to get the plane off," I interrupted them. "I'm going up to the cabin for a rope and then I'll try to catch Shylo. They need boards and help propping up the skis. Try to stay clear of the overflow, Laurie. I think it's a small patch." Darlene and the pilot were not as vulnerable, for their footgear was waterproof, but the rest of us wore my handmade mukluks.

Arm in arm they turned to follow me, faces shining with the thrill of reunion and bubbling over with months of unsaid words.

It was already dark inside the cabin when I opened the door and entered with a white blast of fog. Luke had changed into dry clothes and slippers. He had lighted three tallow candles to welcome the company.

"Are you okay?" I asked softly.

"I was really scared," he told me. "Laurie saved me. I couldn't even get my ski pants off. They were frozen on!"

"But you're all right now?"

"Uh-huh. And I'm making a surprise for everyone."

"I have to try to catch Shylo. The pilot says she's dangerous to him. He's stuck in overflow and everybody will be working very hard to get him out. You'll have to be here by yourself a little while. Promise me you'll be real careful with fire."

"I want the pilot to stay, too!"

"That would be wonderful for us but not for him. Darlene is here and you'll get to see her. She's planning to spend the night and the plane will come back tomorrow."

"I don't want to miss everything!" His chin was quivering.

"I know. But this is really important, and the pilot will be back. Maybe it would be better if we blew out the candles and lit the lamp, since you're alone."

"Don't worry. I'll be responsible," he promised.

The door swung in with another cloud of crystals falling like a miniature snowstorm and the two women entered laughing. They collected the boards and departed for the plane. I set off on a wild-dog chase, leaving the others shoveling slush and prying at the rapidly freezing skis. I despaired of catching Shylo, but thought I might lure her away, and so started for Pike Slough along the old trail. Behind me, I could hear the plane laboring to free itself, the intermittent bellow of the engine throwing instant frostbite at the three people who buckled under the wing struts, pushing.

The willow flats stretched beautiful and wild before me, softened with undulating folds of snow. A gentle breeze had sculpted dunes behind each twig and dimpled hollows along the trailing edge of buried logs. The sun was gone, the sky backlit with a tangerine glow. I labored along the familiar trail, wishing I had taken time to put on snowshoes and down pants. With each step, I punched through the crust to my knee and my toes were beginning to get numb. I wondered if Darlene was dressed well enough and I worried about Tom, thinking that his feet might be wet. He had looked mutely miserable, straining in the terrible prop-wash, his beard a hoary mass of icicles. He was no longer coughing blood but still wasn't entirely well.

Shylo danced ahead, tail waving like a cocky flag, warily out of reach as I plodded. I kept listening for takeoff, but only the sporadic revving and my own gasping breath interrupted the intense silence. At last I could hear nothing. Perhaps the plane had taken off, I thought. In any case the burning cold in my feet told me that I needed to turn back. It would soon be dark. I retraced my steps, feeling tired and overwhelmed. Why did I need to hold my world together with my stomach? I wondered. The cabin seemed very far away, viewed from the foreshortened perspective of snow to my knees. I could see my own tracks with Shylo's overprinting the soft wrinkle of our old trail as it curved over the horizon of dunes ahead.

I reached the plane in time to help push it onto a ramp of boards. The Cessna 185 was tiny but amazingly heavy. The pilot had given up and would stay the night. He covered the engine cowling with a fitted red quilt, drained the oil, and removed the battery.

"I'll put a catalytic heater on it overnight," he said, "and hopefully we'll be able to get it started tomorrow." He spotted the condensation trail of a high jet, a dark line against the fading sky, and pulled a radio from beneath his parka to hail it. Thirty thousand feet above us, a disembodied voice from the other world crackled momentarily in the cold air.

"That was a piece of luck!" Steve grinned in relief and returned the radio to the warmth of his jacket. "If I hadn't been able to close my flight plan, Search and Rescue would've been out here tonight. The radio works line of sight, and I was afraid I'd never raise anybody down in this valley."

"How about dinner?" I asked. "I know you'd rather not be here, but we've got a warm cabin and a little boy up there who is dying to meet you."

Arms laden with boxes and gear, we ascended our hill. It took several trips before the wealth of new supplies and overnight equipment was safely stashed inside. The cabin seemed suddenly very crowded with moving shapes and extra gear. Tom hung the gas lantern from the loft over the table, then lit two kerosene lamps and placed them in corners. It was a grand gesture, for we had been conserving fuel. People sat in garrulous clusters, laughing and talking around the table or on Tom's newly completed wooden sofa.

It was exciting to have company and I realized that I had missed talking with friends. Time came rushing back into our lives as we learned that the other world had not stopped in our absence. I reached for the clock and set it by Steve's watch. My attention was scattered, my mind pulled between the conversations and figuring out what to feed everybody. For the first time, I got a look at our guests. Darlene sat beaming in wonder, one arm around Laurie and one around Luke. It was hard for me to grasp that she was really here, and apparently she felt the same.

Steve Porter was friendly and polite but reserved, overwhelmed perhaps to find himself the one stranger among close friends. He was around thirty-five, a fine looking man with neat, dark hair receding at the temples, trimmed beard and mustache, nice teeth, and clear blue eyes. He was of average height and obviously in good physical condition. He struck me as being energetic and competent. His clothing and equipment were quality and he seemed little bothered by the cold. He mentioned that he had once been a professional mountaineering guide.

Luke was hungry for male companionship and hung adoringly about the pilot, asking endless questions about planes. Steve was patient and went out of his way to be kind, showing Luke the barometer on his watch and taking him out to light the catalytic heater. Steve had taken on Joe's commitments on short notice, he told us, and was not accustomed to bush landings. I could see he was concerned about his plane and he disappeared into the icy dark twice during the evening to check on it.

"We're not out of the woods yet," he said when he returned. "The temperature is down to minus fifty and still dropping." It was as dark as a cave outside with only starlight on the snow.

"Haven't you always wanted a quiet vacation?" I hinted. "We have some great trails around here."

"I know, I saw them from the air. It looked like a whole village. I'd love to see more, but you don't have a fax," he laughed.

"That's why we're here," Tom beamed. "Not many places you can escape them."

"It's tempting," he acknowledged. "I'm in and out of the bush all the time and never get to see it."

"I'm due back at work in three days," Darlene put in. "I was just planning a brief visit if Steve could fit me in, but when he said he needed two trips I decided to spend the night."

"You mean you came five thousand miles for a few minutes of visiting?" I asked, incredulously.

"Oh, it's worth it. I love your place! John came to see me and showed me the pictures he took. I couldn't imagine how you would stay warm with all those cracks between the logs!" She reached out to touch the moss chinking.

"So what's the plan tomorrow?" Tom wanted to know.

"First we have a look at the thermometer. If it's still fifty below . . ."

"Choose a good book," I interrupted.

"Yeah. That's about it. We may be spending Thanksgiving. I hope my wife isn't worried."

"If we have to stay too long, you may as well leave me here," Darlene put in. "I won't have a job to go back to."

"Oh, they'll understand," I scoffed. "Take some pictures."

"No, they wouldn't," she replied with certainty. It was strange to think that being stranded in the wilderness was not a legitimate excuse for missing work. The Arctic wasn't the only unforgiving environment.

We were finishing up cornbread, spaghetti, and leftover Cajun bear ribs, six of us seated on benches around the table. We really had accomplished a lot, I thought, trying to view the cabin as a stranger might. The main floor was finished, as well as half the utility room floor. Our clothes and books were stashed neatly on shelves along the walls. The eight double-glazed windows had sparkles of frost in the corners but were generally free of ice, making the place seem friendly and light when the sun shone. It was warm inside, dressed as we were, and although things left in the utility room would eventually freeze, the large opening between the rooms kept it from becoming dank.

Steve glanced up as he helped himself to more ribs and caught Tom videotaping him. He grinned self-consciously and said, "I know you live out in the bush and all . . ."

I laughed. "We have to play it over and over to see what people look like."

After dinner, I excused myself and left the warm company to search for Shylo. It was black out. I could hear the quiet hiss of my breath freezing—a diagnostic sound of fifty below. After all the excitement, she was going to be hard to approach. I spotted her curled up in the snow a few yards from the cabin, eyes shining in the pale gleam of our only flashlight. The light drained quickly as the batteries chilled. I switched it off and put it in my pocket.

"Come on old girl," I coaxed, walking quietly toward her. She was reluctant to move and lose heat. I wondered how she could avoid frostbite. Her fur wasn't overly thick and the naked skin of her pads and nose provided little protection from such bitter cold.

I stroked her head a moment, then snapped a leash onto her collar. Knowing that she would jerk her head free if I tried to drag her, I lifted her fifty pounds and carried her struggling with panic into the cabin where I tied her to the ladder. She fought to-and-fro in terror, but finding no escape finally hunched up in the corner.

"That puppy of yours sure is wild," Steve acknowledged. "I didn't mean to send you off like that, but I totaled a plane hitting a dog. One time I nearly ran down a whole Iditarod team."

"I'll keep her tied," I said.

Laurie and her mother were deep in a world of their own, talking earnestly together. I felt somehow excluded—not on purpose, just forgotten in the excitement. I was tired from running so hard and feeling responsible for the welfare of all these people. I felt that I had to control and provide for every contingency, and the effort left me drained and frightened. The overflow, the cold, Shylo, what to feed people and where to accommodate them whirled through my thoughts. Yet everyone appeared to be enjoying themselves. Steve had a homestead in the bush, and he and Tom were soon talking about ripping logs for floors.

Luke and the women slept in the loft, laid out like a row of pupating cocoons under down bags, while the men elected to sleep on the floor. I was concerned for their comfort and disturbed them a number of times to ask if they were all right. The cabin chilled rapidly as the fire burned out, and I wondered how our home would stand up to the serious cold of the next three months. Shylo was restless as well, dragging her chain across the floor whenever someone turned over. I slept very little between my own thoughts and Darlene and Laurie's whispers. It was very exciting to have company but disturbing too.

STEVE PORTER WAS UP long before light, anxious no doubt to be off. He was already out checking the plane when we rose. We had shifted our habits with the light, waking and going to sleep late, for it was easier to stay up in a warm house than get up to a cold one in the dark. As light began to filter through our front windows, Laurie stretched and crawled over her mother to snuggle under my bag with me.

She hugged me a minute then said, "I've been thinking all night. I don't know how to say this, but it's time for me to leave."

I bit my lip and said steadily, "I know." It hit me so hard that I couldn't say any more. This was the impending storm I had sensed—the unwanted gift from the sky. After a moment, I turned from her and went down the ladder to make breakfast.

Steve had started the fire and the place was already warming, but for the first time I found ice in our cups. My contact lenses were encased in little white marbles and my hands shook as I melted them free. I felt suddenly shy and wanted to dress before Steve returned. The cabin was soon full of good-natured banter as the others got up.

"Well, the catalytic heater went out," Steve said as he entered with a burst of frost. He stamped the snow from his feet and pulled off his parka. "It couldn't keep itself lit. Now the engine is cold-soaked and it'll take a lot of heat to get it going. Anyway, we're not flying today; it's still fifty below."

I didn't know if I was relieved of not. I wanted the people to stay, but my stomach was in knots.

"How can we support you?" Tom asked him.

"I'd like to pack a runway with snowshoes. It'd be tough getting off with a load in that soft snow. If we tramp it down today it should freeze up nicely overnight. And I want to check for overflow. The stuff around the plane looks real solid now."

"We've all got snowshoes except Darlene," Tom answered. "With four people walking it shouldn't take long."

"You'd be surprised what it takes to pack a twelve-hundred-foot strip with a turnaround at both ends. Then we'll need to come up with a way to warm the plane."

Tom and Steve huddled, inventing a device to deliver heat into the engine cowling, while I fixed breakfast of coffee, oatmeal, and cinnamon toast. I could think of nothing but Laurie. It was like we were the only two people in the room. She was watching me and when I melted in tears, she followed me into the loft. We held each other, our faces all screwed up with grief and sat rocking before the window. The gray dawn outside illuminated long icicles hanging along the back roofline.

"I don't want you to go," I sobbed. "Life without you looks lonely and bleak . . . I feel so vulnerable with just the three of us. What about Luke? I keep wondering how we would have handled the bear. Would one of us have gone out to face it alone or taken the chance of leaving him an orphan here by himself?"

She listened, her good-natured face open and sorrowful, and offered no answers. For there were none.

I blew my nose on my kerchief and looked her in the eye. "I can say these things because we both know you don't need to rescue me. My life will keep turning out as it should. It's just . . . so hard . . . to see you go."

"Oh, Miss Jeanie. You've taught me so much. About being free and releasing those we love. Thank you for sharing yourself with me. It's been five of the best months of my life."

I smiled, then broke into fresh tears. "I'm glad I can trust you to make your own decision and let me handle my emotions. It gives me freedom to express them."

"I'm going to miss you."

"Is it John?" I asked.

"He's part of it," she answered carefully. "And I just feel that it's time. I've grown and changed and I need to go back to that other world."

"I'm glad you were here for as long as you were. We couldn't have done it without you. Not this way."

She looked about the cabin. "It's beautiful, isn't it? I've never loved a home like this. I'd like to come back sometime with a child of my own. Would you be my nanny?"

I nodded mutely and hugged her. "If life in the other world turns out to be a disappointment, come back to us. Denise has our checkbook. Just ask her to arrange the charter."

"I will."

❦

THE TEMPERATURE WAS UP to minus forty by the time we headed for the river. Steve and Tom had already lined out a twelve-hundred-foot runway with a teardrop turnaround at each end. The day was gray and their dark figures drifted slowly back and forth, lifting big feet high with each labored step as they stamped out the track. I left Shylo tied to the sawbuck and snapped on Luke's skis, telling him to stick to the hard trails and not furrow the runway. Darlene was with him, a gentle presence. I was concerned that she might be cold, but she said she was fine. She was obviously having a wonderful time.

Up and down the runway we waddled, each lost in the rhythm of breathing: plodding, dark, anonymous forms in the mist, frosted and hunched against the cold. A steady breeze trickled from the north and we pulled wool scarves over our cheeks against its raw bite. I watched Laurie snowshoe ahead of me, seeing her sturdy legs and the swing of her bulky arms, the familiar wool cap and scarf. My heart was heavy and I knew I had more to say. I stopped her in the turnaround and we stood breathing white smoke into the air, our eyebrows and lashes crusted with frost, noses dripping and tears running down red cheeks.

"I'm feeling angry and hurt," I said. "I need to tell you so that I can release it before you go. You were planning to come back and now suddenly it's all changed."

She said nothing, just watched me through the tears.

"I guess that's all," I said, wiping my nose with an icy kerchief. "I'd hug you, but I'm all frozen and wet."

"So hug me anyway."

And we did, awkwardly straddling one another's snowshoes, there at the end of the runway. It was our real good-bye.

"There's never a separation in love," I whispered reassuringly. "What we love is always a part of us."

❦

I HAD LEFT MOOSE and lentil soup on the stove and a corned moose roast in the oven, so dinner was ready when we returned around dark. The fire was almost out, but the cabin was still warm as again the movements of six people filled the small space. I took a lantern and began sorting through the clutter of boxes in the utility room, pulling out perishable items. I had already discovered a broken bottle—frozen while we struggled with the plane.

"I think there's a turkey in one of the boxes," Darlene told me as I pawed about in the half-darkness. "Denise took vacation time to shop."

"The Warteses have been such good friends," I said, wondering how we could ever repay them. Then I realized that they didn't expect us to. Friendship was not about keeping score. "I'm overwhelmed by the kindness of so many people."

"Wait until you get all the boxes. There are about twenty-five left, mostly from your friends."

"That'll make our Christmas." But Laurie won't be here to share it, I thought sadly.

In the other room I could hear Tom and Steve improvising an engine heater. They used an old five-gallon tin to hold Steve's small propane stove. Cutting out the bottom and punching a hole in the top, they attached a tube of beer cans connected with duct tape to funnel the heat under the cowling.

"I'll have one shot in the battery at starting the engine," Steve was saying, "so we'll want to make it our best. I'm gonna put the catalytic heater on it again tonight."

"See, aren't you glad Ken brought in the beer," Tom teased as I entered the room. "I knew these cans would come in handy for something."

Conversation around the table turned to events in the outside world. New countries had been created and they were already killing each other there. People were still doing unspeakable things to one another all over the globe. Of course, I reminded myself, many were quietly doing beautiful and heroic things as well.

"It's Saturday night," I told Steve. "That means you have to sing for your supper." To demonstrate, Laurie and I crooned a duet of "Some Enchanted Evening," using a metal five-gallon can as an echo chamber. Long out of bourbon, Tom opened a bottle that had arrived from friends. We took our bow to the cheering crowd and yielded the spotlight to Steve.

"I deny any ability to sing," he demurred, "but I can play the harmonica. Unfortunately, I didn't bring one along."

"I have one!" Laurie chimed, jumping up. She reached onto the bookshelf and handed it to him. He examined it skeptically.

"I've never used it," she said. "I was hoping to learn."

"Harmonicas are kind of personal," he admitted. He lifted the little instrument and filled our cabin with sweet rhythm and blues, "Oh! Susannah," and the wail of a train. We sat grinning at one another and tried to sing along. My eyes traveled around the table, memorizing the happy faces by the glow of the lantern. I knew it would be a long time before we had company again.

"Where did you learn to play like that?" Darlene asked Steve when he paused.

Without skipping a beat Luke said, "Oh, just dinkin' around, I guess!" We all laughed, then Luke turned to Laurie and asked, "How come you never played it?"

"Well, I sure can't after that!"

During a lull, Tom inquired if there would be any problem taking Laurie out. We were all aware of the delicate limits of the little craft.

"We'll be a bit heavy for this runway, but I think it'll be okay. She can't bring much baggage."

"I'm just taking my sleeping bag, backpack, and a change of clothes," she said.

"You folks okay here?" Steve wanted to know. "I mean, if I don't get back for a day or so, will it be all right?"

"Oh, no problem," Tom answered. "We're set."

"As long as it's before Christmas," I added. "I think you've got most of the presents."

"Do you have any way to call help if you need it?" he persisted.

"We have an ELT."

Steve shook his head. "To tell you the truth, unless you've filed a flight plan, I don't think they'd respond. There's just too many that get set off accidentally in the back of someone's car. The first thing they do if they pick up a signal is check to see if there's a flight plan."

"We're not going to need it," Tom assured him.

"If you ever do, turn it on for fifteen minutes, then off for an hour, then on for fifteen. Establish a pattern so they know someone is signaling. I still doubt if they'd respond, but it'd be worth a try."

"Have you ever needed to be rescued?" Darlene asked.

"I lost a plane once that blew up. They say you have thirty seconds to get clear after a crash. I was out the door and across the muskeg when I thought, 'My survival gear!' I turned around, and the whole thing blew. But I had filed a flight plan and they picked me up within two days."

"Have you had any other crashes," Luke wanted to know.

"Oh, you stay in this business long enough, you have experiences." He was quiet a moment and I wondered if he too was thinking of friends lost.

THE NEXT MORNING THE thermometer had risen to twenty-three below. We started cuddling before dawn, laughing and talking in the loft. I was feeling emotionally drained and was almost relieved that the temperature had climbed to the acceptable flying range. I wanted the farewells over. Laurie had taken Luke and then Tom aside for private good-byes. I knew that beneath our cheerfulness lay a quiet ache that couldn't be healed by prolonging things.

Despite several attempts, Steve had been unable to radio out again, and he was certain Search and Rescue would be coming if he was forced to remain another day. While I started a Sunday breakfast of homemade donuts, he and Tom began warming the plane. Their invention worked well, pumping heat into the engine, and we took turns watching to be sure that the plane didn't catch fire. It required several hours, and the brief day was already fading by the time it was ready to try. Meanwhile, there had been preparation in the cabin: making a snack, rolling up sleeping bags, last-minute packing, mail, and carrying things down to the river. Steve wrote a flight plan and left it with Tom. He wouldn't have radio contact until he climbed out of the valley.

"I'm going to say good-bye to you now," Steve told Luke sometime after noon. "Once I put the battery in, I'll need all my attention on the plane." Luke threw his arms about the pilot and hugged him. We were gathered on the ice, waiting for Tom to fetch the warmed oil and battery from the cabin. The temperature had dropped steadily all day, and it was now thirty below. Steve kept glancing at the southern sky, which was gray with a coming storm. Our sliver of sun had never appeared and already the light was failing.

Tom arrived carrying the warmed oil and battery under his parka. Steve switched off the heater and pulled away the cowling cover, handing the extra fleece that we had provided to Luke. He was intent, his actions deft and quick as he installed the battery and poured in the oil.

"When you get in," he told Laurie and Darlene, "don't talk. Breathe into your parkas until we're in the air. If we fog up the cabin, I won't be able to see for takeoff. Stay back until I call and look where the seat belts are before you get in."

We stood a good distance away as he entered the plane, leaving the doors open. A few minutes later he yelled, "Clear prop!" and we echoed, "Prop clear!" The engine spun, coughed, and died. We waited perhaps five tense minutes before he repeated the call, but this time the plane roared to life. He let it idle ten minutes and then revved the engine, trying to break the skis free of the ice. Nothing happened.

At Steve's signal, Tom ran forward and heaved on a wing strut. His hood

flew back exposing his face and ears to the thirty below hurricane of winds. I filmed the plane and then Laurie waving good-bye as she ran to get in. Luke broke down and was sobbing "Laurie, I love you!" but no one could hear him above the engine. Then they were boarding and we cleared the strip, Luke with his arms around the blanket of fleece and his eyes streaming with tears.

The plane taxied downstream in a blizzard of snow.

"There's something wrong," Tom said, peering through the perpetual fog of his iced glasses. "He's off the strip and I think he's into overflow!"

We watched tensely. The plane slewed around and poised at an angle to the river for several minutes as if undecided. We could see his lights red, green, and twin white. Twilight was descending with a gray bank of clouds out of the southern evening.

"He's into overflow," Tom repeated. "I was worried about that area, but he checked it and said he thought it would be okay."

"Is there anything we can do?"

He shook his head. "I don't think so."

Suddenly, the pitch changed to a flat yowl that filled our quiet valley, echoing off the bluff at Pike Slough. The plane lurched into motion and plowed toward us, terribly slow it seemed to me. It passed us, laboring upriver in a fog of blowing snow, and disappeared from view.

"He said he'd be off by here!" Tom yelled. "He's not going to make it!"

He's got to stop! I thought, staring hard into the small blizzard that obscured the river. Still the roar continued. I counted the long seconds and watched the trees that loomed like a brick wall at the bend, my jaws clenched in fear. Then suddenly we saw the plane lift ponderously out of the haze, a white smoke of condensation streaming behind the wings.

"He's off!" we both breathed. My heart was hammering. The brave little ship with its precious cargo became a dot in the northern sky, then circled back, high overhead. They passed us with a good-bye waggle of wings and a twinkle of lights that became a star in the stormy south. The last thing to disappear was the drone of the engine, leaving a vast and sad silence.

I turned to Luke and knelt. "It's okay, Son," I told him. "You've got Daddy and me, and we're still going to have a good time."

His wet face framed in icy fur turned up to me in misery. "Not as good as with Laurie," he sobbed.

"I know," I said, my own eyes filling again.

Tom stooped and picked Luke up. "This is a new beginning," he told us, "and we're going to have a wonderful year." He smiled gently and hugged his son. "Let's get warm. My feet are freezing."

Shylo was chained to the sawbuck, a position from which she would neither eat nor relieve herself, but sat glaring dolefully. I snapped off the hated chain, releasing her into the dusk. After she had attended to nature she disappeared for an hour, presumably checking out all the activities that had excluded her. I was pleased to give her the night but had promised Steve to confine her during the daylight hours until the plane returned.

Our diminished family entered the dark cabin and lit the Coleman lantern. We were quiet and somber, but grief has its own course and some things can't be rushed. The thing I remember was how gently and with what love we treated one another. Losing Laurie reminded us of how precious each person is. We were all we had.

"I'd like to take over the dishes," Tom offered as I set the table for three. Luke had climbed the ladder and was quietly digging through his Legos for the first time in weeks. "I'll also handle firewood, water hauling, and slop bucket. I've been thinking that we should let Luke use a bucket at night. It's asking too much to have him go out in the dark at fifty below and sit on that toilet."

"He's been afraid of the meat rack ever since we killed the bear there," I agreed.

Tom put his arms around me and looked into my eyes. "I know you're going to miss Laurie, we all will, but it's an opportunity for us to pull together."

I studied him and nodded slowly. His nose was peeling from frostbite and his face looked pale and vulnerable. It was true, I thought. It had been so easy for me to depend on Laurie that I had fallen into the habit of thinking of her as my major support. Women often have this unspoken harmony of daily movement. But where did that leave Tom? He had never acted jealous. He seemed remote, almost indifferent at times, which prompted me to greater dependence on Laurie. Well, Tom wasn't a woman, yet he was capable of nurturing if I gave him a chance. He just wouldn't compete for my attention.

I laid my head on his shoulder and rested my arms about his waist. He seemed half the size he used to be. "I guess Laurie must have achieved her goals," I said. "Maybe it was time for her to go."

"We planned this adventure before we met Laurie. We're still here and look at the wonderful home we have, thanks to her. I just hope she isn't feeling incomplete. It was a hard choice and a sudden decision."

"It gives us a chance to rediscover each other," I said slowly. He didn't answer, but his arms tightened around me.

After dinner, Tom read Luke a short story and I took him up the ladder to bed. "Do you want me to help you say a prayer to release your feelings about Laurie going?" I asked as I settled him in his corner under the window.

"No. Not yet," he answered sadly, tucking Oliver under his chin. "I don't want to talk about it."

I pulled his covers back from the black window so that they wouldn't freeze into the ice. The small panes under the eave and the door were the only single-glazed windows in the cabin.

"I don't like that window," Luke confided.

"You don't? I planned it as a cozy corner for you, though it doesn't look so cozy right now," I admitted.

"I'm afraid bears will climb in," he whispered.

"The bears are all asleep for the winter, and they wouldn't climb up here anyway, you know."

"I'm still afraid. Will you sleep next to me the way Laurie did? She kept me safe."

"Yes." I thought of Laurie gently soothing him at night when he ground his teeth. She was so patient and gentle.

"I want you to come to bed now."

"We're right below you, Luke. Nothing can happen."

"Please?"

"I'll lay here awhile. Now you go to sleep. You've had a rough three days. We all have."

"What's wrong with Daddy? He makes that wheezing noise." He demonstrated, drawing in a long and noisy breath.

"I don't know. I wish I did." I lay on my back, watching the warm play of light along the ceiling poles. Luke's head was cradled on my shoulder. How glad I was to have a haven from winter, but how I dreaded the dark and cold! It depressed me and made me feel vulnerable. Maybe we should have all left, I thought.

"Does he have the flu or something?"

"No. Not the flu. You have to catch that from people."

Tom still wheezed, especially when he lay down, and his hacking cough persisted. He had completed three courses of different antibiotics and it hadn't cleared up. I put him on Luke's asthma inhalants, hoping to open his airways. At least Luke had shown no sign of problems this winter. For that, I was thankful. I sighed. Even if Tom had TB, he had licked it once without medical help, maybe he would again.

"Is he going to get better?"

"I hope so. I want him to go out to see a doctor when the plane comes back. He doesn't think he needs to."

"When's the plane coming?"

"Probably in the next few days. If Steve waits much longer, it'll be too dark. We'll need to keep Shylo tied until then. Are you looking forward to seeing the plane again?"

"No. It'll just remind me of Laurie going away," he answered, turning his face to the wall.

I stroked his soft hair, smoothing the cowlick. "Tomorrow let's read our mail and see what people sent us. Thanksgiving is in three days. I think the turkey got left for the second trip, but we do have a chicken. And frozen pizza."

"It won't be the same without Laurie."

"No, it won't, but we can still make it special."

❦

OUR SECOND THANKSGIVING WAS subdued. On the bookshelf I discovered a small package and a note from Laurie. "How do I ever thank you for welcoming me into your lives with the same generosity and loving kindness that you have allowed me on my way now," she wrote. "My love for you is tender, appreciative and immense. Gratefully I bid you peace until we meet again. Your Laurie."

I wasn't ready to read the other mail. It had waited months in the Warteses' home and I would have preferred to ration it, like the chicken, after I recovered from all that had happened. Nevertheless, we needed to prepare answers to go out with the plane, so Tom read aloud while I cooked. Our families had contacted one another and exchanged copies of our few letters coast to coast. Everyone sent love and good wishes. Most of the boxes contained groceries that Denise had bought for us, but there were a few presents that we tucked away until Christmas. John had written separately to Luke, sending him a fancy slingshot and a new spring for the scissors of his knife. Luke's playmates, Troy and Michael, had also written with childish hands, proud in their new abilities to print.

The temperature rose and we spent the days tramping a better runway. To keep Shylo from remaining tied, I harnessed her each morning and let her pull a short log about as we worked. Luke came too, a little figure skiing back and forth, the long sleeves of his parka dangling over his poles, hood bobbing and motor running.

"Isn't he ever quiet?" Tom asked as we paused at the turnaround. Luke was a hundred yards away, but his happy noises carried clearly on the still air. With the warmer weather, the chickadees were active and we could also hear them singing back in the trees.

I smiled. "Just think of him like a bird," I answered in my self-appointed role of peacemaker. "It's as natural for him to make his little music as for them." There's an inherent aloneness in the heart of life, I thought watching this son of ours ski toward us. We see one another through filters. My efforts to justify myself or others were pointless. If someone sees you, there's nothing to explain; if they don't, no explanation will work.

Luke drew abreast of us and stopped to gaze down the long runway at the departing sun. In my mind, I could envision the three of us standing alone in this great, white land, an image both beautiful and frightening. It was a privilege to be here and a risk—just like the rest of life. Straight south, the crest of midday sun slid along the distant mountains, casting enormous shadows across the blue snow. It was almost gone. We wouldn't see it again for nearly two months, and I felt a sadness as we watched its fire melt into the land and twinkle out. I could understand how ancient peoples had worshipped the sun—giver of all warmth and life on this planet. To see it vanish and know that it would not be back tomorrow was a poignant experience. The long dark was upon us.

I sighed, wondering how I would fill the cold, black days ahead. Life was always perfect, but it didn't always fit my pictures. Happiness couldn't be held, but was created from finding the beauty in each day, even when I couldn't see the sun. Happiness, I thought, is a discipline as well as an occasional gift.

We kept watch, expecting each day to see the returning plane and anxiously checking the overflow. It would soon be too dark for a flight from Fairbanks. Day by day the runway grew until it was forty-feet wide, twelve hundred feet long, and packed hard enough to walk on. Each time it snowed or the wind blew, we tramped it all again. My mind kept returning to the image of the little plane disappearing into the gray sky and I wondered if Laurie, Darlene, and Steve had made it out safely. If they hadn't, we might not find out until next fall. No, I wouldn't think about it, I decided.

And so we waited and kept improving the runway as the days slowly passed. There was no way of knowing at the time, but we would not hear of them, or the challenges they faced on that flight, for five long months.

First snow, and we are happy to be inside with plastic in the doorway.

Jeanie and Luke read stories to pass the dark days.

Luke creates games during the "way belows."

Overflow inundates the old runway.

Luke skis beneath a winter moon.

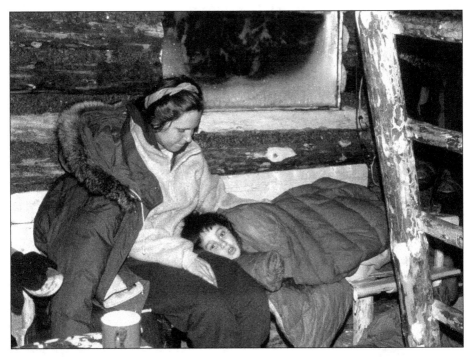

Laurie and Luke snuggle on the sofa.

Downstream travel to the bridge, summer 1993.

Windy day in camp on the Yukon.

CHAPTER 10

I peered between the dark spruce of Daddy's Magic Forest, wondering where Shylo was. Luke and I had been out several hours and the light was beginning to fail. There wasn't enough time to take him home and return and search for the dog, and there was no point in calling for her. She wouldn't come unless it suited her and, like the wolves, Shylo never barked.

We had taken an excursion over to Lake Eugene, enjoying the falling snow and packing trails, while Tom renewed the airstrip. Because of the plane, Shylo was still restricted to pulling her log during our five hours of twilight. It was troublesome keeping her under control but discipline had been good for her. Deep snow had forced her to follow me on the way out. Luke vied for second place in line, but she shouldered him into drifts and ran over him. When we turned for home, Shylo had sprinted ahead on the freshly broken trail and disappeared.

It was the second week in December and the temperature had risen, as it did whenever a storm came, to almost zero. Silently I blessed the warm weather. It was a beautiful, blue-gray day, soft as a dove without shadow or definition; a day like an Ansel Adams photograph, misty and indistinct. Our own clothes provided the only color.

I scanned the edge of the woods for fresh sign, but tracks were hard to discriminate in the falling snow. Shylo could be anywhere and, though I was angry, the image of her snared by her harness back in the trees worried me. The trail followed an old river channel beside the wood. Ahead was a little "ski run" I had stamped for Luke on our way over, a packed loop that ascended the bank. From somewhere back in the trees came the sudden alarm call of a red squirrel.

"Why don't you stay here," I suggested to Luke. "Don't go anywhere; just practice skiing on your new run until I get back."

"Okay."

"Promise?"

"Uh-huh."

He turned onto the path that angled up the bank. At the top he called out to the silent world like a radio announcer, introducing himself as a famous skier about to make a historic jump. Then he plunged down the brief incline and nosed over into fluffy snow. Only the back of his parka marked the spot where he had crashed. A moment later he emerged and started over.

I was reluctant to leave him but knew he'd have trouble back in the dense woods. With a last look, I struck out toward the sound of the squirrel. The soft snow was halfway up my thigh, and it took effort to move off the path. In many ways the land was more accessible now, but one was restricted (almost like a train) to beaten trails, limiting the sense of three-dimensionality that comes of viewing life from a variety of angles.

Tom had discovered this forest last summer, part of the system of old islands with overgrown bars that stretched east to Pike Slough. It was a squirrels' paradise of healthy spruce with interlocking branches. There was a mysterious energy about the place, as if fairies lived beneath the canopy. It was also close and unpleasant when the trees were heavily laden with snow. Every step brought fountains of crystals onto my head as I plowed on, ducking under the heavy boughs.

I quickly left the open behind. Gambling that the squirrel would continue his angry tirade, I wove toward the sound, accompanied by a constant deluge of snow. The forest was dark and it was good to know that I would be able to follow my own laborious trail back. Beneath the trees, the snow was peppered with shredded cones and tunnels attesting to the recent activity of squirrels. They were awake periodically throughout the winter, especially when it warmed.

Abruptly the clamor ceased and I peered up in time to catch the flash of a little body outlined against gray sky. Another movement arrested my attention, and there was Shylo. Her harness was wrapped about the trunk of a tree and the log was snugged up tightly on the other end. I plowed toward her on my oversized feet. She was totally unrepentant and lunged after the squirrel the moment I released her to untangle the mess. However, I was ready, having threaded her leash through the harness and onto the collar to keep her from wriggling free. I had schooled under a sterner teacher than Shylo, a nasty gelding who left me with a permanent rope burn across the back of one hand and a respect for the cunning of an unwilling animal.

Slowly we made our way back through the forest. I forced Shylo to walk behind me on the leash, pulling her log. She was sullen but bided her time, treading on my snowshoes occasionally to contest. I was happy to emerge in the open and see Luke, looking like Frosty the Snowman from his numerous spills, cycling on the ski run.

I stood catching my breath and watched a troop of crossbills work the tops of the spruce. There were perhaps a dozen birds and they blew like autumn leaves in a singing crowd from tree to tree, picking the tiny seeds from the cones and coincidentally knocking the tops free of snow. The spruce seemed to welcome the attention, their top cones arrayed in offering. The light was fading and I called Luke. He took the lead going home while I kept Shylo tethered behind me in disgrace.

As we plodded through the silent land, I wondered how I found myself the uncontested gardener of this vast wilderness. True, most people didn't want to be here. Many viewed the Arctic as wasteland or as raw material for development. They didn't look for the countless facets of God: the way everything is interconnected. It wasn't simply a matter of saving land for the future, I decided, but of beliefs about it. You couldn't put a price tag on it or claim ownership. As Chief Seattle said 150 years ago, "The earth does not belong to us. We belong to the earth." I thought about the Buddhist philosophy that said life could be lived as a walking meditation. Every movement can be sacred, every thought, a prayer. Karma Yoga it was called, where "the chopping of wood and carrying of water (quite literally in our case) becomes a conscious celebration of Spirit."

I felt like a junkie, drying out from my cultural addiction to stress, the cerebral process, and the need to produce. Surely, there must be more to life than production and consumption of products, but I didn't know how to get out of the cycle except by leaving it altogether. Leaving wasn't the ultimate answer, but it provided a context for gaining perspective. Enlightenment seemed possible here, where the very land shaped the mind in natural, harmonic patterns. This winter landscape with its austere colors and dearth of sound lent the perfect simplicity for exploring a different level of seeing.

For twenty years I'd been continuously doing, never finding the time to just Be. So here I was, remote from race mind, seeking serenity and inner light. Here, at the end of the twentieth century with all its complex problems, I had been granted an unusual share of beauty and solitude. I smiled to myself as I walked, enjoying the rhythm of my own breath, the crunch of snow, and the misty world of swirling flakes outlined in dark trees. I needed time out but I had business in that other world too. Somehow I would need to learn to balance myself in both.

❧

"I MANAGED TO STOP the drip," Tom told me as I stepped from the blue twilight into the warmth of the cabin. Already a lantern burned on the table. "A dam of

ice had built up along the edge of the roof. That west side is just too flat to drain well. I cleaned it out, but ended up tearing the plastic. I probably should have left it alone."

"Basic design flaw," I said balefully.

"It isn't a big deal," he reassured. "We'll put a bucket under it. Anyway, it's not dripping now."

We had awakened that morning to a soggy bed. Water was seeping down the inside of our west wall and onto the loft. It left me feeling peculiarly vulnerable. For me the loft was a safe retreat, and I didn't like being reminded that only a thin piece of plastic held out the winter.

The icicles had started in October, crystal stalactites growing from the edge of the roof whenever the weather warmed until they finally touched the ground. I had worried about them, but Tom had seen only beauty in their gradual encroachment. Now it had reached the point where they were losing their charm, even for him.

It's hard to fathom the inexorable power of ice. There's no force on earth that can match the gentle fall of snow. Silently, it accumulates, delicate crystals adding tons of weight with such precision that a feather of moss or a footprint will emerge undisturbed from four feet of snow in the spring. Yet the relentless power of frozen water cannot be stopped. It surrenders each summer as long as the balance is maintained, then a year arrives when the ice begins to win. Season by season it grows and moves, locking up the earth's water, flake by tiny flake, until it buries continents under thousands of glacial feet, carving deep into the bedrock, gouging out valleys and depressing the very mantle of the earth. Between the dance of sunlight and ice does all life exist.

I busied myself making potato-cheese soup and moose bacon sandwiches. We had fallen into the habit of eating when we were hungry and sleeping when tired. It seemed only natural, for here the day itself changed dramatically with the season. I generally went to bed early and woke early; Tom was the reverse, and so we acquired privacy in a small space merely by separating in time. It was the kind of adaptation many species devise to share the same resources.

As I cooked, Tom shuffled the cards for cribbage and dealt hands for himself and Luke. He had hauled water for baths and the big kettle on the back of the stove was full and already hot.

"How's the creek doing?" I asked.

"Looks pretty good. I thought we'd lose it during that last cold spell, but it's still flowing."

"Can I make you a cup of coffee?"

"Poof!" said Tom, just like Laurie used to.

Luke raised his face and grinned. "And life goes on," he remarked.

It does indeed, I thought. Tom had been particularly tender to both of us since her departure. We were discovering that life was still good. Ours was one of contentment and ease. With only three there was a geometric decrease in interactions, but a quiet strength had grown from our unity. Luke received a great deal of affection and seemed to be doing well.

"What's infinity plus one?" he asked, thumbing his cards.

"Calculus," I answered. Luke looked at me quizzically. "It's still infinity," I told him, "but you're not supposed to think about it for a few years."

"How can it still be infinity?"

"Well, if infinity goes on forever, then you can always add one more to it, right? So infinity plus one is still infinity."

"No, it's infinity plus one," he persisted.

"Are you gonna count your hand?" Tom asked, drumming impatiently on his cards.

I smiled to myself watching the homely scene, faces out of a Rembrandt painting in the glow of the lantern: Luke's fresh as a peach, his expression serious and mouth working silently as he pondered his cards; Tom's relaxed and thoughtful, a crinkle of laughter in the corners of the eyes. What a gift this year had been for each of us!

It was getting dark. I set a tallow candle on the counter and lit it from a long splinter thrust into the stove. It still amazed me that I could release sunlight stored in moose fat. For that matter, my own fat would give off this golden light. We shared this energy cycle: sun, tree, moose, and I.

After dinner we slipped on parkas and went down to see the river, as we always did. When I turned her loose for the night, Shylo became a different being. In a demonstration of reckless power, she sped in great loops about us, darting in and out of the trees like a spirit of the twilight. It was no longer snowing and the clouds had lifted in a sooty band above a strip of periwinkle sky. It was a signature color, sky darker than the snowy mountains, that I've only seen in high latitudes. Through the black trees we could see the full moon rising, a great golden sphere along the silver flank of Mount Laurie, shadows marching before it across the pale snow.

We saw more of the moon as winter progressed. When nearing full, it rose higher each night, until it circled the sky for twenty hours, dramatically lighting the valley. Night was almost as bright by that full moon as it was during much of the day now, but our adventure with the bear had left me with a lingering unease. I spoke of taking a moonlit hike yet I wasn't really comfortable with the idea. Fear of the dark has ancient roots, and between the energies of fear and quest did my own life balance. I had yet to make peace with my bogeymen.

Out on the river, Shylo swam through the snow, waves of it billowing about her leaping shoulders. She should have been born a wolf, I thought, watching her. How she loved to run free! The cloudy sky glowed brighter than the forest, giving a strange daylight cast to the land. Clouds alternately screened and revealed the moon, while on the ground all was quiet. Delicate "fairy snow," half the width of my thumbnail, six-sided and perfect, sifted down in shimmering flakes. They sparkled in the moonlight, accumulating in a fluff so light that a fragile inch was only a few flakes high.

I still missed Laurie. Many animals experience themselves as a group, and I wondered if that wasn't true of me. I remembered walking through the pines one Arizona evening, baby Luke on my back, Tom and my aunt and uncle beside me. As we crested a hill we spread out among the giant ponderosa, young and old traversing the ridge together. I had a sudden feeling of transcending millennia: this was my family tribe, those I could depend on and who depended on me. The image brought a sense of deep contentment and connectedness. It had been written in my genes. Here was a void that a myriad of social contacts could not fill. I realized that this closeness was integral to our current odyssey, and part of my feeling of loss at Laurie's departure. I didn't miss "people" but members of my clan.

We stood for a long time gazing at the velvet evening. Somewhere upriver a great gray owl called into the stillness and was answered by another over at

Pike Slough. We hadn't heard wolves since early September and I imagined they had followed the caribou into Canada. As the moon cleared the peak, a strange whisper of wind touched the trees, causing them to creak like stiff old men as they gratefully shook off the weight of new snow.

"I was saying a silent prayer of thanksgiving," Luke told his father. "Aren't we lucky to be here?"

"Yes, we are," Tom agreed. He had his arm about his son's shoulders. We watched the moon rise in the cold, clearing sky.

"I'm done now," Luke said. "Do you want to go in? I can stay longer, if you like."

"No, I can go in now," Tom replied. Hand in hand the two turned back up the trail and I followed them, Shylo at my heels.

Ahead our cabin appeared, blanketed in white and striped with moonbeams. Candlelight beckoned from the windows. I felt a rush of joy at the sight of it. Somehow the act of pulling these logs together had given me a feeling of wonder and pride, where the world of earthmoving machines always left me feeling puny. This was a scale of human accomplishment that my mind could grasp. I never tired of its moods. On cold nights, frost glittered like diamonds along the bottom of the windows. By candlelight it seemed magical, a woodcutter's hut sprung from a storybook in sepia tones of gold and brown. It was a living (and biodegradable) home, and we often heard the faint sound of larva eating their slow way through the logs. Sometimes they would pupate, small, black beetles falling onto the table, out of sync with the rest of the Arctic.

Tom and I now took turns putting Luke to bed. He had developed a disturbing fear of bears since Laurie's departure and insisted that someone remain in the loft. One of us always lay beside him until he fell asleep.

"I'm afraid of bears coming through the window," he whispered as I tucked him in that night. It was warm in the loft, but he pulled the covers up to his neck. I had zipped our bags together into a big quilt and he wrapped it tightly about him.

"I understand how you feel," I said, peeling the covers back and handing him his blanket and teddy. I leaned on one elbow and kissed his cheek. He smelled clean and his hair was still damp from the bath. "When I was your age, I was afraid of men hiding under my bed at night. Even after I looked, I was still afraid. All I can tell you is that it's only a fear. You know why bears won't climb through that window?"

"It's too small," he chimed, exposing his two new teeth.

"Right. And what else?"

"It's winter and they're sleeping."

"Good. Anything more?"

He thought. "Well, it's too high up."

"Uh-huh. So you already know that it's just a fear. It feels real, but it's not. Don't cover up; it's too hot up here." He was again pulling up the sleeping bag.

"But I'm afraid of bears," he said reasonably.

"Covers won't protect you. You'll just sweat."

"They help. I can hide."

I thought a moment, rolling onto my back to stare up at the rafters. They were streaked by the drawknife and had a random pattern of worm furrows. From below came the soft hiss of the gas lantern where Tom sat reading. I started on a different tack. "Here's old Oliver," I said patting the little white bear. "He'll protect you."

Luke studied the benign creature thoughtfully and shook his head. "I don't think he can."

"Maybe you need a large bear for an imaginary friend," I counseled. Zaza had disappeared late in the summer (mean tricks and all) and nobody missed him. "Once there was a little boy . . ." I began.

I was to tell Luke stories for much of the winter until they became a saga. At some point he took charge, and his fantasy world evolved into a far grander and more technical arena than I had created. My homely cabin in the woods was transformed into a crystal palace staffed with armies of willing servants and throngs of helpful bears, all flying about in immense planes at a hundred times the speed of light. Such are the ways of progress.

When I had finished the first tale, we lay quietly together. His eyes were closed and I thought he had drifted off.

"Do you think Santa will find us?" he asked.

"Oh, I imagine so."

"What do you think I should ask for?"

"A bicycle. Like you got last year."

"Mama, I'm serious. What do you think I should ask for?"

"Well, what do you want?"

"I don't know. That's why I'm asking you. Something we could use up here. Not a bicycle! Maybe a sleigh."

"Why don't you just leave it up to Santa? He's pretty wise you know."

"I was thinking of sending him a message in my mind. Like I did the Tooth Fairy. I don't want him to bring something I can't use. Maybe he could bring Daddy some different medicine."

"Daddy's doing better. I think he may get over whatever it is yet." I reached across and stroked his forehead. "I love you, Bukie."

"I love you too, Mama Lama." He kissed my cheek and then rubbed it in with his pudgy hand. "Sometimes I say, 'I love you' just to hear you say it back," he confessed. "So I can feel special and valuable."

"A lot of people do that. It's very common."

"It is?"

"Yes. I've done it. But I'll tell you a secret: you're the one who creates the experience of being special and valuable. It's a gift you give yourself."

♥

"Zoom! Pow! Boom!"

I came slowly to consciousness to the patter of light thumps and wiggles from Luke and a whispered barrage of "Clomp! Clomp! Clomp!" Pearl-gray light filtered dimly through the windows and I knew it was about eleven. The cabin was cold and my nose told me the temperature had plummeted again during the night.

"Can't you hold still?" I whispered in exasperation.

"I'm having a fantasy," he informed me. "It's my first real one."

I didn't ask him why every morning began this way. "You could go down and start the stove."

"It's cold."

"I know. That's why it would be nice to have the stove going." I rolled toward him and gave up sleep. "Whisper, so we don't disturb Daddy."

"Tell me about when you were little."

"Me? I was never little. I was born forty-two-years old."

"No!" Luke started to giggle and put his hand over my mouth.

"My mother was so disappointed," I pulled his hand away and propped my head up. "She was expecting something small and pink."

"Mama, stop it. Really." He was laughing now.

"Shhh . . . you'll wake Daddy. When they handed me to her she said, 'What's this old lady?'"

By this time Luke was giggling so hard that Tom couldn't resist joining. He rolled over and snuggled warmly against us, our sleeping bags a big pile of fluffy down.

"Daddy, it's important that you always find women who can handle an ax and use tools and fix things," Luke informed him.

"Why is that?" Tom wanted to know.

"Otherwise you can't go to the Arctic."

"Now, Luke," I amended, "some men know those things too."

"Like me!" Tom said defensively.

"But that's because Mama taught you," Luke said roguishly.

When they reached across me to tickle each other, I extracted myself from the middle. "We'd better get up in case a plane comes today," I told them.

But it didn't.

✿

STARING OUT FROM THE cutbank at thirty-five below, it was hard to remember how the valley looked in summer, or indeed to believe this was the same land. I had joined Tom at the Overlook, a point south of our old camp. The runway stretched below us, written in thousands of snowshoe tracks. Luke was becoming very proficient on his little skis and was practicing runs up and down the trail to the river. Shylo was out on the ice pulling her log in the pastel dawn.

"What do you suppose happened to him?" I asked, gazing into the empty sky.

Tom was bundled in the green down parka and mukluks that I had made so long ago. His face was framed in frosted ruff and his glasses were frozen. Tusks of ice hung from his mustache, but his gaze was peaceful and far away.

"I suppose it just got too late in the season," he answered. "I imagine we'll see him when the sun returns, but it doesn't hurt to keep the runway open—just in case."

"It's hard to let it go," I sighed. "I was counting on Christmas presents for Luke."

"I know. If he doesn't make it before Christmas, I'd just as soon he saved us the money."

"It's only money," I reminded him. That was something we had often told one another in the past, but it seemed particularly apt from this perspective. Neither of us had mentioned money in a long time.

"We can make presents," he went on. "I'm planning a beaded leather holster for Luke's knife so he can wear it on his belt. We'll have a second Christmas when the plane comes. And there's always Santa."

"I want Christmas to be special for Luke this year."

"I agree. Do you think we should have a tree?"

I considered it a minute. We had always bought living ones and planted them afterward. "He's made all those ornaments," I answered. Luke had been making them for weeks, his own project. He began by sawing round slices from the ends of sticks, then drilled holes for string to hang them by, and colored them with his crayons.

"We can thin one from a clump and explain to Luke that it'll help the remaining trees," he answered.

"It's gonna be kind of a bare Christmas," I admitted. "I had counted on presents from friends and family."

"I don't think that'll matter if we make it special." His eyes crinkled lovingly at me though his lower face was a mask of ice.

"I have a secret hope that Laurie has decided to return after a long visit with John," I confessed. We were quiet awhile and then I added, "My secret fear is that they all died going out."

"Whatever happened, it was long ago." Tom put a big, fluffy arm about my back.

"It's like we're frozen in time," I said. I remembered reading newspaper packing from one of the boxes and telling Tom that this was what it was like to die: the world goes on without you. There was a certain relief in discovering that my presence wasn't necessary.

My feet were getting cold, but I stayed. These days of lingering twilight were as beautiful as a symphony. In the perfect silence I could almost hear George Winston playing classical piano. It was a land of dramatic changes, of sky, snow, and aurora borealis. The colors were often unreal: mauve, violet, and smoky blues so deep you would disbelieve them in a painting, or soft and seductive, glowing with an internal radiance of the day unborn.

"Funny," I mused, "there really isn't that much to see, and yet I never tire of looking at it."

Tom was quiet awhile. "I have moments each day of sheer exhilaration," he said slowly. His white breath smoked into the still air. "It's so silent, all you can hear is your heart. I didn't know you could hear your own heart. I never dreamed there was this kind of quiet."

I nodded. "I sometimes feel like I'm right on the verge of something. A doorway I can't quite remember."

"I come down to this lookout several times a day and just stand here," Tom agreed. "I never get enough of it. Often I have a rush of pure joy, like nothing I've ever known. Just to be here. Yet sometimes it strikes me with a deep sadness, and that's what I don't understand."

"A melancholy. Yes, I know."

"It's almost too beautiful. So beautiful it hurts."

"Maybe that's because you can't ever quite grasp it," I offered.

"I don't know why," he repeated. "It's just that way. This land is full of questions. I'm not sure that the answers are important. Each answer only opens new questions. It challenges you to be responsible for your own life and your own vision of life. There's no one to judge you or cover for you."

"My feet are cold," I said, picking up my snowshoes and starting for the trail. "I'm gonna walk the runway."

"I'll join you, but I want to get water first." Our little finger of the creek had finally frozen, but Tom had discovered thin river ice near Clam Springs, which would give us easy water much of the winter.

The runway had evolved into a piece of art. Tired of simply trudging back and forth like a miniature steamroller, Tom had begun walking intricate patterns into the snow. It now spread before me like a giant quilt. As I huffed along in ever decreasing rectangles completing the north end of the pattern, my breath lined out behind me in the still air, remaining in a vapor trail as definitive and almost as lasting as my tracks.

There was something freeing about creating an act of art with no enduring product. It was pure process, unmarketable and therefore playful. The next wind or snowstorm would bury it. I felt the same way about our trails: their very impermanence added to their appeal. With my feet I could manufacture a wide, smooth boulevard over which I passed with ease, but add sunlight, and presto! Not a mark would remain of my labors. It was the ultimate in recyclable architecture. That brought me again to the definition of art, not as something you do but a way of Being. Ultimately, one's own life was the real artistic expression. It was possible to live creatively without leaving monuments, to touch the earth softly.

At the bend in the river I spotted our cow moose foraging along the base of a cutbank, her dark form blending perfectly with the blotches of exposed earth. She seemed to have become accustomed to our presence, for we had sighted her on several occasions. I stood watching as she moved like a ship, plowing steadily through the deep snow, only her head and upper body visible. Sometimes she disappeared behind the dunes so that only the hump of her back and ears remained. She was dainty in her habits, brushing the snow from twigs with the flexible tip of her nose, spraying it around her in white plumes. I wondered if she were the same animal I had spared the previous fall.

I was discovering a preference for gentle interactions. Even meat seemed distasteful, particularly after my messy bouts with the large, dripping quarters in the half-darkness of the cabin, but I drew no general conclusions. What was appropriate for me, might not be for another, or even for me at a different time. Balance was an individual matter; certainly it couldn't be attained by judgment or passing more laws.

"I'm going in," Tom said as he came abreast of me and stopped. "It's too cold." A fit of coughing hit him.

"I think you should." We had been plodding up and down the runway for much of an hour, ships passing in the twilight, each in the world of his own thoughts. I pointed to the moose and he nodded. Halfway down the airstrip we could hear Luke puttering like a lawn mower. He was on skis, wearing adult snow boots over layers of socks as he did in very cold weather.

"I'm almost done. I'll be in soon," I told him, wiping the frost from my crusted lashes. "Ask Luke if he wants to join you . . . turn this way . . . let me look at you."

"What's the matter?"

"Looks like you froze your nose again." The tip of Tom's nose had turned a sickly white. "Put your hand over it."

"Don't stay out too long." His voice was muffled as he thawed his nose. "I'd rather we stuck together when it's this cold. It's just not safe."

❧

I FOUND MYSELF DREADING the cold and dark of deep winter. It wasn't the cold as much as the dark that I minded. There was an essence of unreality for me in the prolonged night. It felt as if my sight were failing as I groped about with lanterns and candles trying to find things and cook meals. Time itself became dreamlike, with no distinct memories or sharp edges. It made me realize how much the very process of memory was visual for me.

A dreamland, I thought: that was my experience of arctic winter. There was a fuzziness to time itself. It was hard to remember the other world. I felt surprised that I had ever been anywhere else. That other life seemed vague, its memories locked in separate rooms of my mind where people and situations remained as I had last seen them. My night dreams confirmed this, for I never dreamed of the Arctic now, though I often did in Arizona. It was as if I lived parallel lives and bridged them only in sleep. When I returned, I knew there would be another shift in consciousness and this cabin would become unreal.

The cold was a constant threat and encumbrance, curtailing our time out-of-doors. When temperatures plunged to fifty below zero and stayed there for days on end, life became a grim siege. Just dressing to go out was a major endeavor. Fifty below is an enemy, a temperature that can kill the foolish or unprepared in minutes. It is almost a hundred and fifty degrees lower than body temperature—a gradient that sucks heat away like a vacuum.

In the cabin the stove was kept stoked. The lower walls behind food canisters glittered with frost as warmth radiated through the logs faster than it was produced. Overhead, ice accumulated between the rafters. We burned piles of

J. ASPEN 94

wood during the cold spells and spent the warmer, snowy days gathering more. It was as important as food to our well-being. When it became obvious that I was not going to complete the small meat house I had started, and Tom was not up to helping me, we cut those logs into firewood as well.

As we neared the end of the year, I held on to the thought that it wouldn't get much darker; soon the sun would begin its return. However, the brunt of intense cold was yet to come. There is always a lag in the seasons, the great mass of our earth taking time to heat up in summer and cool in winter. Early man must have watched the skies much as we did now, yearning for the return of light, warmth, and the promise that life would go on. So it was that we approached the Solstice with thanksgiving, accepting on faith that soon our planet would grandly commence its ponderous swing back into life.

I spent the long evenings reading to Luke in exchange for his efforts at schoolwork. We had finished many of the children's classics. Boredom can be an ally, a door to growth and imagination. There is an inner resourcefulness that only germinates in the soil of unstructured time, and it was gradually taking root in Luke.

He invented a variety of ways to pass the long hours inside. Often he would put on a show for us, asking me to announce him, then appearing from the utility room playing "rock and roll" on the harmonica to the stamp of his feet while we clapped. He performed simple experiments like freezing colored water in various containers. After a bath he would run outside to freeze his hair.

He cut crayons and melted pictures using the heated skillet over foil. He made a plane from wood chips and flew it about with much buzzing and bombing. Sometimes he played jack-in-the-box in an empty garbage can, or chased the dog around on all fours under the table until I had to throw her out.

❧

WE PUT UP OUR Christmas tree on the eve of the Solstice. We had started the day with a special breakfast of powdered eggs, toast, jelly, and the one package of pork sausage that came on the plane. Tom said a lovely prayer, but Luke was impatient and disruptive and it ended with a sense of loss.

"It isn't easy for me to express my feelings," Tom told him. "It has always been hard."

It may have been the first time Luke realized that adults have feelings too. He thought about it much of the morning and later apologized on his own, requesting another family prayer.

Being human, I thought, is never easy. It reminded me of a conversation I had with Luke the day before. I was bringing in loads of firewood as Tom split them when Luke had approached with a stick in his hands.

"I want to show you a new game I invented," he told me. "It's called Bing Whopper." Bing is family lingo for the end of a dog's nose, the part that resembles a black cherry. "First you take this big stick with a hook on it . . ."

"And then you sneak up behind this big ol' bear who's digging roots . . ." I interrupted.

"No. Then you catch the hook over the clothes line . . ."

"And you haul off and 'Whop!' him across the bing!"

"No! Then you take a little stick, like this dowel pin . . ."

"'Ow! Ow!' cries the bear," I grabbed my nose and hopped about, 'Why'd you go and do that for?'"

In spite of himself, Luke laughed. But he was upset too. "I don't like it when you tease me," he said.

"Oh, Luke, lighten up. I'm not poking fun at you; I'm just playing."

"It's just that I sometimes feel like you won't let me finish what I'm saying. You just talk right over me and don't listen."

That really caught me up short. Perhaps he was right. "I'm sorry, Luke. I'll try to stop doing that," I told him.

Raising kids keeps you on your toes, I thought, because your relationship with them is always changing as they grow and acquire new stature. It was a perfect example of letting go of the answers when the questions reappeared. If one was to maintain a healthy, honest relationship and raise a self-regulating human being, there was a fine balance between setting the framework and claiming expertise in another person's life.

❦

OUR CHRISTMAS TREE WAS a scrawny little spruce cut from a cluster on the willow flats near the delta. The day was stark and clear, a landscape of blue and gold with the sky reflected on silent waves of snow. It was forty-nine below zero as we trudged through the soft drifts. We selected the sleeping tree and Luke cut it with the handsaw. Tom carried it gently home, for at that temperature the twigs are as brittle as glass, and we let it warm much of the day before putting it up. Then Tom fitted it through a hole drilled in a flattened log that he nailed to the floor in the corner.

We shared a special dinner of shredded moose burritos and plum pudding with hard sauce, then spent the evening stringing popcorn to decorate the tree. We added tinsel, the few Christmas balls I had brought, and Luke's little wooden ornaments. When we finished, we set out our two presents, for which I had some lingering disappointment, and sang Christmas carols until bedtime.

"It's the nicest tree we ever had," Luke confided as he hugged his father good night. I noticed Shylo had her eye on the popcorn strings. Having no attractive alternatives, she had become remarkably meek and compliant since the onset of serious cold weather.

Late that night, Tom and I stepped outside for a moment before going to bed. It was fifty-three below zero and there was no moon. The inky sky was alive with a grand display of northern lights, sweeping recklessly across the stars. It took my breath away! No matter how often I saw it, I never got used to it. We laughed and pointed as the flames danced and rippled overhead. The sky seemed immeasurably deep with curtains of light streaming downward like sunbeams penetrating the depths of the ocean. There was nothing but a few molecules of frigid air between us and the Milky Way, and I marveled we didn't fall off.

"I think I've discovered the secret of a good life," I told Tom after the cold had driven us back inside. We entered with a burst of frost falling about us in a tiny storm. Tom's glasses instantly froze white, like cartoon eyeballs. He exchanged pairs before cocking a curious eye at me.

"If I can only remember it," I grinned. "I believe that reverence is the yardstick by which to gauge my intentions. If the physical universe is a dimension of God—which I believe—it's up to me to see beauty in every situation. This is easier in Nature," I admitted, "but God must be present in the works of man as well."

Tom mulled this around for a moment.

"There are three principles," I continued, ticking them off on my fingers. "Treat yourself and everything else as sacred. Practice Joy. Seek simplicity."

"I think there is a fourth," he told me. "Integrity. You need to keep your word and remain consistent with your own moral standards."

I started to laugh. "Isn't it some sort of cliché that hermits go off to seek the meaning of life? And I was just saying there are no answers, just questions."

"No, you were saying that the questions remain and the answers keep changing. This is a valid answer for you now, but don't carve it in stone; you may want to grow beyond it."

❦

CHRISTMAS DAWNED AT FIFTY-TWO below, a temperature that had held for days. Sometimes I felt like the thermometer was frozen. Luke awakened early and crept down the ladder in the dim light. He crawled back into bed a few minutes later, eyes big with wonder and fingers cold.

"Santa brought me a little sleigh!" He whispered as he snuggled like a chick against the warmth of my body. "There were other presents, too! And all the stockings are full!"

Then, as a measure of his maturity, he remained very still and allowed me to doze for almost an hour until it was light enough to get up. Even at noon I had to put my contacts lenses in mostly by feel. I rose when I heard the guilty crunching of popcorn and tossed Shylo out. It was too cold to worry about keeping her tied. No plane was coming today and I knew she wouldn't go far.

"I'm glad your stockings contained real goodies, too, not just nuts and apples like usual," Luke said as we shared Christmas morning together. "I must be very special for Santa to be so nice. Isn't my sleigh beautiful! I've already thanked him in my heart."

The only store-bought present he received from us was an orange Frisbee, but he thanked us for it and all day proudly wore his knife scabbard and the mink booties I made. We put on our best clothes and ate tenderloin, the last of the chicken, mashed potatoes and gravy, fresh rolls, and cherry pie (made from a can that Denise had sent). Luke wanted to hitch up Shylo and see how the little wooden sled worked, but it was too cold. We celebrated by lighting two lamps. Tom remarked that we were halfway through the dark days and had used only a third of our fuel so we could afford to relax. It made the day more cheerful.

I felt privileged to be here this special Christmas Day, sharing the wilderness with my family. My happiness would have been complete, had it not been for Tom's persistent cough. He was getting worse again, there could be no doubt, coughing blood once more and occasionally chunks of peculiar stuff that looked like moldy sponge. I didn't know what to do. I could resort to antibiotics, but that hadn't cleared it up before and I doubted it would now. Yet what else was there? I looked at his bony chest and wished I had X-ray vision. What was going on in there? The old question, "What happens if someone gets sick?" was coming back to haunt me, and I didn't have any answers.

CHAPTER 11

The Australian aborigines believed that everything was created during the Dreamtime: the time before the beginning. And the earth was without form, and void; and darkness was upon the face of the deep. While God dreamed, totemic Beings arose and wandered the land, singing it into existence, making paths, rivers, and mountains and performing ceremonies to call forth Life: the known from the Unknowable. In the beginning was the Word, and the Word was with God, and the Word was God. Something from nothing. Substance from Intention. Matter from Consciousness. That is the act of Creation, the timeless dance of Being.

Like the first aborigines, we moved in an insubstantial world, awaiting light and the sound of the Master's Voice. It seemed a time of incubation, an embryonic age spent together around the flickering lamps in our tiny cabin or walking the vast quiet of a frozen planet where nothing else moved. There was a quality in the unborn dawn as we stood gazing over our valley, of an orchestra poised, a hundred violinists with their bows in the air, awaiting the signal. To stand in that silence as the sun returned was to witness at the dawn of Creation.

Time seemed insubstantial. It was not linear at all, but expanded or contracted with the details of life. Just as space shifted for me when I stepped out of the cabin, so too was time now compressed for its lack of embellishment, one day blending into the next. We performed our little chores, enjoyed family life together, and watched the birth of the year.

The New Year came, but that seemed of little importance: ours had commenced with the Solstice. Each day brought expectation and joy as more light appeared. The biological new year depends on where you live, I decided. In many parts of the world, life returns with the monsoons. I realized again how the landscape shapes our thoughts: whether we feel it or not, we are inseparable from the planet.

It had warmed to around twenty below zero after Christmas, and for this I gave thanks. There's a world of difference between twenty and fifty below. To a great degree one's experience of cold is a matter of attitude and having the right clothing, but there are levels of cold that must be zealously guarded against. When the weather first drops to minus twenty, it seems serious, but when it later warms to the same temperature, the air feels almost balmy.

Tom's lungs continued to deteriorate. He was weak and suffered from night sweats. When he began coughing up bloody green phlegm and feeling sick again, I put him back on antibiotics, switching to the Terramycin powder I had bought at the feed store.

"If I can just make it until spring," he told me, "I'm sure I'll be okay. Breathing this cold air makes me worse." We were facing each other over breakfast dishes. Outside in the snowy morning we could hear Luke chattering like a squirrel as he whacked icicles from the wood stacked against the front of the cabin. There was a sound like breaking glass as the crystal stilettos fell away.

"You were better when it was really cold and you stayed inside," I reminded him. "I know you hate to be housebound, but I'd like you to just take it easy. I can haul water and split wood."

"Those little chores don't hurt me," he replied. "I can't stay inside all the time."

I took a deep breath and forced myself to go on. "This is hard for me to talk about, but I've been wondering what I'll do if you die."

"I hope you'll go ahead and enjoy the summer with Luke," he said reasonably.

I thought about the scenario. I'd have plenty of food and a good home. Luke and I could take hikes. "I don't want you to die," I said bluntly, "and I'm not sure that I would enjoy being here if you did." In spite of myself, I felt my chin quivering.

"You've always told me that death is as natural as birth," he replied gently. "It happens to all of us."

"I know… I just don't want to face it here."

"I'm happy here," he answered. "I'd be disappointed to miss the end of the story, but I'm not afraid." He reached across the table and brushed a strand of hair back from my face. "It's okay," he told me softly, "you'd do fine."

I couldn't say anything for a minute, just sat looking at him through my tears. "I take you for granted a lot," I said at last. "I just always expect you to be around."

"I know," he smiled. "The only thing that worries me is Luke. When my dad died it left a big hole in my life. I don't want that to happen to him, but maybe it can't be helped. I'd like to think you'd marry again, if you found the right person, someone who could be a good father."

"I can't even imagine it at the moment."

He nodded. "It takes time. But Luke is still young and you are too."

"You've been sick for two and a half months, and I don't know what to do." I cradled my head in my hands and looked at him. "If the plane comes back, I'd really like you go into town." For all my talk of simplicity, I thought, healthy people our age didn't die of chest infections in that other world. Nature is a ruthless weeder. It was an ancient concern. I thought of the taboos, religions, and even science that had developed to ward off catastrophe. Always behind the creative force was this sudden, inexplicable power that could rend one's world asunder.

Tom took a deep breath. "Let's just see how I am when he gets here," he temporized. "Maybe this course of antibiotics will do the trick. I'm afraid if it's TB they might keep me."

"If it's TB we could all come down with it," I reminded him.

"I've worried about that," he admitted.

"I'd be a lot better off alone here with Luke, knowing you were getting help, than watching you die."

"Okay," he consented. "If I'm still sick when the plane comes, I'll go. I'll be back as soon as I can, or I'll try to send someone."

I packed Tom a bag with a change of clothes, the mail, and all those documents that control life in the other world, but the plane didn't come. I kept him on antibiotics for three weeks, and gradually his condition improved, though his cough never completely cleared. I think we both knew the issue had merely been postponed.

☙

WHEN THE NEXT DAY dawned clear and ten below, I decided to take Luke out on his sled. Although it was almost noon, Venus shown bright in the southern sky as I stepped from the cabin doorway. It was a glorious day, pink clouds in an ocean of baby blue, moon still high in the northeast. The sun would return soon, perhaps within ten days.

A noisy group of white-winged crossbills came flitting high overhead and landed in the nearby spruce tops, their sweet garrulous voices calling to one another (and I fancied to me as well). I whistled back and soon had a cheerful crowd dropping cones on my head as they worked the trees above me. Although they ate spruce seeds and didn't benefit from my presence, the little red birds clustered about, seeming to enjoy my company.

I harnessed Shylo while Luke pulled the sled down to the runway. Keeping her tied had become a real chore. With warmer temperatures, she could only be captured before leaving the cabin in the morning.

Tom had coughed much of the night and agreed to stay quiet a few days. Over the river the sky was going burnt orange with clouds like plumes of smoke rising gray out of the sunset. Luke said it reminded him of a volcano. Our family of ravens was playing king-of-the-mountain on the tallest tree of Topo Island, using their raucous voices. We hadn't seen them for some time and I was pleased to welcome them back. They are called "the largest songbird," sounding like a harp when it pleases them, but today they yelled like crows.

The fluted snow along the bank was printed with wandering tracks of ptarmigan, fox, and martin. Even our moose had meandered aimlessly through the willows. Like the birds, perhaps she too was beginning to feel the promise of life returning. From the thickets near our old camp I heard the cackle of ptarmigan. Searching the bushes I spotted them, white grouse balanced on twigs or shuffling about on feathery feet.

When all was ready, I called Luke over to the sled. It was designed for a smaller child and it wasn't easy for him to get in and out. Candy-red slats curved behind his back and his feet protruded over the front. He giggled with delight as Shylo threw herself into the traces and bounded after me onto the runway. I was no match for her, even with a weighted sled, and was soon left puffing behind. She pulled well on the packed surface but found it boring and soon quit. When I tried to take them up the creek trail we ran into problems, for the sled repeatedly plowed off at the turns and was buried in snow.

"This isn't working," I told Luke as I unhitched the dog and snapped on her leash.

"Santa must have meant for me to use it," he insisted, frowning. I couldn't argue with that. His rosy-cheeked face peered up, hurt and defiant from the soft frame of parka ruff.

"Well, I'm sure you'll be able to use it," I stalled. "You can pull things behind you and maybe I can make a slide somewhere, but it just doesn't work with Shylo."

"It's got to!" His voice held a note of desperation. For days he had harbored fantasies of zooming over the snow in his one-dog-open-sleigh. He yearned for power and speed.

"She can't pull you on a trail," I said reasonably. The sled was tilted and bogged in snow. Shylo was frustrated and had simply given up, refusing to go further unless dragged.

Luke was crushed at my words and remained stubbornly seated.

"I've got an idea," I told him. "Do you think you can ski behind her?"

He brightened immediately and crawled from the wreck. We pulled the sled home and Luke put on his skis. Back on the runway, I snapped a sling through a carabiner and onto the metal rings behind Shylo's harness. Then I handed the sling to Luke.

It soon became clear that I couldn't keep the dog on a leash while she pulled him. "Try not to let go," I warned as I threaded the sling and leash into Luke's mittened hands. "We can't catch her if she gets away."

I stepped back and Shylo realized she was free. She shot forward like a race horse, jerking Luke onto his face and dragging him some distance. He was screaming with rage and his skis stuck out like anchors, but he grimly hung on until she stopped. I caught up and righted him, and they were off again. We repeated this ordeal until Luke's face was scrubbed red and his collar was packed with snow.

Gradually, he began to spend as much time gliding happily along the airstrip, shouting "Faster! Faster!" as he did plowing the field. Unfortunately, when Shylo tired of the sport, she whipped about in a circle, ensnaring him with the sling and jerking him over. Then she yanked this way and that while he shrieked and pummeled her with impotent fists. They were both glad to see me come panting up. Luke wanted to stay out until he mastered this new sport, but I figured we'd all had enough.

❦

ANOTHER BOUT OF WARM weather brought snow and the drip began again. We awoke to the sound of it splashing steadily onto our bed, and looked out to see large icicles forming along the eaves. I spent much of the day fighting ice and mud, ripping my mittens and nearly freezing my fingers as I tried to ferret out the problem under the sod. Another leaky night proved that my efforts had accomplished nothing, so we did a major overhaul. Tom pulled off much of the lower sod and chopped away the ice, then rested in the cabin while I patched and replaced the sod. That seemed to do the trick.

The problem would have resolved itself anyway, for we awoke to forty-five below. About noon we went down to the river to pack the runway after the last snow. From the south end of the strip, Luke was first to see the sun. He yelled and beckoned for us to hurry. Tom and I made the sweep, plodding down the river like matching tractors, our lashes crusted with ice as we watched the southern horizon. Flames spread along the ridge, bleeding into the deep blue sky and setting the fringe of low clouds afire. Suddenly a bright twinkle of golden light stabbed north over the frozen land and my heart flooded with thanksgiving. Singing praises to God, I thought, was the most natural thing in the world. As if on cue, a flock of small birds flashed by, high overhead, welcoming the dawn with a joyful noise. Surely, they too reached out to celebrate the blessing of sunlight after fifty days without it.

◆

WINTER WAS FAR FROM over. Except for a brief rise in temperature, the remainder of January and into February hung in the "way-belows." Forty, fifty, sixty, sixty-five below zero, day after day, kept us huddled in the cabin. It was hard to prevent frostbite in such temperatures. At sixty-five below, one can do little but den up and wait.

The nights were still very long. I felt threatened by the extreme cold which layered crystals up the walls and smoked in from the blackness whenever the door opened. The cold was something to be endured. The first few days of the way-belows weren't bad, but as the spell wore on, it was harder to keep the cabin warm. At these temperatures the heat escaped through the logs at an alarming rate. It took all day to warm the walls and we lost ground at night. I reminded myself that it couldn't last forever.

The sun climbed rapidly, rising about a degree a day as it rolled along the southern hills. Soon it could be seen from our cabin, twinkling between the trees and streaming through the utility room windows. Somehow I didn't feel as cold or cabin-bound now that the sun penetrated the building. We went out each day, if only to haul water and restock the wood box. Sometimes Luke remained in the cabin while we did these chores. We would return with buckets of icing water on the sled to find him in the loft, armed with slingshot, snow goggles, Frisbee, and stick, pretending to tease the invisible bears.

Luke and I passed the cold weather on schoolwork. Fortunately, we had received a box of children's books from Annie in November. Luke had finished his reading texts and started over, delighted to sail through the first one in a couple of days.

"The difference between your first performance and now is practice," I reminded him.

We were all seated around the table sharing the yellow circle of lantern light. Tom was reading to himself while Luke and I studied. Blue evening shown through the windows where a waxing moon illuminated the frost between the panes, causing it to sparkle. It was the fourth of February, and the sun was already fifteen degrees above the horizon at noon, shining for five hours as it slid west along the southern mountains. Though still very cold, the daytime temperature had begun to fluctuate a few degrees. Because of the lingering twilight, we now had ten hours of visibility and our schedules had gradually shifted accordingly.

We were dressed warmly, for it was around fifty inside despite the blazing stove. Luke was wearing a wool shirt, jacket, and his mink house booties. Tom was comfortable in a down vest and his new "minkies." I had double lined them with felt and fleece then added a foam insole and leather bottoms. The thermometer outside our frost-coated door hovered at fifty-four below zero, up six degrees from the day before.

Luke was dawdling over the final page of subtraction problems in his second grade math book. I had promised an apple pie and an evening of family board games when he finished the book.

"I feel like I'm dragging you through this," I told him.

"Maybe we can just have the party and then I'll finish," he suggested.

I shook my head. "You can be done in ten minutes or take all night. Stop putting your energy into resisting and just do the problems."

He had managed to complete the first grade in three months, working one or two hours a day. I was curious what schools did with the rest of their time. It occurred to me that people would be a good deal more contented and productive if we organized our schedules around goals instead of time. Most of us serve time from kindergarten to retirement and then have no idea how to use what's left.

"I want you to learn something many adults have trouble with," I told Luke. "Completion. Do you know what that is?"

"Well," he answered, "it's when you finish something."

"Yes, and more. For some reason people often stop just before completing things. They do almost all the work and then quit. It's very unsatisfying."

"Okay. I'll do it if you make me," he said truculently.

"No. You don't win that way."

"You know that 'regrouping' is very stressful for me." He looked up, big eyes sad as a basset hound. "I haven't told you this because I thought you'd laugh, but math gives me a tummy ache."

"Tell you what," I said, trying not to laugh. "I'll help."

I knew it wasn't the math, but being required to do it, that disturbed him. He would sometimes "trick" me by doing his homework when I wasn't looking, but he was unbelievably stubborn if he thought someone was "forcing" him. He could count to a hundred by twos, threes, fives, nines, tens, and elevens, and do a geometric progression to 256. He knew "regrouping" addition and subtraction to three places as well as some multiplication. I had even made a game of graphing quadratic equations—failing to mention that it was higher math.

I sat next to him and made up a chant about each problem, and he churned out the answers without a mistake, faster than I could sing. It became a challenge match, my voice against his pencil, stomachache forgotten.

"In life either you set your goals or someone else does," I told him when he had finished.

"What do you mean?"

I took a deep breath and thought. "Life is your school," I said slowly. "You do your best because it's your life. The only discipline is self-discipline. To be free, you must choose your behavior because you choose it, not because someone makes you or because you'll get fired. Do you understand that?"

"But I don't like school and you're making me do it," he argued.

"It would be easier on both of us if you chose to do it."

He didn't look convinced and I could sympathize with him.

"Get used to it, Kiddo. Nobody said life was easy, but it'll be a lot more interesting if you take control instead of being dragged along. Freedom comes from choosing your responsibilities. You can be herded through your education and into the workforce, or you can find directions that interest you. It's up to you."

I rose from the table to knead the bread, setting two loaves above the stove to rise. Then I made hash with chopped roast, potato cubes, powdered onions, and dried tomato paste. Coming up with a varied diet continued to be one of my biggest tasks. We were running short of some items (coffee, peanut butter, margarine, candy, fruit, oatmeal, and toothpaste) but still had plenty of other supplies.

While dinner cooked, I soaked dried apples for Luke's pie. He had his crayons and paper out and was working patiently on the deck of cards he had decided to make, cutting out and coloring fifty-two of them.

"Remember reading about Kipling's poem, 'The White Man's Burden?'" Tom asked suddenly. "Well, here it is tucked away in volume two of *The History of Western Civilization.*"

"For such a small library, we see that a lot," I commented.

Tom leaned back and stared out the darkening windows. "When I went back to college," he said, "it seemed that no matter what courses I took, they were related; like all knowledge was tied together in some unfathomable way."

"Wasn't that the original idea of a liberal arts degree," I asked, "to have a broad enough view that the universe would begin to make sense?"

"The Renaissance man and all that?" He nodded slowly. "Well, if wisdom is the ultimate intention of education, I think it only comes when you have an appreciation for the whole picture."

Luke had set down his scissors and was listening, his face a study of concentration.

"It is all connected!" Tom stated, eyes intense as he groped for words. "You just keep picking up the pieces and the pattern keeps developing."

"Yeah. Forever."

LITTLE BY LITTLE THE thermometer began to ascend, fifty-one below, forty-six below—not exactly a heat wave, but surprisingly more comfortable than sixty-five below. By the second week in February it soared to ten below and never dropped into the way-belows again.

It was a beautiful time of year, as clear as a cut diamond, every tree delineated by a slanting light so pure it vibrated like music. Days were usually cloudless and calm, with widening diurnal shifts in temperature. The low sun glistened for hours off the painted snow and we spent many happy days outside, working the runway, stamping in new trails, and exploring our valley. Tom was feeling better, able to take short hikes with us, though he was still using the inhalant. He wasn't as thin, but still tired easily and his feet got cold.

With the returning sun, the wildlife became more active, their stories written in the deep snow wherever we traveled. Small bands of caribou were again migrating through, headed back to calving grounds in a never ending cycle. Unlike moose they traveled together, often stepping into a single set of prints.

Luke was gradually becoming proficient at skiing behind the dog. On hikes he sailed ahead of us like some miniature musher with a team of one, silhouetted against the rosy snow, calling out "Faster! Faster!" It was an important win for him, this mastery over the beast, and he reveled in his role of king of the wind, at home in his world of ice and snow. Shylo didn't appear to mind the extra load, perhaps preferring it to her log. Luke had little control, but the deep snow limited them to trails, and she couldn't run off with him. He had learned to crash into drifts whenever he wanted to stop, using his body as a sort of anchor. When the path forked, however, we would often arrive to find him sputtering with rage and buried to the eyeballs but gripping the sling, where he had tried to go one way and she the other. Perhaps I imagined it, but at such moments Shylo seemed to be laughing.

One afternoon found us a mile up Luke's Creek. We had been extending our trail, the world smooth and unreachable ahead. It was a slow business but satisfying. What a joy it was to visit our old haunts after all this time, and how different they appeared! I wished Laurie could see them. As we turned for home, the new trail wound like a highway before us. Blue shadows waved over the dunes and spokes of light radiated like a crown from King Mountain where the sun had just disappeared. The sky was clear, but sparkles of fine ice twinkled softly about us, condensing from the air as the temperature fell.

I smiled fondly after Luke. He had quickly dwindled into the distance when we turned back, his happy voice ringing up the valley. Tom had his shoul-

J. ASPEN 94

ders bunched against the noise. I laughed suddenly realizing I was living my dreams of twenty years before: myself in this wilderness with a child of my own. I wondered how often we get our heart's desire and fail to recognize it because it looks different from what we expected.

I fell into step behind Tom. The trail was four feet wide and ran along the creek bottom in gentle curves. Its width was a concession to Luke, for it took balance and good reflexes to charge over the terrain behind Shylo. Breaking new trail was an endeavor of considerable effort now that the snow was deep. One had to lift the snowshoe up to thigh level before stepping, and there was no bottom from which to push. Tom and I walked in tandem like duel graders, one offset behind the other, returning the same way to smooth the trail. If it wasn't well packed the first day, it would always be lumpy.

Suddenly a cackle erupted to our left and a flurry of ptarmigan burst from the willows, flying low and fast down the valley. I counted eleven. It was our home flock.

"Eleven," Tom confirmed. He was wearing his purple sweater with the hood back, ears protected by a woolen headband I had knitted. At twelve below it was too warm to hike in a parka.

I nodded. "They've all made it."

"You can tell them apart by their tracks," he said pointing. "Look at that fellow. He always drags his tail when he lands. That one plops right down. There's one that slides."

Animals, I thought, are all individuals just like people. They are curious and changeable and they make decisions based on experience as well as instinct. The tracks of our moose followed the old section of our trail, wary of stepping on it. I could see where she had pushed her nose into the fresh snow, brushing it aside to catch our scent. To honor life, I realized, we need to see the uniqueness of each living thing and at the same time appreciate the unity of all, for they are kin to us.

A howl brought me out of my reverie. Luke was down and Shylo was sailing free, skimming over the trail with never a look back. When we arrived Luke was crying so hard he was hiccuping.

"She . . . she . . . she . . . ran away!"

"It's all right," I soothed, pulling him out of the drift and dusting him off. I unzipped the front of his parka and emptied out the snow. "She can go. It's too late in the day for a plane."

"But she left me!"

"You may have to ski home on your own," I said, trying to sound sympathetic.

Tom had already passed us, ears flattened against the noise. With the beauty and silence of the Arctic stretching out in all directions, he found it hard to commiserate.

Shylo had raced out of sight, but finding herself alone came pounding back along the trail. She avoided Tom by lunging around him in the deep snow. Hoping to zip by me on the wide trail, she dodged past at Mach speed, but I dove for the trailing sling, jerking us both up short. Luke's tears cleared instantly and he aligned his skis. I handed him the sling and with an imperious "Go!" he was off. Tom barely had time to leap to one side as they flew by and the words "Faster! Faster!" drifted back over the stillness of the wilderness.

❦

SPRING PROGRESSED RAPIDLY AS we gained ten to fifteen minutes of light each day. Already the sun stayed up eleven hours and we spent much of our time outside. Snow was melting like cotton candy from southern exposures and icicles festooned cutbanks. A shiny glaze reflected from the mountains and we took to wearing sunglasses. Tom hung a moose antler in the tree outside as a bird feeder, offering moose cracklings to the gray jays. The spruce were alive with squirrels and Shylo rushed from trunk to trunk, staring up. We even had a martin that visited occasionally.

I was busy thawing, slicing, and drying endless meat, but at least the cabin was now sunny and bright. We had started preserving meat for summer some weeks earlier, wanting it all handled before the bears came out of hibernation in April. The rafters overhead were hung with strings of jerky and sausages. In the oven a pan of shredded, boiled meat was always drying, a summer staple that reconstituted in hot water.

I woke one morning to the sound of wind. I had heard it begin in my sleep. I could sense the heavy thrumming against the cabin and the loft shuddered with the gusts. I thought of the runway. It would be buried beyond recognition. I wondered again what was keeping the plane and if he was coming at all.

Quietly I crawled over Tom and descended the ladder. With the returning light, I was again getting up early. I enjoyed starting my day alone by the stove, sipping coffee and meditating. I heard Luke stir and sleepily roll next to Tom. Out the window, clouds scudded like pink smoke from the clear western sky. Through the trees I could glimpse snow pluming in a rooster tail hundreds of feet off the trailing edge of Annie's Peak. I was glad I wasn't up there.

The roof was dripping again, and I listened to the sound of water plunking into a bucket upstairs. All summer we had worked to build a safe nest. I had believed that if only we had a solid home, wood, water, and food we would be safe and happy. Let it snow. Bring on the cold and dark. We didn't have to fight nature, just be prepared. You couldn't control this land, but you could learn to work with it.

However, nothing stops ice, I thought, pondering my personal glaciers. The drip was more than an annoyance: it made me feel insecure. I, who had tried to control every detail, had made a mistake in the design and no amount of patching was going to cure it. I remembered telling Luke that worry was negative. "While you need to be aware of dangers," I had said, "fearing them has no value. In fact, it's apt to cause more problems." He had considered this for several days then quoted it back to me as I fretted over the roof.

I smiled at the memory, but he was right. The worst that could happen was a mess. What I needed to heal was my attitude. My home wasn't perfect, but it was my anxiety rather than the roof that needed fixing. Perhaps that's my lesson here, I thought. Again it wasn't the one I wanted, but such are life's gifts. Maybe I could apply it to Tom's lungs as well. He didn't fear his infection. Perhaps I wouldn't either in his place. I didn't fear death for myself. It was the thought of losing those I love that haunted me.

"Good morning, Papa," I heard Luke whisper.

"Good morning, Son," Tom replied softly.

Little bare feet appeared at the top of the ladder coming down one rung at a time. In his arms Luke cradled a pillow on which Oliver was lying, wrapped in the old blanket. Luke would soon be seven. His childish enunciation had cleared, though the recent loss of his top incisors caused some backsliding. His face looked very different with them gone and I could see his jaw spreading daily to accommodate the big, new teeth. From months without the sun his smooth skin was light and his long hair dark and glossy.

"Good morning, Snags." I said as he joined me by the stove. I usually had pet names for him, and Snaggle Tooth had arisen after he lost his top front teeth. He put up with most of them but told me he didn't care for "Woofles."

"Good morning, Woofles," he said mischievously.

I smiled and said, "You should have put on your slippers."

"It's not cold. Will you wrap Oliver? I never get it right."

I took the bear and bundled him snugly. "Do you remember hearing the wolves last night? I woke you up to listen."

He thought a minute and then his face lightened. "Yes! Even when I was asleep, I heard them. They circled into my dreams. It almost sounded like someone playing a piano, all different notes. Plink, plink, plink," he demonstrated.

We were quiet together, listening to new birds declaring their territories in exalted trills outside the sunny cabin. I watched the treetops sway and bob through the front windows.

"You're getting freckles on your nose," I observed. "I thought people got freckles from being in the sun."

"And you're getting gray hair," he said seriously. He reached up and gently stroked my head. "Mama, your pretty hair, all gold and silver," he said tenderly.

"It's all right to get old," I smiled. "There are many gifts you can only get by living a long time."

"Like what?"

Like what? I thought. Like the mountains, my body had become rounded and creased with the seasons, but it was an old friend. I no longer strove for physical perfection but was content that it ran well. I knew its weaknesses and how to get the best mileage. And relationships: Tom and I had come to respect one another as people with differences. Like two old draft horses, we knew how to pull together with minimum strife. We could communicate and we knew when to leave one another alone.

Tired of waiting for an answer, Luke had picked up the book we were reading, *Lassie Come Home.* "How come stories are always sad?" he asked on a different tack.

"Well, it makes them more interesting. Life's that way too."

"You mean God makes people unhappy on purpose?"

"I think you wouldn't learn as much if you didn't have to deal with some conflict," I answered slowly. "It's not an easy question. It comes down to your image of God. Do you think of God as an old man in the sky?"

"Well, you say God is everything. I believe what you do."

I smiled and shook my head. "At some point you'll have to discover what's real for you. Some people believe in good and evil: that there's a kind of war going on between a good god and a bad one. In that case, God is not all powerful; He may be stronger, but He's not the whole enchilada. Follow me?"

"That's the Devil, right?"

"Right. This is the way they account for the unpleasant things we have to deal with. If God is good and kind, how come people are unhappy?"

"Yeah, that's what I wanted to know," he reiterated.

"I don't see God as a personality," I told him slowly. "To me God is a vast, creative energy that evolves into everything we know in interwoven patterns like ripples in a stream. There is no death, only change. God experiencing God. Look at the wonderful diversity of life, growing, fading, exploring new avenues and disappearing. And yet life goes on."

Luke knitted his brow, thinking hard. "What about us?"

"We're part of God too, each very special. In order to experience life, we take on form and the belief in opposites. What we see as negative is really an opportunity to grow and experience Who we are. That's how we learn about ourselves, which is the purpose of the journey. And like your book, if it were always pleasant it would probably be pretty boring."

I smiled and rocked back on the bench. "It's early," I said. "Why don't you go back upstairs and snuggle with Daddy?"

"Do you want some private time?"

"Uh-huh."

"Okay." He tucked Oliver against his chest and ascended the ladder, bare feet disappearing over the edge of the loft. I heard him settling in. The heating stove ticked and I reached out to stir the morning's cereal.

Perhaps that's why we're drawn to hardship and risk, I continued to myself. I thought of people jogging before dawn and mothers going back to school. The act of discipline strengthens us and feeds a spiritual hunger. The Quest forms a rite of passage for a young person and allows continued growth as we get older. It's a choice to participate in living rather than watch it on a screen. In self-discipline the unsung battles are won.

What about me? Certainly quest was part of my reason for being here, but had I also been trying to re-create my past? Like my mother, did I define myself dressed in the Arctic? Growth means releasing one's past, yet how did one know when a particular path was over? I thought of something Tom had said the day before. I had mentioned my other cabin and he had told me, "I hope this year will allow you to let go of your past. I feel like I've lived with it for twelve years; now I'd like to move on."

He had never expressed this before, and it took me by surprise. Tom had encouraged me to write about my previous life and later supported me in lecturing. With never a murmur he set up the slide projector and dealt with people who mistook him for Phil. "You didn't have to endure months of cold and deprivation to woo me away from my past," I had joked. But Tom hadn't answered, and I wondered if maybe he did. Perhaps he, in quiet wisdom, had chosen this way of solidifying our relationship. If so, it had worked, and now the Arctic had become part of him too.

꿏

By Luke's seventh birthday, February 25, the runway had flooded. It had been clear of water since December, but I knew it couldn't last. For days the overflow poured invisibly onto the ice, saturating the snow. I felt guilty, as if I were responsible for the weather and owed it to our pilot to hold back spring. At first the packed strip withstood it, the runway becoming a deceptive island, but as I walked the outline I found myself sinking in slush to my knees on weighted and freezing snowshoes. Within days, it soaked through in teal green, buckling the foundation under its massive weight. There was nothing we could do to save the airstrip. No plane could land now.

Shylo told us when the wolves returned. She was tied one morning when we went down to the river for water and she lifted her voice in a mournful wail as I departed. From far away came the haunting answer, musical, wild, and remote. She stood transfixed and listened, the call reverberating deep within her memory.

As spring advanced Shylo became wilder. No longer seeking the warmth of the cabin, she was difficult to catch. I was rapidly losing what little control I had over her. She roamed the valley and was often gone much of the day. The squirrels were mating, and the sight of them fighting and racing up and down trees made her restless and aggressive as she stalked silently through the forest, her mind set on murder. Her interactions with Luke had also deteriorated, and I found I could not trust them alone together. When I let him out the door, she would attack unprovoked if someone wasn't there to guard, taking out her pent-up frustrations and wild eagerness to sink her teeth into something. Twice she had drawn blood, knocking him over and biting his arms and face.

On March 2, Shylo disappeared. She had spent the day away as usual and I didn't think much about it when she failed to return. I had another problem, for Tom had relapsed, with all the old nasty signs. I started him on his fifth course of antibiotics and hoped for the best.

"This sounds gruesome, but I've been wondering what I'd do with your body," I told him, when the subject of death raised its grim head again. Luke was asleep above us and outside the stars were just appearing. "The ground is frozen. I could pack you in snow on the north side of the cabin, but the ermine might get at you. The toilet hole seems disrespectful . . . and I don't want to draw bears . . ." I found I was blushing and looked away.

"You could put me on the roof until the ground thawed," he said helpfully. "You'd want to keep enough of the body to get me declared legally dead; otherwise you'll have a great deal of difficulty with social security and IRAs."

"Like what? Teeth and claws?" I asked dryly.

"I think the whole head would be best."

"Forget it. They can dig you up themselves."

"I suppose they would fly in here and dig me up. You could videotape things."

I sighed. "Your family would never forgive me."

He laughed. "No, they wouldn't."

Poor Luke, I thought. This was not the kind of memory I had in mind for him. "If you die, think how Luke will remember this year," I said miserably.

"I know," he said heavily, "but I don't think it'd be any worse here than someplace else. At least he wouldn't feel shut out. When my father died, I was bundled out of the way. It was all very unreal."

"If it gets really bad, would you consider using the ELT?"

"We'll see . . ." He shook his head. "Maybe it won't come to that."

We both sat looking into the flame of the lamp. I couldn't help imagining the grim scenario, seeing if I was up to my part. Tom's last days, could I carry him up the ladder onto the roof? No, the snow behind the cabin would have to do. The snow would be gone before the ground thawed. That would be unpleasant! Better wrap him well in a tarp. Closing up the cabin, then hundreds of miles by canoe . . . I replayed the memories of the lower river: rapids, rocks, sweepers, wind. It was no place for handling that big canoe with only a child to help.

"I feel like everyone is leaving!" I said, starting to cry. "We were supposed to be this big jolly crew, helping each other. Then, one by one, everyone goes and Luke and I are left alone!" I put my head on my arms.

"Come here," Tom said gently. He moved onto the sofa and indicated his lap. I felt awkward, heavier than my husband now, but I climbed into his arms and he held and petted me.

"I feel like a little waif in a storm. All my old childhood stuff about my parents' divorce and being fostered out. Decisions I made when I was three years old. You can't trust anybody; in a pinch they're all gone!" I took a ragged breath. "I guess I still have some feeling about that," I said in surprise. "I thought it was all handled. But now everyone's leaving again!"

Tom didn't answer, just held me and listened. What was there to say? Then the main question I couldn't even voice: what would Luke do, if he lost me? His earlier fears coming to pass despite all our preparation and assurances! For that matter, what would I do if I lost him? The two of us alone here didn't look like a very strong arrangement. It wouldn't take much for the family dream to disintegrate into a nightmare.

Was there a way to hold life, I wondered, where I didn't have to keep shoring it up, healing each fear as it arose? Like it or not, there really wasn't anything to hold on to. You could devote your life to prudence and still lose it all. Industries throve on selling the illusion of security.

"If you get too bad, I can use the ELT whether you like it or not," I told him defiantly.

"Don't put your hopes on that one," he said gently. "You know what Steve told us about flight plans. Besides, there's no place to land now."

I took a deep breath and relaxed in his arms. All we ever have is this moment, I thought. How many times had I agonized over something that hadn't come true? Life viewed as an endless series of battles against the inevitable looks grim, but if I held it as a Spiritual Quest there were gifts even in the parts I didn't like. I had chosen this time of solitude and personal growth. Nobody said it would be easy. Somehow I needed to learn to release those things over which I had no control.

CHAPTER 12

Luke grieved deeply for Shylo. She hadn't been much of a pet, but she was a member of our small clan and now there were only three of us.

"She was never really ours," I said gently as I sat with him on the sofa. He wasn't crying, his face set and remote, but I was. "She was always Shylo the Magnificent, her own person. We'll all miss her." I didn't mention that considering their relationship, it was probably better this way.

"She'll come back," he declared staunchly.

I shook my head sadly. "I don't think so. It's been two days now and no sign of her."

"When she sees us get in the canoe to head downriver next summer, she'll be here," he insisted. "She's just running with the wolves."

I didn't have the heart to answer. She may have been Shylo the Magnificent, but wild animals live on the edge; she didn't have a chance out there. She was too wild for our world and not wild enough for theirs. She couldn't make it on her own and there was no tribe for her. My throat constricted at the thought of this being who didn't belong in either world. I grieved for Shylo, but I also grieved for Luke and his dream of friendship that had never turned out.

I thought of life, wild and free, and what it really meant. Day after day the wolves must hustle. Most didn't survive to reproduce. Nature prunes ruthlessly, continually molding life to fill every possible niche. Existence has always been uncertain, especially where conditions are harsh. Barry Lopez speaks of the Eskimo concept of living with sudden, violent death. Perhaps I carried the modern man's naïveté about life, thinking I could assure my family a happy and successful sojourn. Obviously, I did believe this or I wouldn't be here. Even so, there was always the random bear, the cabin fire, the river.

I remembered fishing from my father's home along the Arctic Ocean the fall I was fifteen. I worked with my sister and two older Native men. We laughed a good deal as we pulled the nets from under the thin ice of the Colville delta. One day we got word that a young relative of theirs had gone through the ice of the Koyukuk River with a sled and full team of dogs. It was eerie how my friends sat up all night chanting together, sharing their grief. I felt somehow alien, like someone from another world who did not belong. What, after all, did I really know about this land?

❧

A FEW DAYS LATER, I was standing at the Overlook when Luke ran up and threw his arms around my waist. Below us the river ice glittered in tones of white and jade.

"I miss Shylo," he told me softly.

"So do I," I replied. "So do I." I pulled his head against me, smoothing back the ruff of his parka. That seemed to handle it, for he played and sang happily while I hauled logs, often giving him a sled ride on the return trip. Tom was too weak to do much and spent most of each day resting.

The ice was changing before our eyes. Much of the river was submerged under two feet of slush, but the airstrip and adjoining trails still supported our weight. The trick was in knowing where to walk. Beneath an inch of snow lay a snaking pond that often saturated the surface, coloring it milky green. The weight of seeping water had caused large fissures and buckles, chasms the span of my hand that disappeared into black ice. We had come to think of the river as substantial terrain, and it was an unsettling reminder of impermanency.

Hoping that the plane might still come for Tom, I decided to make a new runway along the bar of Topo Island. The new strip had the advantage of being above the water, but it was poorly aligned for landing and somewhat short. How I hated listening for planes! I had listened all winter until my ears heard a perpetual hum of faraway engines.

Still weak and clammy from his recent bout with infection, Tom joined me in compacting the virgin snow. The weather was gray and without definition as we traveled back and forth, dark figures floating in a white haze, while Luke played along the bank, burrowing and rolling.

By the third afternoon, Tom's stamina gave out and he returned to bed while I finished the narrow strip. Twilit sky expanded overhead when I finally climbed the hill. A half moon gleamed golden through the periwinkle mists of evening. Venus shown like a beacon directly west in the peach sky, while Jupiter hung bright and low in the deep violet southeast. The constellations had rotated westward and higher as the Earth's pole swung toward summer. An auroral display like a galaxy of green flame spiraled to the north over the river, rolling above the snowy crags of Flattop. For the first time, I noticed that twilight extended north in a pale band: a sign of coming summer.

✺

SPRING WAS RUSHING UPON US. Birds now sang continuously throughout the daylight hours. Owls called much of the night, and the ravens were very active. An immature bald eagle had returned to the area and we would often see it high overhead and hear its piercing chirps. The ptarmigan were pairing off and dispersing to the high country where occasional patches of ground showed. Without the menace of Shylo, our red tree squirrels soon became quite bold. Tom set up a feeder stump and put out sunflower seeds. "Tippy" was the tamest. She was easy to identify by the split in her tail and the scar through her left eyelid. She and "Quester," a male, waged noisy warfare over our roof and up and down the trees.

As the snow retreated we began cleaning up our area, carting bones and meat scraps across the river for the wolves and throwing Shylo's droppings into the toilet. The moose hides were dragged to the far side of the river for animals to eat and we dismantled the meat racks, freeing the patient trees. We deliberated long about the bear skin. We couldn't carry it in the canoe and leaving an untanned hide in the cabin would only invite trouble. One must set free that which no longer serves, I thought, as I pulled it across the river to join the others. Dust to dust.

Luke had received a large nylon kite for his birthday, and as spring advanced we spent many happy days on the old runway. The ice was brilliant and white peaks blazed in a cobalt sky. Our cabin with its many windows was now bright and cheery. We went about in shirt sleeves and often left the door open. I tried to do most of the cooking at breakfast, allowing the cabin to cool before bed. We took to hiking in the evening when the snow crusted, and packed a picnic for cutting firewood. Luke pulled the gay little sled loaded with food, tools, and cameras. He told me he would have to replace Shylo.

March temperatures ranged down to thirty below at night and soared to ten or twenty above during the long days. The old runway skinned over, but its surface was hard to gauge, even from the ground. Ice is surprisingly plastic. The overflow was strange, amorphous stuff, often appearing solid, but continuing to well up from below in blisters, cracking and distorting the foundation. Tinted milky turquoise, dove gray, sky blue, and emerald, the river ice glistened like open water sprinkled with delicate feathers of frost.

As the day warmed, trees released their winter loads of snow with a sigh, and most of the spruce were soon free. Where snow remained in branches, it looked like soap suds, big disparate globs stuck randomly on limbs and trunks. It may only have been the angle of sunlight, but the forest appeared different, less somber. Only the month before it had seemed dark and drab, but now there was a definite green glow to the trees, as if they also were awakening.

The snow was changing daily, becoming granular and coarse. Open areas took on a pitted, glazed appearance, shining in the heat of the day and feeling slick underfoot. Tracks melted, becoming vague and diffused. Caribou droppings, sprinkled like chocolate chips, cut tiny shafts as the sun warmed them. Icicles festooned the cutbanks like jewels.

It was easy to see why Eskimos had numerous words for snow—this magical, ever-changing substance with very different properties as time, wind, and temperature work upon it. Our own vocabulary seemed colorless and inadequate to describe it. Its ephemeral beauty, like wildflowers, is precious because of its transitory quality. Ice touches the essence of Creation, which is always in process: The God Force within life and within oneself.

※

WE AWOKE TO A snowy morning, the world retouched in perfect white. Our colorful old runway was freshly painted, its blemishes treacherously concealed. We spent a quiet day inside. Tom was in the utility room making a wagon for the water buckets, while I stood at the counter cutting meat. We were tired of the smell of boiling and drying moose, but were nearing the end. All those big, bloody pieces had been dried and packed away in five-gallon buckets.

My moose, the older (and because of the rut, stinkier) was quite infested with muscle parasites. It was perhaps well that we had eaten most of it in the dark. I had decided to heal my attitude toward meat and schooled myself to think of it as sunlight. I blessed it, parasites and all, as I worked. Eating and drinking are a communion with life, I reminded myself, and therefore preparing food is a sacred trust.

As I worked, I thought of how ideas arise and become part of a culture. Years before, I had learned to hang jerky by sewing strips of meat onto a string. Early people would have discovered how to tan skins, make snow houses, arrows, cooking pots, boats, tents, and needles. They would have guarded this precious knowledge and passed it on: which berries were edible, how to deal with condensation, how to conserve body heat, and how to approach the mystery of Life honorably.

Nearby on the sofa Luke was teaching himself to read, working at it several hours a day. He resented my interference in his education, preferring the

Calvin and Hobbes do-it-yourself approach. Despite my help, he continued to plow diligently forward on his own. As I sliced meat my reverie was frequently interrupted with questions.

"What does I-R-O-N-I-C spell?"

"Ironic."

"What does it mean?"

"Well, it means something that contradicts itself in a funny way."

"What does 'contradicts' mean?"

"To do something the opposite of what you say. Like if I told you never to go near the river and then sent you down there."

There was a moment of silence and whispered readings, then a giggle. "What does S-O-P-H-O-M-O-R-I-C spell?"

"Sophomoric. It means someone who thinks they know a lot, but they don't."

I worked in silence for a while and then realized that Luke had set down his book and was watching me.

"I wonder where Shylo is," he said sadly. It was the first time he had been willing to talk about her.

I rinsed the blood from my hands and joined him on the sofa. He seemed quiet and wistful.

"I thought she'd come home today," he confided. His eyes filled with tears. "Why did she go away?"

"She always was wild, you know," I told him gently.

"If she comes back, will you tie her up?" he pleaded.

"No," I answered. "I won't keep living things chained."

"I don't care if she bites me or knocks me down," he sobbed. "I just want her to come back."

"I know. But I don't think it will happen. Don't hope too much."

I thought about Luke and Shylo. She had shown him no affection, but despite the attacks he had seen her as a friend and protector. Although Shylo was a far greater danger to him than bears, she was a known danger. He accepted bruises and an occasional bloody cheek as part of his relationship with her. Now that she was gone, bears were even more on his mind. He imagined them waiting for him in the loft and insisted that someone precede him to kick them out.

"Move over bears," I would say as I climbed the ladder.

"No, not over. Out!"

"But they're so sleepy and warm up here," I would plead.

Nevertheless, the bears had to go. There would be no mercy. He knew their shadowy forms weren't real, but they had a certain substance nevertheless.

When Tom or I lay beside him, it was our physical presence rather than logic that pushed back the dark, hairy phantoms and gleaming eyes. Danger wouldn't enter if Mama and Daddy were there. During Tom's bouts of illness, I found that I also took comfort from Luke. His sweet warmth made me strong, reminding me of my obligation to be his rock.

I needed that reminder. I was frightened by my own phantoms. Like my son, I had set my hopes on an event that was not going to happen. For whatever reason, the plane wasn't coming. I had to release that hope and go back to my own power: the power to find beauty in each day, to take Luke on short walks, and to celebrate the spring. It was curious how my world turned upon my thoughts. When I practiced living in the moment, our life was rich and full, but as I lay awake and worried, the Arctic seemed a perilous trap. I thought of the old-timers whose trails I had found in this country, most of them killed by the land. Why had they stayed year after year, knowing it would get them in the end? Perhaps because life is for living, not for saving up.

❧

GIVING UP ON THE plane released me. We continued to maintain the new strip out of habit, but I no longer felt obligated to stay near the cabin, and I quit listening for the sound of an engine. To my great relief, Tom was getting better with the spring. It was good to see him enjoying life again. He gradually took over his old chores, saying that he didn't want me to feel like a drudge (which I did). To spare my hands, he also volunteered to do all the laundry.

There was a cold snap in mid-March that froze the overflow into a smooth highway. Our stretch of river was transformed into a beautiful mosaic of colors. The textures ranged from veined marble—polished to a mirror surface—to great blisters that split and sent frozen cascades of water like candle wax snaking away from a black hole. Much of the surface was decorated with exquisite frost ferns.

In the evening we usually went down on the river to play. We slid and laughed and called one another to come and see. It was indeed a magical land. The line of trail marker sticks now marched through gleaming ice, each rimed with delicate tracings of frost and reflected in the smoky surface as in a deeply waxed floor. This lasted perhaps a week before another snow powdered the world with an inch of minute crystals as fine as cornmeal. The old runway was again solid (if hummocky and very slick). We outlined it and Tom tramped out big letters I-C-E.

I had started wearing Laurie's clothes, feeling close and missing her. Luke had outgrown most of his pants and I sewed wedges of extra material up the sides or back and lengthened the cuffs. I also repaired his boots where Shylo had bitten through. He looked healthy but very rustic, like a child in an old photo. Others might see the patches as signs of poverty, but to me they were badges of love, representing hours of careful stitching.

ONE NIGHT AS I put Luke to bed I asked how he was feeling. I had been keeping a close eye on him, fearing that he might come down with Tom's infection.

"Okay," he answered. "Well, I have some pain here," he said, pointing to his upper chest.

"Your lungs?" I inquired.

"No."

"Your stomach?"

"No. Just let me talk. My life space. My loving." His eyes filled unexpectedly with tears and he turned away.

"I don't understand," I said with concern.

"Sometimes I feel like you and Dad act like you love me, but you really want to hurt me."

I was taken aback. "Can you give me an example?"

"Like Dad burning me this morning," he said. Tom had spilled water on the hot stove, spattering Luke with fine droplets. He had been more frightened than hurt.

" Luke, that was an accident."

"And yesterday you left me for the bears."

"I don't remember," I said, still trying to puzzle out this turn of events. "You mean when we were hauling logs?"

He nodded. "Yes. You could have left someone with me!"

"You could have chosen to come along," I countered.

"And you know I don't like moose sausage, and tonight you put some on my plate," he accused.

I laughed. "Sausage? Luke, are you serious?"

He laughed too, then turned away in tears. "I feel like you're hurting me when I'm vulnerable. Like I did to Dad," he sobbed.

"When was that?" I asked, still trying to clarify what this was all about.

"When he said the prayer." It was back at the Winter Solstice when Luke had been disruptive during Tom's prayer. He had a way of processing things at his own pace.

"I'm sorry, Luke. I didn't realize. Come here." I cradled him a moment then said softly, "You know that Dad and I love you very much. We may not always do everything right, but our intentions are good. If you start collecting evidence, you'll prove whatever you believe. That's the way the mind works."

I hugged him and realized how each day Luke became more his own person and less my child. I could no longer smooth over his concerns with kisses. He too would need to grapple with the complexities of human existence and find his own answers.

"When you feel hurt, you need to talk to Dad and me," I continued. "Find the right time and be brave enough to say how you feel. I have to do it sometimes too."

"What if you don't listen?"

"That's the risk you take, isn't it? But what are the alternatives? To never let anyone in?"

"I want you to stop teasing about the bears in the loft," he said suddenly. "It's time to let go of them."

"I think that's a good idea," I answered.

❧

EVERY EVENING WE WENT down to the Overlook to sit on the old stumps and watch the river. The sky over Mount Laurie would gradually deepen to a smoky blue-gray while peach and rose tinted the snowy cliffs of Flattop. The sun would swing north below the horizon giving the distant sky and mountains the appearance of dawn at the seacoast, yellow and rose bleeding into aqua above. Along the sweep of ridges the panorama gradually reversed tones, going from peaks silhouetted against a pale wash in the north, to light lavender mountains dramatically painted on a flinty sky in the south.

"The earth is singing," Luke told us one evening as we watched the show. "Sometimes I can hear music and voices."

"Me too!" Tom chimed in.

I also had heard it, strange ephemeral sounds that seemed to originate inside my head. When the auroras were out I was certain I heard notes. I knew the Van Allen Belt is hundreds of miles away and that the solar wind is a silent stream of charged particles—but I still heard it.

The first willow buds sprouted early in April and we cut a bouquet to grow in a jar on the counter. The snow crusted and became too soggy to walk on during the heat of the day. Animal tracks were everywhere: lynx, martin, wolverine, wolf, crisscrossing the land. We shared their desire to be on the move and took to using the river as a highway. For the first time we were free to travel for miles upriver, walking the frozen overflow to watch spring progress.

Late one afternoon we were startled in our walk by a blue-and-white Comanche. The small plane arrowed down the valley at two hundred miles per hour, a few feet off the ice. It rounded the upstream corner and shot by so fast we hardly had time to wave.

"I don't think they saw us," Tom said. The whole event had taken only a few seconds.

"Maybe it's my brothers," I speculated. Not many people knew where we were.

Luke was hopping up and down with excitement. "Do you think they'll land? Do you think they'll land?" He and I had turned and were hurrying back toward the cabin.

"No, Honey," I consoled him. "He couldn't even throw a note out the window at that speed." The Comanche is built for speed and could no more set down on our little airstrip than a 727.

The plane made a wide sweep and took another run toward the cabin, pulling up before he reached us. "He didn't see us," Tom repeated.

The third swing was again from the north. It rounded the bend and laid over, wings perpendicular to the ground. As it shot past, I caught a glimpse of tiny figures waving from the cockpit.

Then they were gone. Tom was again headed upstream, but Luke and I stood gazing after the vanished plane. A brush with that other world had left me feeling somehow lonely and a bit dowdy. Up in that climate-controlled, upholstered machine, whoever-they-were had been comfortable and well-groomed. Up there were carpets and plush seats. Perhaps it was better, I thought, that we only waved from our separate worlds.

❧

By April 9, my forty-third birthday, new overflow was creeping down the river, pouring noisily into a crack near the delta. I baked myself a cake and Tom gave me a rolling pin he had carved. We played on the river, splashing and crunching in the shallow turquoise stream that was again flooding the ice. Luke built slush castles with sopping mittens where water welled from a crack forming a series of sunken "bathtubs" below the cabin.

Two days later we celebrated Easter. Luke had spent much of the previous day cutting up paper streamers to turn a clear plastic container into an Easter basket. We had been out of candy for some time, so it was with much excitement that he rose early to see if the Bunny had found us.

"He gave me more than last year!" he whispered excitedly as he climbed back under the covers and plastered his little, cold feet against mine. His breath smelled of chocolate. "He must have known we really needed it!"

The following day Tom turned forty-seven. We decided to postpone his cake because we had eaten pie the day before. His birthday feast was warmed-over rice with meat gravy and some particularly bad bread. I had just placed it on the table when I caught the distinct buzz of a Cessna!

It had to be Steve Porter! I bolted through the door and down to the runway, arriving in time to see him make a flyby. He circled back over the new runway as I ran out to plant the wind sock. He came in low over the trees, touched his skis, and was off again.

"He's getting the feel of it," Tom said as he and Luke joined me. I was grinning from ear to ear.

Luke was hopping up and down. "Oh boy! Oh boy! Oh boy!" he laughed.

Again the plane swung around, doing another touch-and-go. A late afternoon crosswind was beginning to kick up, making the approach tricky. My stomach knotted as he lined up yet a third time.

"He doesn't like it," Tom said, soberly. "Wind's wrong."

The plane looked huge as it dropped onto our short, skinny strip. He must have thought so too, for at the last minute he gunned it. Again and again he tried until I was almost in tears. "Don't do it, Steve," I whispered under my breath. "Don't risk your life."

"I can't watch!" I told Tom. "I'm going up to put on my boots." I was shaking as I climbed the hill. I could hear the tortured whine of the little engine as he skidded down the short strip and took to the air another time. He circled to check other places and even tried to land downwind as the minutes ticked by. Sometimes he made wide sweeps around the valley, seeming to wander like a lost bird with no place to rest. He would be running short on fuel soon and need to turn back.

"Are you okay?" Tom asked when I joined him.

"Yes. I'm just very disappointed. To have him be so close and try so hard. Why couldn't he have come a week ago?" I thought of the Christmas presents and food that might be on board and of mail from friends. I found myself crying.

"It's all right," Tom said, placing an arm around my shoulders. "Just seeing him up there lightens my heart. It means they made it out safely. That's worth the charter money to me. Here he comes again . . . Just stay down . . . stay down," he whispered to the plane.

At the last second the plane was airborne again, engine bellowing as he pulled up to avoid our bench. "He's not going to make it," I said, sadly. "If he hasn't made it in nine tries, he won't. He's been at it an hour."

Luke was looking from one to the other of us. "You mean he isn't going to land?" he asked in dismay.

"I don't think he can, Honey. Look, there he goes, back to Fairbanks." We gazed up and I sadly raised my hand and waved. "Good-bye," I said softly. The little plane wagged its wings in farewell and slid away south. Tom headed for the cabin while Luke and I remained on the riverbank looking wistfully south.

"I don't want him to go," Luke said, chin quivering.

"He can't land," I told him gently.

"He's coming back!" Luke said.

"Oh, I don't think so."

"Listen!" We couldn't see him, but the faint hum of his engine shifted as he banked. "He's coming back!" Luke shouted, running for the cabin to get his dad.

I almost wished he wouldn't. He came blazing past a hundred feet off the ice. "He's going to drop a message!" Tom shouted above the roar. "His arm's out the window!"

For a moment I saw a dark glove flapping wildly, then it was fluttering onto the river. I raced out and picked it up. Inside was Steve's company form in triplicate. For a crazy moment I thought, "He's dropping the bill?!" With shaking hands I pulled it out and found a scrawled message on the back. It said:

"Wind from wrong direction for landing. Strip orientation marginal for C-185. Be back in 1-7 days (please indicate # of feet of snow depth spruce bows in snow). Give one arm wave for all okay!"

I felt confused. Spruce boughs? How? If we stuck them in, he wouldn't know how deep. Write numbers? I ran back to Tom and he was as confused as I. Meanwhile Steve had already turned for the flyby. "Let's run out and stand!" I shouted. "Luke, you stay here!"

Together we raced for the new runway, and while I stood on the packed snow, Tom ran a few steps into the knee-high drift. We both waved one hand then Tom raised his arms, palms up, in a shrug.

Steve later told us it was that gesture that did the trick, as if Tom had asked "What else do you want?" While we were explaining to Luke that the plane would come back later (though how that would help, I couldn't say), Steve lined up and set her down. He whirled toward us as usual but didn't gun it, slowing, slowing, and then sliding off the shoulder, listing to a stop. We splashed across the new overflow and ran to greet him.

"How you doing?" Tom called.

"Oh, not too good. I think I'm stuck," came the unhappy reply. Steve looked as handsome and neatly dressed as before.

"Really? Need some boards or something?"

"Well, maybe buckets of water to build an ice ramp. How much snow do you have here?"

Tom shrugged. "Two feet."

"No, I mean how deep is the snow?" Steve was on his knees, digging. "Hey! There's ground under there! We're not on river?"

"No, it's all gravel," Tom assured him. "That's why we put the airstrip here."

For the first time Steve smiled. While I sealed letters and hauled packages back and forth, the men tramped a path to the old runway where there was room along the edge for a short takeoff.

"A little overflow won't hurt me," he assured us when I pointed it out. "I've even landed on water using skis; it'll hydroplane, but you have to get to shore before you stop!"

"Where's our turkey?" Luke asked as we off-loaded boxes and drums of fuel from the cockpit.

He longed for Steve's attention, but it was already evening, and the pilot was running late. I tried to interest Luke in transporting boxes to the cabin while the men dug out the plane, but he ran after them through the overflow trying to be noticed until he fell in. He was crying when I took him up to the cabin and insisted that he eat something before putting on Tom's rubber boots and dry pants. When the men arrived, Luke heaped the pilot's hands with Easter candies from his treasured stash while Steve shared the news.

"I thought you guys had ten or fifteen feet of snow," Steve said, politely eating one of the sticky chocolates. "I was afraid I'd get stuck. It's been quite a winter. Serious winds up north and heavy snows in the Interior. I don't know how you missed it. I met a trapper out of Bettles who saw what he thought was a wolverine swimming through the snow. When he got close, he realized it was the head of a moose! I was gonna come back with someone to kick your stuff out the door."

"It would have landed on solid ice," I said, wondering what that did to supplies. "Tom, are you going back with him?"

Steve raised a questioning brow.

"No. I'm gonna be fine," Tom answered. "I had a bit of trouble with my chest last winter," he explained to Steve, "but I'm okay now."

"Why didn't you come back?" Luke asked, plaintively. "We waited and waited." It was the question we all wanted to ask.

"Well, you remember that night we left. We didn't make it out. Got weathered in at Coldfoot for a few days. Then it just got too late in the year," he explained.

"And that's why you didn't come back for five months?" Luke persisted. I had to admire him. Much as he idolized the pilot, he pressed for clarity.

"Then this spring has been one thing after another. To tell you the truth, I just didn't think I could land. In deep snow that tail wheel'd sink clear to the feathers and maybe flip me."

Soon Steve headed out the door. "You guys got all the food you need?" he inquired as we loaded our winter clothes and spare rifle into the plane. "You're set for the summer?"

"We've got food," I assured him.

"Mostly beans and dried moose," Luke answered. He wasn't a fan of either.

"Hey, you don't know what's in the boxes," Tom grinned, pulling him close.

As the plane roared to life, Luke stood calling "good-bye," and waving sadly. He was wet again. "It's just like when Laurie left," he said and then burst into tears as the Cessna bounced over the rotting ice and into the air.

Tom picked him up and Luke clung like a monkey, sobbing into his father's neck while ice water dripped from his soggy clothing.

"Come on," I said. "Let's get home and see what people sent us."

❧

I SLEPT LITTLE THAT night, my brain reviewing all that had transpired. Our touch with that other world had again left me empty and frayed.

Throughout the next few days we quietly read the mail and opened our packages. Many had been shipped in September. This was how people lived a hundred years ago, I thought. We opened each present tenderly, conscious of the love of our family and friends. We were not alone, after all. The turkey hadn't come, but we had been sent a great diversity of things, mostly special foods, toys, books, and some clothes. Luke received badly needed summer shirts, and Tom got real coffee mugs and plates. There was even toothpaste.

Winter made one last stand a few days later, snow falling steadily over the dark spruce and soggy ice. It melted the next morning, leaving a smell of wet trees. It was a scent, Luke pointed out, that had been absent all winter. The river looked innocent, but the ice was undercut and one could hear the rush of water in places. Though still four feet thick, it was "candling" into a matrix of long, vertical crystals, thin as pencils. Warmed by the sun, our marker sticks were plunging through like hot knives.

One could still see stars around midnight, but it no longer got dark. We started putting cardboard in the windows to keep out the early morning sun. Our roof was bare of snow. Tom pulled the Plexiglas out of two windows and installed mosquito netting. When flies emerged, I corned the remaining roasts. The snow was too slushy to walk on even in snowshoes except at night.

Luke was enthralled with spring. "Just look at this!" he said breathlessly as I walked with him up the creek. His hands were filled with candling ice. "It's like a forest." He twisted until the crystals disintegrated in a faceted spray. "See all the cells? If you squeeze, you can hear them. I just love ice!"

A moment later he had dropped to his knees where snow had melted from the base of a tree. "Isn't it wonderful to see the ground come back to life?" He grinned. "It was just a vast white plain, but suddenly bushes and bare earth are popping to the surface!" He pushed his nose into the turf, greeting the plants. "See! Moss, blueberry bushes. It smells so good! Would you like to hear a poem I made up?"

"I'd love to," I answered, and seated myself beside him on the patch of bare ground.

His voice became soft and far away as he said:

The door is opening,
It is snowing out.
The door is opening
Into spring.

He was silent awhile. "I just opened another door. With Dad. I asked him to be more patient with me."

"What did he say?"

"He said he'd try. Then he asked me to be more willing to do what I was told and not talk back."

"And what did you say?"

"I said I'd try."

ONE MORNING WE AWOKE to a gentle rain that turned snow to the texture of knee-high mashed potatoes. The ice was pitted and slick with puddles and the sound of running water could be heard almost anywhere. Then came a cold spell and the snow crusted enough to hold our weight in the early mornings. It was sculpted into waves like a frozen ocean and our trails stood up in high relief, their edges carved into ribbons of stiff lace. We often wandered up the creek, Luke scuttling, rolling, and sliding as he crossed the country in the most difficult and interesting ways, his enthusiasm spilling out as happy noise.

The creek was suddenly running, jade water flowing over and under the groaning ice and pouring onto the river where it disappeared into the snow. The first goose came honking up the valley and my old friend the white-crowned sparrow could be heard in the thickets. An otter appeared in the "bathtub" of open water that formed on the river and remained several days while the hole grew into a creek running down the edge of the ice. Our wolves had found the scrap pile and we often saw or heard them.

Tom spent much of each day out alone with the camera. He would return happy and share his discoveries. Yet against all my hopes, he was again coughing up blood. Although he didn't speak of it, I knew he felt weak and tired easily. He didn't want to abandon our summer plans of exploring the valley, but I could see no reasonable alternative. He was quiet and introspective much of the time, preferring to be left alone.

I put up an old hammock and Luke spent part of each day swinging and making up little songs to the squirrels. Tippy had become quite tame, climbing onto the feeder as I scattered pumpkin seeds. As I filmed her eating, Luke carefully put out more. Soon she was taking them from his fingers.

"I don't know if that's such a good idea," I warned, but was so intent on filming this special moment that I ignored my common sense. Suddenly Luke was in tears, gripping his bloody hand.

"She bit me!" he whimpered, shocked and embarrassed.

I ushered him into the cabin and examined the wound. Two cuts slashed through the tips of the first fingers of his right hand.

"I feel betrayed." His eyes looked hurt and confused. "I trusted her and was kind to her."

"I don't think she meant to," I reassured him. "She can't see where she's chewing." I washed the hand thoroughly and milked the fingers before putting on peroxide. Then I looked up "animal bites" in my various medical books. The news was not reassuring.

"Tetanus is almost always present in animal mouths," wrote one. Luke was probably okay there, I decided. Another book described the progress of rabies in horrifying detail. All of my books warned that any wild animal bite required rabies vaccine unless the animal could be captured. Rabies was especially carried by skunks, squirrels, bats, and foxes. Squirrels! Cold fingers of fear gripped my heart. I looked up rabies in the *Health Guide for Rural Alaska* and discovered that it was prevalent here. I kicked myself for my stupidity. Well,

Tippy appeared healthy and we could keep her under observation for the critical ten days, I decided. By then the ice would go out and we could head downriver. It wasn't such a bad idea considering Tom's condition.

TWO DAYS LATER LUKE woke me in the night, vomiting spaghetti into his pillow. I spent the next day cleaning and airing our bed, consumed by a growing fear. I approached Tom about the idea of using the ELT, but he reasoned that a plane couldn't land now. The ice would go out in a week and we would leave.

I looked at my beautiful child playing peacefully, the familiar curve of his cheek, his gap-toothed grin, all so painfully dear. If I only knew what to do, I would use any means to save him! The two little bites were healing nicely. If it were Tom or me, I would take the chance, but Luke?! One book said that symptoms appear anywhere between ten days and two years (!), the average time being fifty to sixty days. Once they appear, rabies is inevitably fatal. What would I do if he came down with it on the river?

Taking my terror out on the delta, I prayed to release it and tried to turn Luke over to his Heavenly Father. I need not play out these awful fantasies, I reminded myself. As I sat meditating, the first seagull appeared overhead, dazzling white in the blue sky. Wheeling close it circled me, voicing the sound of the sea. Was it a sign, I wondered? That evening as I stood on the point, a lone goose passed up the valley, calling, calling. The next morning we awoke to a sky filled with geese winging their way north. I felt my throat constrict and my eyes fill with tears at my own helplessness and the preciousness of life.

THE TENSION THAT HAD been building in the land now erupted. I watched it all from a distance, feeling frightened and remote. The sound of running water and singing of birds bridged the twilight hours. Flocks were arriving hourly, scores of new voices echoing and reverberating through the forest. Within three days, the snow melted from the delta and the creek freed itself. It was odd to see the vestiges of our old trails lying like white ribbons over the familiar terrain of last summer, and to have our ancient footprints emerge like fossils in the mud. Tea-colored water rushed along the edge of the rotting river ice, breaking off large floes that jammed and swirled against the shore.

Tom's condition was rapidly deteriorating and we had no more medicine to help him. He became shaky when doing even light chores and nights found him sweaty and fevered. I took over hauling water again. I should have worried about Tom, but I had lived with my concerns for so long that I was worn out. It was Luke, healthy and strong who filled me with foreboding. When Tippy suddenly disappeared, I felt a knife twist inside. I searched for her everywhere, but she was simply gone.

Tom and I took turns watching and filming from the Overlook at the building power of the river. It cut channels of brown water and surged along both shores carrying stray blocks of ice. We were all there when it started to move the morning of May 15. Our runway was so well-packed that it slid quietly past, hardly cracking. It was strange to see the trails and landmarks glide by amid a thumping crowd of lesser bergs.

It was a lazy breakup, stopping and starting as blocks the size of rooms piled up at the curves. For three days we had runs of ice as higher tributaries broke free one by one. Because of the wide bend, we missed the dramatic rush and thunder of ice. It was more like the LA freeway—sometimes stalled, bumper-to-bumper, at others the pack hurrying along with a constant swish and thump of tons of candled ice. The roar of the creek could now be heard, drowning out even the song of birds.

"ARE YOU STRONG ENOUGH to canoe out?" I asked Tom bluntly one evening after Luke was asleep. The river was a swollen torrent of mud. Jumbled blocks of ice jammed the banks, but the major runs were over.

"I don't know," he answered simply.

"I've been thinking of what it will take to paddle hundreds of miles down this flooded river with a sick man and a possibly sick child, and it doesn't look smart to me."

Tom didn't answer. He looked wan and clammy.

"I want to use the ELT," I stated. "The river is high, but a plane could land now. It's embarrassing to call for help, but I'd go through any kind of hell to make sure Luke and you are safe."

To my surprise, he agreed.

That night I slept little, thinking of what needed to be done to evacuate the cabin: bring in cached clothing, cover the windows, put valuables upstairs safe from bears.

I was up early the next morning, planting the wind sock. Luckily the delta was not yet under water and I laid out our orange tarp, weighting it with rocks. The day was cold and windy, and I spent much of it down there, turning the ELT off and on in a regular pattern, feeling foolish and desperate and terribly tired. I hadn't really slept in days and could hardly bring myself to eat. I was blind to the beauty of spring, praying only to see my family safe.

By evening I turned on the little transmitter and left it running. I was too exhausted to stay with it. The sun rolled below the horizon for the 15,665th time in my life, uncountable billions since the formation of my planet, in a Universe where time itself loses meaning. It was all too big for me.

"I don't think anyone is coming," Tom said when I entered the cabin at twilight. "We may as well bring the ELT in."

"I'm just going to let it run all night," I answered.

"I think tomorrow we should head downstream."

My head ached with fatigue and worry. "We can turn it off two hours before we leave," I told him. "That will give them time to get here, if they're underway."

I couldn't even think of the trip out. I would need to repack for a long canoe voyage. The shore was rammed with ice. I thought of the rapids and the wind. I thought of finding camps above the high water. Of my family. That river was no place for sick or exhausted people.

❦

NEAR MIDNIGHT WE WERE jerked from sleep by the drone of a small plane! Pulling on jackets and rubber boots, Tom and I rushed down to the delta and lit our signal fire. The sky was burnt orange, but the land lay in deep shadow. The fire gusted brightly, blowing sparks across the sand.

Spent from this small exertion, Tom returned to bed with our sleeping child while I watched the plane transect the valley in a hunting pattern. Finally it turned toward us. Shivering in my night clothes, I lay on the tarp, holding my hands over my head to indicate that I needed help. At last he spotted me and began to circle.

I could see that he was on wheels, but I tried to indicate with gestures that the river was our airstrip. A streamer on the ground caught my eye in the twilight. I ran to pick it up and found a small plastic bottle tied to one end! I hadn't seen it fall. Inside was a note. With shaking hands I opened it and read: "Hello from the Civil Air Patrol! We have notified the State Troopers that you need help. If you need immediate medical attention split your fire in two. You can turn off your ELT now."

Immediate medical attention? I wondered. The word "immediate" was the problem. I didn't want food dropped, and I didn't want help next week.

I made up my mind and split the fire. It turned out to be the wrong answer, but as I'd told Luke, sometimes you make decisions without all the information. You do the best you can.

I returned to bed but not to sleep. They had come! My family would be all right. I must have dozed, for my dreams included a familiar chop-chop-chop sound, growing insistently louder.

"Helicopter!" I yelled, bolting upright, my heart pounding. It was twilight, the sun not yet up. I slid on my down vest and rubber boots and rushed for the beach where a large, serious-looking army helicopter was settling in a tornado of sand. Two olive clad men with a stretcher ran toward me.

"We heard there was a guy with a heart attack!" one of them said as we met.

I felt bewildered. "We're expecting a floatplane," I began. "My little boy was bit by a squirrel and we're concerned about rabies, but my husband is too sick to canoe out. I think he has TB."

They led me to the chopper where I again yelled our story to the grim looking pilot and copilot. The four men shut down the engines with a slowing whine of blades then followed me across the delta, shiny black boots sinking into the mud. It all seemed very unreal. Realizing the expense and trouble this trip had entailed, I was embarrassed that a Medevac team had come. The men were tired from the long trip and lack of sleep. We were beyond their normal range and they had taken out the rear seats to load extra bladders of fuel.

Within our dim cabin the medic examined Luke's fingers (now almost healed) with a flashlight. Then he listened to Tom's chest with a stethoscope and asked him questions. The men had a whispered conference and one of them said, "You definitely need medical treatment and should both be seen by a doctor, but this isn't an immediate emergency. It'd be better if we called someone else to come for you." We later heard that private ambulance and charter companies resented lost business.

"That's fine," we agreed, "but we need to get out soon." I gave them the Warteses' phone number saying, "Tell the pilot the river is high but clear of ice."

They said they would radio in flight. With that they were gone, leaving me feeling like Alice in Wonderland. I had reached a state where nothing seemed real.

"Do you think anyone is on floats yet?" I asked Tom as the staccato of the chopper died away.

"I hadn't thought of that."

"Well, it's out of our hands. Even if it takes two days, it'll be a lot faster than the river. And safer."

"I know," he said, softly. "I couldn't sleep last night, thinking of the river. In my shape we might have all been killed."

The day slipped by in a strange, tired daze as I completed preparations and fixed meals. My stomach ached and I had to force myself to eat. Feeling dizzy and weak, Tom remained in bed. Luke was subdued and quiet.

It was late afternoon before a white-and-green Cessna 180 on floats passed close over the cabin, circled once and landed. He came to shore just below the main creek, grounding between the chest-high blocks of rotting ice. The river had been rising steadily and already much of the bar was underwater. There was no place to tie the plane, so the pilot stood in hip boots, holding it in the current while we closed the cabin and brought down our few things.

Our friends had spent the day locating a pilot who was on floats. Don Ross was a quiet man with a gentle smile. He was somewhat older than us, tall and lean with reddish hair and fair skin. He had flown for Fish and Wildlife for years before starting his own business. He'd been around awhile and nothing seemed to faze him. His plane looked old and well-loved, the upholstery stitched in places. He loaded us aboard and set off down the torrent, dodging driftwood with easy confidence. For the first time in days, I relaxed. I took a deep breath and watched the banks slide past with a childish sense of wonder and trust.

Don drove his plane like a boat down to the tight inside bend where he swiveled around and guided it deftly under the high cutbank—aligned for a straight shot upriver. His left wing was practically touching a sweeper, one of those dangerous trees that falls into the river as the bank is undercut. He idled there a moment, warming the engine, then poured on the power. From a side window I saw the brown floodwater and trees flying past, and felt the slew of the pontoons as we curved with the river and gained the step. Then we were airborne but still below the trees, wending up the middle until we could climb above them. As he banked over the still frozen Horseshoe Lake, my heart filled with thanksgiving. It was all going to be okay.

❧

WE STAYED IN FAIRBANKS a week. The Warteses welcomed us home as always. Denise scheduled an appointment at her clinic where Tom and Luke got immediate attention. We were much relieved to find that Luke didn't have to undergo the rabies series. After questioning him closely about the squirrel, the kindly physician's assistant, Mr. Rogers, explained that while there was indeed a high incidence of rabies in the Arctic, foxes were the main carriers. Squirrels died rapidly of the disease.

Tom was diagnosed with mycoplasma pneumonia.

"Pneumonia?" I asked, incredulously. "For eight months?"

"They used to call it 'walking pneumonia,'" he told us. "He's got a lot of consolidation down there. Listen, you can hear it when you thump his chest." Mr. Rogers demonstrated, using his fingers to percuss Tom's ribs. He smiled and shook his head. "Sounds like you tried every antibiotic except one specific for this condition."

Tom was put on a new miracle drug—six pills in all—and told it would take three months for his lungs to clear entirely. Mr. Rogers gave him an extra course, should he need it, and resupplied us with other antibiotics.

Six little red pills, I thought. Could it really be that simple after all these months of worry?

I visited a dentist who replaced the temporary filling Tom had put in when I broke a rear molar earlier in the spring. My stepmother, Martha, took Luke to buy toys and jeans. Tom bought a new fishing license. We also phoned those we loved, telling them only that we were visiting town briefly, for Tom didn't want to worry his family. When I reached Laurie we exchanged laughter and tears across the miles. She was working at her old job and didn't think she could get away for the summer. In the complexities of that other world, her relationship with John hadn't worked out.

Before we left for the bush again, I found our turkey still in the Warteses' freezer and we shared Thanksgiving dinner with them. It was fitting that we should.

❦

THE RIVER COVERED THE delta when Don set us down beside our old camp. The snow was gone and most of the ice had disappeared. Our cabin was just as we left it: quiet and cool inside, sunny outside. Mosquitoes drifted about in token numbers, parents of the coming swarms. Standing beside the flooding river, we waved good-bye as swallows streamed like smoke from under the cutbank. Our lives had been renewed, and for that I would always be grateful. I could view Luke without a cloud of fear and, though not yet well, Tom was improving daily. A second chance, I thought, to cherish each moment and a reminder that we don't have forever!

Watching the plane depart, Luke was subdued and sad. "I didn't want him to go," he said as we ascended the familiar hill.

"I know," I answered, "but I promise we'll have a wonderful summer. Much better than in Arizona."

"What about Fairbanks?" he asked. "We could have stayed with the War-teses." There was a note of pleading in his voice. He had joked about discovering root beer and pizza, yet I knew it was people that he missed.

"Just think," I told him, "they'll be waiting for us when we get out."

We went to bed early and slept peacefully in the stillness of our cabin. I lay listening to my family breathe as I watched the sunset glow that Luke called his "golden light" creep along the wall. From beneath the floor came the minute squeaks of baby voles. Perhaps I would never understand the miracle of life. Maybe living it was enough. To hold our precious children (all children!) and see God in their eyes; to sing and praise Creation, to honor my body and rejoice in my every breath—this was worth the ride.

CHAPTER 13

The Australian aborigines saw the land as routes or "songlines" rather than space. Originally created by song, the earth is re-created by walking it. Even today these people may suddenly lay aside their tools, step out of their clothes, and go "walkabout." For them, it is connection with the earth rather than getting somewhere that matters. I've always felt a kinship with this idea and a love of walking the planet. In the age-old balance between the Quest and the search for security, we leave our comfortable surroundings and place our feet upon the unknown path.

As Tom's strength returned, we loaded our packs and set off on our own version of walkabout. He had crafted an exterior door that he nailed shut, leaving the hammer and a note under the eaves. He covered the windows with split logs driven onto dowels. Bears will often go to great lengths to enter a cabin and some people simply leave the door open to minimize structural damage.

It was a warm day with popcorn clouds scattered over the sky. We hoisted our packs and set off parallel to Luke's Creek. Tom and I each carried around eighty pounds, while Luke had fifteen. We planned to follow the creek into the mountains and onto the high ridges where snow still mottled the ground. The stream was loud and brutal, impossible to cross, so we followed the rocky bench where birch, spruce, and cranberry prevailed. This was broken with occasional muskeg, but for the most part the walking was fairly easy.

I was feeling old and soft beneath the heavy reality of my pack as I lurched and staggered over the uneven ground, sinking shin-deep in a wet carpet of lichens, mosses, and stunted bushes. Luke found his own pack uncomfortable and frequently swung it off. I walked behind him, tripping whenever he halted to pick flowers. Only Tom seemed in good form, stepping easily ahead, feeling better each day as his chest cleared.

The land was still brown with bright new leaves just breaking out, but perennials were already rocketing into bloom. Cranberry plants were hung with tiny pink urns, and spikes of bell-heather, like miniature pine trees, sprouted little white bells. Clumps of narcissus-flowered anemones were everywhere. Rusty-looking Lapland rosebay bushes wore masses of large, magenta blossoms and the showy pink stalks of woolly lousewort speckled the ground. Blueberry bushes in tender red-green leaves were decked in minute red buds. With stained fingers and knees Luke enjoyed grazing on overwintered berries as we traveled.

Without a watch, and with the sun going around the compass over new and changing landmarks, it was impossible to determine the hour or how long we walked. It was June and the sun only dipped behind the peaks around midnight. Gradually the valley closed about us and we angled higher onto the encroaching mountain to avoid the tumble of rocks and brush. The roar of the creek was a constant and wearing presence. I trudged along, swimming through alders with my heavy pack. Luke kept up a stream of questions and observations as continual as the roar of the creek below.

"Do you think we could make a steam engine with our cooking pot?" "Could a person explore all the Brooks Range in his lifetime?" "How do geysers work?" "What's on the other side of the universe?" "If light went a trillion times faster, could it cross the galaxy in a second?" "How come species can't cross-mate?" "What's the opposite of yellow?" "How come animals are afraid of us?" "Do you think I could ever make friends with a bear?" "I don't have many mosquitoes on me, but when you come up, you're like the white man bringing diseases to the Natives." Then with a twinkle in his eye, "Mom, you sure carry the bugs!" With this he began smacking Laurie's old Smokey-the-Bear hat, which I was wearing. Luke and Tom had on baseball caps and wore their hair long on their necks as protection from sun and bugs.

We reached the first tributary late in the day and named it "Janet's Creek" after my aunt. It poured in a loud torrent down a steep gully that was choked with boulders and streaked with shadow from the overhanging trees. We had passed Annie's Peak and entered between the mountains. An eagle's nest hung from the cliffs above. Crossing Janet's Creek seemed out of the question, but Tom discovered a place where a dead tree had fallen, forming a railing. While I filmed from the steep bank, he edged his way through the rushing ice water and climbed the opposite bank. There he left his pack and returned for Luke. Timidly I followed.

🦋

THE NEXT MORNING MY pack was heavier, for I had filched some of Luke's load to quicken our pace. He bounded along, bubbling with questions while I stumbled after. At one point, half the hill had given way, exposing a bare seep that we picked our way across.

"Wheeeee! Quick sand!" Luke said, jumping forward with both feet. "Arugh! Quick mud!

"Tell me about the water cycle again," he began as we fought through the tangle of slide alders on the far side. Their hanging branches were loaded with pollen and he swatted them in delight, inundating us in pounds of pale green dust. "Why does air get cooler as you go up?" "What's the name of that flower?" "Why do I have to go to school? You can teach me at home." (To which I answered that I was tired of the struggle.) "But I'll change," he promised earnestly. "I already have changed; you just haven't noticed." "How old do you think that tree is?"

It was late afternoon when we reached a second major tributary, dubbed "Bert's Creek" after my uncle. It was obvious even to Tom that we were not going to cross this one. We set up camp near the junction, as far back from the merging creeks as possible.

"The noise wears me out," I told Tom as I dished up bowls of rice and dried meat from my place by the fire. We could see birds flitting through the forest, but their song was buried by the thunder of water. "It's like living with heavy, earthmoving equipment."

"It is heavy, earthmoving equipment," he stated. He finished breaking up a pile of firewood and joined us on the ground. He looked happy and at home.

I smiled across the smoky blaze at my family. For weeks I'd been processing thoughts about what I perceived as the "dark side" of Nature, those forces that randomly tear life apart. We had found a drowned moose calf, no bigger than Luke. The thought that God would create this beauty just to throw it away filled me with a sense of fear, as if life itself had no meaning. Somehow, I had to resolve this issue; I couldn't always be trying to shore up my courage, always watchful and afraid.

Destruction, I suddenly realized, is the left hand of Creation. Both are necessary to the miracle of life! Cataclysms, fires, plagues, floods, volcanoes, glaciers, and even winter, are a cleansing force. They wipe the slate clean. "Behold! I make all things new!" It could not happen without death and decay. If the energy of Life is eternal, there is nothing to fear.

THE FOLLOWING DAY WE trudged up Bert's Creek, ascending a steep canyon where snow lay plastered between the rocks. Already my clothes felt loose and I was better able to manage my pack. Above us, the canyon ended in a dramatic amphitheater, peaks standing hard against the blue sky. Leaving the trees behind, we climbed through waist-high dwarf birch toward the ridge where we planned to camp.

The mosquitoes were worse now, but a breeze helped to keep them at bay. Spring was just arriving up here. With catkins erect, arctic willows no taller than my finger netted the ground. White-crowned sparrows and Lapland longspurs sang in the late afternoon sun. We waded through rushing snowmelt until we reached a protected saddle overhung by a rocky cliff. Here a series of ponds fed both directions. The facing ridge rose above us, splotchy with snow, and across the steep canyon King Mountain loomed.

In the saddle we found the only bit of dry and level ground in miles and put up our tent. To either side the ridge climbed into the sky, inviting us to explore on and on, which we did until dark clouds drove us back to the small refuge of our leaky, yellow tent. We were using my old backpacking tent, and Tom tied our orange tarp over it to keep out the rain. There we hunkered against the thunder and wind. Clouds streamed over the cliffs, while isolated shafts of sunlight stabbed like searchlights along the far peaks. In the steep valley below, we could see a snowy owl riding the updraft, white against the black storm.

❦

THE MORNING WAS BRIGHT and gentle as we set off along the alpine ridge. We walked the roof of the world, canyons dropping away on either side. Here minute plants with beautiful flowers bravely bloomed with the valley spreading below. Slabs of rock tilted into the sky wore flowers planted along their seams: yellow anemones, arctic phlox, and tiny clusters of purple mountain saxifrage of rich hues. The rocks themselves were works of art, sculpted and colored with lichens. Marmots lived among them, whistling alarms at our approach.

Storms blow up from nowhere on those exposed ridges and move with terrifying speed. Soon a wind tore at our clothes and black clouds ripped through the pass behind us. Lightning stabbed along the ridge. It was no place to be caught in a storm. Pulling on rain jackets, we plunged down the steep slope, tearing through chest-high bushes as a wall of hail descended.

Luke no longer asked questions. Like a frightened rabbit, he scurried ahead of me, his little form squelching through the wet thickets and slipping on the balls of ice. Within an hour the hail had turned to drenching rain, but lightning still cracked about us as we raced down, down the open ridge, aiming for the shelter of the forest. Water poured off the mountain beneath us.

Janet's Creek had been transformed into an uncrossable flood. Luke and I were both very tired, but Tom wanted to push on. After a brief rest, we descended the drainage until the creek narrowed between cutbanks. Tom suggested we build a bridge and we gathered small dead trees and dropped them across. When there was a sizable bundle, he wrapped them with a piece of cord, then crossed the torrent and secured the other end. Tom transported the packs across and returned to help Luke. After I was over, he retrieved his rope and we continued on.

It stormed again that evening, and the next day we turned for home. Spring had changed to summer in the low country. Alder and willow were in full leaf; blue arctic lupine, wild sweet pea, and showy oxytrope had burst into bloom.

When we arrived at our cabin, Tippy greeted us, demanding sunflower seeds. Her babies were old enough to be left and she was hungry. The mosquitoes had hatched en masse. Gratefully we closed our door on their numbers and unpacked our wet and filthy possessions. Tom hauled muddy water from the river and we all had a bath. It felt wonderful to sleep in our clean, flat loft.

❧

TEN DAYS LATER WE were off again, wanting to see more of the country before we started the six-hundred-mile downriver trip that would take us back to civilization. It was the middle of June, and already the brief summer was passing. Our crossbill family was learning to fly and the yard was hopping with young squirrels. The haunting melody of my "cathedral bird" once more echoed through the twilight. Flowers were everywhere, beautiful and profuse, the loveliest I could remember.

This time we headed north, lining our canoe upstream. The river was still very high and muddy and the going difficult. It was turning into a rainy month, storms rolling in almost every afternoon. As we rounded the first bend, I noticed clouds building over Flattop. Lake Eugene was completely thawed, a yellow mass of marsh marigolds waving along one edge. The bluff was clothed in the blossoms of kinnikinnick, prickly saxifrage, and beautiful Jacob's ladder. Lupine, wild rose, northern oxytrope, and death camas lilies made a carpet of flowers against the sky.

The day was hot and the mosquitoes thick as we labored, pulling the canoe with our outfit and Luke aboard. Just as the flowers were prettier this year, so too were the mosquitoes far worse than the previous summer. With the high water we were forced to work our way along broken cutbanks overgrown

J.ASPEN 94

with willow and matted with driftwood. It often took our combined efforts to get around obstacles and I found myself yelling at Tom in frustration above the sound of the river.

"Dad and I aren't mad at you or at each other," I explained to Luke during our brief lunch break. "We're just tired, hot, and sometimes scared. It'll be awhile before we get our act together."

Luke didn't seem to understand. Maybe I'm expecting too much of him, I thought as we continued on. I was thrashing through a tangle of brush, waist deep in rushing water as hundreds of mosquitoes swarmed around my face.

"How do helicopters fly?" he asked from the rear seat, yelling over the roar of water and bugs.

"Luke, I can't talk now!" I snapped back (. . . ease the bow line off, let the current catch her a bit, keep up momentum to get around that snag . . . Damn!).

"I mean," he continued, insistent as a mosquito, "how do they go up?"

When we were even with Wandering Slough, we worked our way beyond the head of an island and climbed aboard to cross again. "Paddle, Luke! Paddle!" I yelled back. I could feel us losing ground, being sucked down the center channel.

"I'm saving my energy for when we go where I want to," he replied.

"This isn't a contest," I bawled. "We're all on the same side!"

Wandering Slough emerged clear and reddish, like tea water, into the muddy river. "I don't think this goes through," I told Tom doubtfully as we entered it.

"Oh, you're so negative," he replied. "Look at the map. It's a shortcut." The slough supposedly rejoined the river within three miles, but we needed water if we were to take the canoe.

"It's an adventure," I agreed. I just wasn't sure if I wanted one right now. I was feeling tired and irritable. The bugs had followed us across the river and joined fresh troops on the far side. Maybe I wasn't cut out for this life anymore, I thought. Slowly we paddled up the slough, gliding easily over the dark surface. It was lovely in the late afternoon, snaking away from the river. Soon we hit a riffle of fast water, but easily lined up it. The slough became a small creek, often only a few feet wide, interspersed with long, shallow ponds and gravel bars. We spotted two dozen fish of an unknown type and Tom eagerly got out his pole but failed to catch one. To his surprise, I declared that I was ready to camp and soon found a place in the narrow belt of spruce that lined the slough. It was all I could do to help set up camp and start dinner amid the constant mosquitoes. Even the fire failed to deter them, and they rained into the pot as I cooked.

"I forgot bowls and plates," I said. I felt ready to cry.

We ate macaroni and cheese from the blackened pot and crawled into our small, yellow tent, thankful to escape from the bugs. Clouds of them covered the screen and their whine filled the air. I had difficulty sleeping with the sun in my eyes and my head downhill in the crowded, bumpy tent. My contact lenses were again pushed to the side. Finally I turned head-to-foot with Luke and slept fitfully.

❧

"I DON'T THINK WE can get out this way," I reiterated the following morning as we continued up Wandering Slough. "The water is the wrong color."

"I know you don't," Tom agreed. "You're such a pessimist."

The little stream soon narrowed to a winding cut not much wider than our canoe. I hauled and lined the boat with Luke aboard while Tom fished ahead without success. Soon the clear water diverged from a muddy slough and climbed in a fast, rocky creek away to the left. The main channel was not flowing. Within a short space the water ended in a series of muddy ponds interspersed with grassy bogs. As we heaved our craft overland between water holes, I suddenly pictured myself as Katharine Hepburn in *The African Queen*. Finally the tract degenerated into a twisted ravine strewn with rocks and the debris of flood. Hot and tired, we portaged the last stretch, unpacking and carrying our possessions and canoe out to the broad sweep of our big, muddy river.

That evening we located a decent camp back in the trees through some old willows. The ground was dry and mossy and there was shade from the morning sun. The bugs were as fierce as ever, but I was able to sit and cook a meal of potatoes, dried moose, and chicken soup.

Luke joined me by the fire. "I like to catch mosquitoes and pull their beaks off," he confided as I handed him a cup of cocoa. Swarms of them were probing over his legs, and his face was speckled with welts.

"They do drive you crazy," I acknowledged, "but it's important not to enjoy the suffering of anything, even a bug."

"But they torture me," he said reasonably.

"It's okay to swat them, but don't pull off their beaks, even though it seems deserved."

He looked unconvinced.

"What you do matters, even small things," I went on. "It's the actions you take every day that make up your life. I used to think there was some great, heroic thing you could do that would change the world . . ."

"Like in my fantasies," he interrupted.

"That's right. But life is just what you do each moment, the little decisions you make.

Luke sat on a plastic five-gallon bucket and sipped his cocoa. We were silent, watching the fire. Nearby, Tom was staking out the tent. He had emptied the canoe and pulled it high above the river, flipping it over and tying it down. The sun hung low in the north behind a solitary cloud, turning it to flame. Its nimbus radiated beams in all directions.

Maybe the world doesn't need changing, I thought. If God is all there is, that must include people and their crazy civilizations. Thinking back on ancient history, I wondered if our problems were so different from those in Egypt and Greece. As individuals, we still dealt with war, politics, art, religion, prosperity, and the cycle of birth and death. The overall scheme hadn't changed: infinite variations on the same old lessons. As I told Luke, my power lay in how I participated.

But what of our planet? Unlike the Greeks, our civilization seems to threaten the Earth itself. Could we really destroy this grand old planet, or were we also part of a natural cycle? Maybe we were the next cataclysm, like the asteroid that wiped most species from the globe and ended the dinosaur era. Oh, we might make it unfit for ourselves and higher life for awhile, but given time, Life would express in new creations of strength and beauty.

Ours is a very exciting and scary moment to be alive. I had always yearned to make a difference, alternating between running away and poking my small finger into the dike, yet watching that radiant cloud—a random act of splendor— I realized that the Earth didn't need me. It was still crucial to live consciously, even if it made no real difference in the grand design, for that is our individual purpose, but the outcome was not in my hands. One way or another it was going to be all right.

❧

As we approached our old friend, Flattop, its contours changed. Soon it looked like "Pointy Top," as Luke said. I was reminded of what two-dimensional creatures we are—we who look into space and see "constellations" on a flat plane and name mountain features from our limited visual perspective. Daily, a spectacular show of enormous clouds loomed above us, their frightening black masses adding depth and contrast to the sky. You never realize how big the sky is until you live under it.

Our soggy boots were falling apart and usually full of sand from splashing along, and we were always wet to the crotch. The river was dropping, leaving gravel bars. We would rest on the warm gravel at lunch and watch those clouds, bigger than mountains, take shape above us, grand and terrifying in their splendor. By afternoon, the wind picked up, blowing cold and dangerous out of the towering clouds, and we sought refuge in the trees until the storm blew over.

We took turns pulling the canoe except where the conditions required both of us. Luke rode or walked as the mood suited him. The journey was hard, but good for us. I was becoming stronger, though certain parts were wearing badly and I feared would not improve. My heel tendons were swollen and had distinct knots on them, causing me to limp. Both of us were having trouble with our arms falling asleep at night. Our skins took it the hardest. They were cracking and mask-like, weathered to leather under the onslaught of sun, wind, smoke, and bug repellent. Even Luke was wrinkled.

Most days we traveled but sometimes we stayed over to explore, returning to our little camps at the end of the day, grateful to find them unmolested. It was not an easy land to walk through and often left me feeling small and ineffectual, still it drew us on. Its secrets beckoned as we traversed ridge and marsh accompanied by the shrill piping of upland plover and yellowlegs or the song of the white-crowned sparrow—and always clouds of mosquitoes.

❧

One afternoon found us battling our way up rapids. Camping spots were harder to find now with forests located back from vast gravel bars. The water was clearing, going from brown to gray-green, but an icy wind poured off of the peaks ahead as the high country opened slowly before us. The upper river had become a swift, braided, snag-riddled, and dangerous place, requiring all our energy to breast.

Evening came on and we were very tired as we searched anxiously for a place to pitch a camp. The sky had a gray cast, and wind whipped spray from the rapids back to where Luke huddled in his wool jacket and life preserver, chapped hands gripping his little bag of trail mix.

"Why don't you run ahead and see if you can find a place at the base of that bluff," I suggested to Tom. "I'll hold the canoe here. If there's nothing, let's go back to the last creek. It wasn't great, but at least we'll be off the river." I had reached the stage of fatigue where I couldn't make decisions, and I knew Tom wasn't much better. Sometimes there are no right answers, I thought. Pick one, just don't dither. To vacillate is to lose all power to the situation.

I grounded the canoe on the rocks. Luke's cheeks looked raw and his eyes were squinted into the wind, but he was singing:

> "Oh, I don't want to go up river anymore, I just want home,
>   that's all.
> I don't care if there's boulders under me, sticks or stumps
>   or holes.
> Oh, I don't want to go up river anymore! I just want home,
>   that's all!"

I smiled and leaned over him, hair whipping into my eyes. "Me too, Kiddo. You're a brave little guy. We'll camp soon, I promise."

When Tom returned to report no camping spot ahead, we climbed stiffly aboard and quickly relinquished a hard-won half mile. We came ashore in a broken and boggy tangle of dying trees. The bank was wet and frozen beneath the hummocky moss; half the trees were dangerous snags, but we tottered about on numb feet making a much needed home. While I prepared dinner, Tom put up the tent, stringing our leaky tarps over it. It stormed much of the night and the sound of crashing trees disturbed our sleep.

"It's not fun anymore," Tom said the next morning as we ate breakfast of pancakes and fried mosquitoes.

"Then it's time to turn around," I replied. That was our agreement: we would travel as long as it was fun. "I don't like the look of this river."

Luke glanced from one to the other of us. "I don't want to turn back," he insisted. "I want to see the glacier." We had talked of hiking over to an ice field created by a spring. For several days we had speculated while slowly approaching the white patch. It now lay across the river and several miles up a valley.

"I'm sorry, Luke," I told him. "We can stop where the creek comes in, but I doubt if we can walk up it."

We loaded the canoe and in no time were erasing days of hard work. Zipping down the wicked little river, we dodged sweepers and tried to recall the channels we had come up. It's surprising how different the view is when you turn around. We spotted the small creek entering between high banks and swung in. The stream was swift and clear, the banks perhaps ten feet high were fringed with trees. We pulled the canoe up the winding channel a few yards to where it opened, giving us a small, lumpy place to camp. There was a lovely view showing the northern amphitheater of Flattop and the encircling arms of a new mountain.

We were weathered-in the following day, which gave us a needed rest. The mosquitoes were still so bad that no one dared exit the tent in the night. They bit right through repellent, and the fire did little to deter them. We ate them by the dozens with every meal.

The next morning we set off wading up "Bright Creek," as we called it, a sunken highway between banks of muskeg and dwarf birch. I carried Luke across the deeper holes to keep him from getting wet to the armpits. The creek had a sandy bottom, and as we climbed toward the mountains it became a swift stream. We entered an impressive gorge, a raw place rapidly eroding under spring runoff. Thickets of willow lay buried in gravel, while water cascaded over boulders and under towering banks of ice. We decided to leave the creek, scaling the canyon rim to look back upon the country we had traversed. It seemed a miracle that we had so easily crossed this difficult terrain.

At last we saw a band of white shining through the trees ahead. A great upland bowl had been carved by the ice, devoid of vegetation and floored in large, broken rocks of many colors. Striated in bluish bands, the "glacier" had melted until it was only a dozen feet high but covered many acres. A strange path wandered up the middle like the Yellow Brick Road. As we followed it, we could hear the gurgle and drip of water in the broken rocks beneath our feet. Behind us spread a wild panorama of tundra, marsh, lakes, forests, and mountains. The sun blinked under a cloud and a cold wind whispered over the ice field.

Chased by the storms, we cut across the ridge back to Bright Creek and had a quick snack by a fire in the shadows of the gorge. We donned our wool jackets against the scattered raindrops before heading back to the friendlier regions of sun and sand. It rained hard much of the night.

WE AWOKE TO A WET LAND. The sun was out and mist rose in ragged streamers along the mountain gullies. Gradually, we got our things stowed and ate breakfast. We loaded the canoe and dragged her down the creek to the river, pulling her over the shallow bed. The river had dropped more than a foot and cleared to jade green. The channel was surprisingly low and sluggish. It seemed ironic that we should have battled so hard to get up this river and now faced a stiff headwind and a slow trip home.

As the day progressed, we found ourselves paddling steadily to keep headed into the eighteen-inch waves and prevent the canoe from being blown upstream. Black storms climbed the peaks, and the wind increased. Along the shore, clumps of poplar thrashed and spruce bent in the blast. Clouds of sand whipped across the open bars. Slowly we counted off our previous days' progress: there was "Forest Island Camp" where we slept on moss among the waxy flowers of wintergreen; there was the place we had stopped for lunch in the scent of wild sweet peas.

Flattop gradually resumed its familiar shape, and we could recognize Mount Laurie and Annie's Peak. We passed the dry beginnings of Wandering Slough and paddled down the long bends of muskeg where high cutbanks caved into the river with sudden "whumps!" as the mud thawed. Once we startled a moose, still covered with old patches of last year's coat.

We stopped at Wandering Slough to warm up while Tom tried to catch a fish for dinner. To the north, the sky was black as night; the wind was gusting so strongly I was afraid we might not get home. I was very tired from paddling against the wind. Cold and wet-footed, I searched the uninviting bar for something to burn. Luke was running and playing, involved in some fantasy.

"Why don't you help me!" I called sharply. "Get some firewood, Luke. I need your help!"

"I'm running to warm up," he answered.

"Well, get some wood as you run and we'll both warm up."

He disappeared angrily into the willows. I carried my sticks down to the mudflat by the canoe and managed to kindle a fire. I could see Luke peeking through the bushes.

"Come on down and get warm," I shouted above the howl of the wind. "Bring what you have."

Tom appeared with a few branches. "No fish in this wind," he told me. "I think we should sprint for home."

I agreed. Luke reappeared empty-handed, just as we quenched the fire. I carried him out to his seat to keep his feet dry. Then I squelched over the slippery stones to push the bow out.

"I did get some firewood," he told me, "but I hid it, because I was angry."

"Well, good for you," I answered without looking at him.

"Don't you care?" he continued.

"Luke, right now I don't care what you do," I said. I climbed in and resumed the battle for home. I was seething. He still thought life was a contest! He had reacted to my words as a challenge and never heard my need for help. As I fought the wind on our final leg, something inside me shifted and I realized that it was time for a change.

We rounded our bend of the river and I tried to see it as a stranger might. This was just another bank, another bar. Those were just spruce trees—but they weren't. Every beloved curve of the familiar shore sang "home" to my heart. No sign of people or cabin, and yet . . . how could anyone miss the golden light that seemed to emanate from the very mud of the bank? There was a poignancy in knowing that we must soon leave it for the long journey back to that other world. But for now, it felt good to come home!

CHAPTER 14

"We need to talk," I told Luke the next morning when he joined me downstairs on the sofa.

Tom was still asleep. The fire crackled softly, heating our morning coffee and breakfast cereal. Tippy was on the woodpile staring through the front window and calling for sunflower seeds. She did everything but handstands to get my attention. She had galloped over the roof much of the night, chirring, squeaking, and whining. We had created a monster. It was lucky that we'd be leaving in time for her to lay up a winter supply of cones.

Luke curled up beside me and gave me his attention. His skin was peeling from windburn and there were crow's-feet in the corners of his eyes. "I've been at fault," I said, "for treating you as an equal. You are equal in value, but to have a vote you must make a contribution. If you want a say in where we're going, you need to help get us there. You can't sit in the wagon cracking the whip and yelling 'Faster! Faster!' as your parents pull it."

To my great surprise, he didn't argue but listened attentively. There were tears in his eyes.

"I realized yesterday that I was disappointed in your behavior but had never communicated my expectations. When we first canoed down this river, all I required was that you be agreeable. We're still operating at that level, which was appropriate when you were four but not now. You are seven, and I expect some help, especially out on the river. When we come to shore, you can gather firewood. You can help carry things to camp. Be appropriate with your questions. 'Could a rhinoceros ride a pogo stick to Mars?'" I mimicked.

A smile twitched his lips and I knew I'd scored a hit.

"Furthermore," I went on, "I expect courtesy. Dad and I don't sass one another and you don't get to either. I expect you to do your studies well and without being obnoxious. And you're to pick up after yourself."

"But I like it the old way," he said, tears spilling down his cheeks.

"Luke, I love you," I replied softly, "but you cannot stay a baby. No one can. Privilege and responsibility go hand-in-hand. I think you'll find there are benefits to growing up, as well."

Then I hugged him and read him a story.

Over the next few days there was a decided shift in Luke's demeanor. He offered to help haul water and went to the toilet unescorted. He stopped whining and making unreasonable demands. He seemed to stand straighter and his manners improved greatly. He got dressed without being nagged. It was as if he had known the next step all along and only waited for me to signal my readiness. I had prolonged his babyhood beyond where it served either of us, and we needed to relinquish it together. It was my job to keep my expectations high, I realized, for Luke was up to them.

AT HOME NEW FLOWERS were in bloom, the earlier ones having faded to obscurity among the general green. It was as if someone had changed the decor. A fluid quilt of overlapping colors washed the land. Beaches blazed in pink clumps of wild sweet pea and Eskimo potatoes. In the forest, shrubby cinquefoil winked bright yellow on gray-green bushes, bunches of white Labrador tea blossoms gave off the smell of spice, alpine arnica looked like yellow daisies, and the blue flowers of monkshood rose on tall stems. We even found occasional lady's slipper orchids in the shady woods.

The creek was again small and friendly with yellow Indian paintbrush poking between the willows. The marsh marigolds were gone, but little bog violets were in bloom, as were the tiny white stars called grass of parnassus. The delta had reappeared with its new-old shoreline. The river was down perhaps five feet and still dropping. Along the gravel bars of Luke's Creek large rugs of yellow dryas were in bloom as well as the magenta of dwarf fireweed. Asters and hawksbeard dotted the beach.

Three weeks after we returned from our upstream trip, we were ready for the long journey out to civilization. We'd spent the intervening days repairing the roof, rafting down extra firewood, filming, and taking hikes. Luke frequently accompanied Tom on fishing trips. He proved to be a reasonable partner, paddling hard and remaining cheerful despite the long walks through muskeg and bugs. He was also learning to fish.

Before we left, we burned empty containers and worn-out clothes. These treasures are apt to become garbage, strewn by bears. It was a hard decision in a land where each item is bought with great effort, but we wanted to leave the area clean. We donated Shylo's dog food to the wolves. Likewise, we burned our

J. ASPEN 94

remaining gasoline, fearing that it could leak and contaminate the ground. At the same time, we prepared our cabin to be a refuge in an emergency. There would be a fire laid in the stove, hundreds of pounds of dried food in closed containers, maps, and a manual of information. It was unlikely anyone but us would ever need it, but in the odd way circumstances unfold, many lives have been saved by old cabins.

Most cabins in this country date from the thirties. Here one sees life at its simplest: eight-by-ten-foot unpeeled log structures with a tiny door, tin stove, dirt floor, and one window notched into a single log for light. Very few seem homey; they represent survival with no frills.

Looking at our cabin, I realized that our life here had not been a statement against technology; we weren't seeking hardship for its own sake. Rather, this year had been a chance to explore possibilities and discover our own answers. Living here had allowed me to step back from my culture and view it. Technology was not the problem, I decided, but technology that does not serve our higher selves. If we could learn to honor our human Journey, the results would be quite different. Hitched to fear and money, our machines have become tyrants, yet they are only tools. What is the point of "progress" that creates a dreary and limiting world? By trying to escape discomfort and death, we have enslaved ourselves to commerce. Yet we can always choose again.

I was ready to go back to the other world, though saying good-bye to this one was hard. It had been a mixed blessing for me: beauty and fear, joy and loneliness. As Kahlil Gibran wrote, who can depart from such a gift without regret? I didn't know if I would return, but for now my direction lay elsewhere. It's too easy to become a prisoner of self-image. If I settled comfortably into a niche (any niche), I would eventually cease to be an artist. Unless I followed the Quest and was willing to risk, I would lose the spark that made life, if not safe, at least interesting. I'm not sure if it ever gets easier, but experience had shown me that a path would open if only I had the courage to set out. Real freedom means having the discipline to be happy wherever you are.

***

IT WAS A COOL summer and looked like an early fall. Smoke from forest fires somewhere to the south often hazed the valley. The river was muddy again, and had begun to come up, taking back the delta an inch at a time. It rained many afternoons, black sky punctuated with lightning. Trees cracked under the wind, while blowing sand thundered down the open bars. We usually took our baths down on the delta, but it wasn't a prolonged or leisurely experience. Though Luke still splashed until he was as cold as a fish, Tom and I did not join him.

We had been waiting for warm weather to begin our voyage, but realized that it might not arrive. Already the blueberries were getting ripe, a bumper crop hanging like jewels about our knees as we walked. The mosquito population dropped from intolerable to merely bad. The birds were mostly silent now, although I still heard the cathedral bird on occasion at night. The yard was full of robins, jays, crossbills, white-crowned sparrows, and of course squirrels. Young ravens cavorted over the river, proud and free on their new wings.

By mid-July it was time to go. We each said good-bye in our own way. Luke spent hours in the lower branches of an ancient spruce near the cabin. With his arms encircling the big trunk of our "Grandfather Tree" and his face looking sad, he made up quiet songs. Tom stood on the Overlook and watched the river coil past. He was already talking about what he'd like to do when we came back. This year had gone too fast, he told me. Next time he wanted to stay longer.

We sorted, packed, and labeled our belongings, trying to find room for the things we wanted to take. The trip downstream would be complicated with a variety of extra possessions: chain-saw, video equipment, rifles, books, clothing. Anything left at the cabin risked being destroyed by time and animals. In addition, we would need our camping gear and 250 pounds of dried food for the trip. The pile was truly staggering and I was worried about fitting it into the canoe.

I felt sad as we covered the windows and hung the bedding from the ridgepole. Tom and I sealed the cabin while Luke hauled gear down to the river. He had tearfully hugged each tree good-bye and was now excited about the coming adventure. When all was in readiness, we stood before the door and held hands for a final blessing. It was Luke's idea.

"Strange," I said wiping tears from my eyes, "I didn't feel this way when we left Arizona." I looked over at Mount Laurie. "Perhaps more of my heart is here." The thought of our cabin, dark and cold, filled me with melancholy. The country didn't need me, I reminded myself. Yet our love had made this pile of logs, this bend in the river, special, at least to us.

It was a dreary day, the river brown and sullen under a leaden sky, as we descended the familiar trail for the last time. The canoe was weighted with gear and sitting low in the water, our outfit piled two feet above the gunwales. There was about seven hundred pounds of gear arranged in awkward layers with the waterproof items on the bottom. These included plastic buckets of food, grub box, cooking pots, rubberized duffel (with tent and sleeping bags), rubber clothing bags, and ammunition box. Over these sat canvas duffel bags, rifles, lunch pack, folding shovel, backpacks, small ax, fishing rod, jackets, grill, extra paddle, tarps, video equipment, tripod, and snowshoes.

Everything was lashed aboard in case we capsized. Our biggest danger, short of drowning, was in losing our outfit and being forced to hike for weeks through this country without provisions or shelter. If we capsized, I was to get Luke; Tom would stay with the canoe and try to work it ashore. We each wore a life preserver, matches, knife, mosquito repellent, hat, and sunglasses. I carried a folded map in my shirt pocket.

"Let's paddle upstream to get the feel of the load," I said. "If it doesn't ride well, we can get back to shore and leave stuff in the cabin."

We shoved off and climbed aboard. I sat in my old position in the bow, Luke on the seat behind me, then a mountain of gear, and finally Tom in the stern. There was little room for our feet. We took a few tentative strokes upriver. She was heavy and sluggish, but rode the water like the freight canoe she was.

"What do you think?" Tom called.

I took a breath and nodded. "Let's do it," I answered.

With a few strokes, Tom turned the bow into the brown current. The river caught hold and swung us from shore, our familiar beach receding rapidly behind as we came around to face the future. The cutbank spun past, swallows billowing from it in a living cloud.

"Good-bye!" we called to each passing landmark. "Good-bye, Topo Island! Good-bye, Pike Slough!" Our family of ravens, usually so aloof, rose from the trees and sailed out to greet us, circling close overhead and crying. "Good-bye," we called back softly.

Our attention returned to the river. It moved us right along, and we soon left our familiar world behind. Apart from the subdued light and colors, it was a fine day to travel, for there was no wind and the clouds kept us from sunburn. We made good time in the high water, scooting over the rapids with hardly a problem. I say hardly, for I lost my nerve once at the sight of waves and chose a shallow channel where we went sideways on the rocks, crashing and yelling as we fought to regain control.

Gradually the overcast lifted, and by evening when we stopped on a little island, it was sunny and lovely. Above us hung new mountains, green against a gentle sky printed with herringbone clouds. Already Annie's Peak and Mount Laurie were far behind. We liked to name our camps and called this one "Emerald Isle." It was a beautiful spot, open yet sheltered by big trees. A carpet of moss ended with a short drop to the gravel bar that sloped into the river. On the beach, a great purple bear flop heralded the berry season.

Although it meant a great deal of work, Tom and I agreed to unload our craft each evening, stashing our possessions safely back in the woods and hauling the canoe up beside them. We were taking no chances in a land without alternatives. Our upstream travels had served as a shakedown, and we set up camp with practiced efficiency. The tent would go here, the kitchen there, dig a toilet hole over that way. Still, it took considerable effort at the end of a long day.

❧

THE NEXT FEW DAYS were rainy with clouds misting gray over the peaks and wind ruffling the water. Wearing wool jackets and gloves we traveled hard, stopping only to eat lunch on rocky bars or set up wet camps at the end of the day. It felt as if autumn were close on our heels, chasing us out of the mountains. We often descended a hundred feet and more in a day. The river was shot with rapids and took constant attention, for the water was dropping, sprouting rocks and shoals as it cleared. As we dropped in elevation the land changed, becoming more lush and closed in, the trees larger. The ridge of green mountains that slid past on the right was now clothed in dense alders.

Soon we drifted into my past, entering the area where I had lived those many years ago. It was strange how every curve of the land was etched into my memory. The morning was bright and windless, the mountains hanging green above us in a blue sky, when we paddled down my familiar "Deep Mile" and ran aground on the rock reef in front of my old cabin. There among the tall bushes it stood, looking like a hobbit hole growing from the face of the steep hill. The logs had mellowed to a red-brown and broken windows showed black in a sunny face. A thicket of young trees and flowers sprouted from the overhanging roof.

I had not been looking forward to this visit. There's a sadness about old cabins (and about one's own past) that is difficult to face. Perhaps because of the sunshine, the place seemed quaint and less forlorn this trip. Also, I knew what to expect and was at greater peace with history. But perhaps more than anything, the year I had just spent allowed me to climb the bank with a steady heart. I was grateful to Tom for helping me realize my own strength and regain a sense of belonging in this land. This was just a place I had lived; it wasn't me.

The door had again been broken open and bear hairs were on the counter. It was littered inside with squirrel duff and scattered items, many that other people had left, still I recognized most of the furniture. I saw my knitting, books, and old clothes. The floor had continued to shift as the frozen hill flowed glacier-like into the river. The rafters were rotting and would cave in someday. Surely, the most respectful thing would be to dismantle and burn this place, I thought, but the wilderness was at work on the project already.

Looking about, I discovered that even my past was no longer mine. I was a stranger here, unaffected by what I or others had done. Luke surprised me in being quite sentimental. He examined every cranny and inquired about my life. He wanted very much to take something away and chose an old enamel mug, a blue one that reminded him, he said, of sky reflected in a lake. I recovered one of my grandmother's spoons; Tom took a Jack London book, warped and mildewed.

After lunch we decided to camp on the crowded bit of sloping shore. We unloaded our outfit and set off for Chris Olson's place, a mile away. This was a collapsed old cabin that Phil and I had discovered the first year we spent in this country. Arriving in this valley with only those supplies we could pull upriver in a canoe, we had been aided by a man, long dead, with his gift of ideas and tools. Unlike most who had come to this land, Chris Olson had made it home.

The day was quiet and muggy. Mosquitoes droned as Tom, Luke, and I traveled the well-remembered trail that I had put in twenty-one years before.

The trees were bigger now and some had fallen, but the path was visible for one who knew the way. Chris Olson's clearing retained a clean and friendly feeling. Even in decay, the place exuded an air of love and good craftsmanship. Constructed more than sixty years before, his cache was still snug and tight, though tilted off its short posts and resting partly on the ground. We spent a delightful couple of hours poking about. Before we left, Luke picked flowers and laid them on the old man's grave.

BELOW MY OLD CABIN stretched several days of rapids, one right after another. The water continued to drop, turning to jade where boulders now peppered the swift channels. Often there was no good route through the stones. This was complicated by traveling into the sun, making it difficult to see. Our canoe was soon leaking as rivets popped up from smashing into rocks and the bottom was dented and scraped. It was a harrowing way to travel and, by the time afternoon thunderstorms drove us ashore, we were usually staggering with fatigue. There, Tom would tighten the screws and caulk the leaks with silicone.

The valley slowly broadened. The mountains pulled back and took on an aloof aspect, more gray than green in the distance. The river was gaining size and seemed less personal, but it was still braided, splitting and joining in a network of channels that rushed over drowned trees and through dense thickets. With the mountains, though, went the teeth of the rapids. They became "haystacks" of fast water rather than rocks and shoals. The storms now hung back along the peaks, watching us from a distance as we paddled on under a burning sun. Sometimes we stopped for lunch on an open bar and stripped for a bath. The water seemed tepid down here, the sky flat and faraway.

"Let's play awhile," Luke often entreated as we dressed by our noon fire.

"I wish we could," I told him. At the moment it looked like summer would last forever. "But I think we should make time while the weather holds."

"When it's cold you want to hurry because winter is coming," he answered angrily, "and when it's sunny you hurry because the weather is nice. All we do is travel."

"We have a very long way to go," I told him. "You may as well try to enjoy the trip."

"I wish you were younger," he said wistfully.

"Why?" I asked.

"Because you'd want to splash and play. You and Dad could toss me back and forth in the water. You just want to bathe and get dressed."

"My dear," I said, drawing him down onto my knees and combing out his dark, wet hair, "you need friends. Parents have a different role. Soon you'll have friends again." I smiled and winked, "but you won't have this river."

It was muggy and in the nineties, and the sun beat upon our heads and reflected from the blue-green water as we traveled on and on. Despite hats and sunscreen, our skins were turning to cracked leather and our eyes were squinted red from staring into the glare. Good camps had become more difficult to locate. We often had to climb a ten-foot cutbank and make twenty trips to unload the canoe. It was important to get back into the trees away from the constant sun. Because it circled the horizon, the shade moved too.

We paddled on into a land of recent forest fires. It was disquieting to drift by a patchwork of charred bluffs and see how the blaze had arbitrarily spared one tree and burned a neighbor. Smoke hung heavy in the south, and a smell of soot permeated the air. Bald eagles rose into the sky screaming an alarm at our approach, and kingfishers shot by low and fast with a loud, clacking call.

One day we found our first garbage and knew we were entering the domain of man. We burned it and set up our tent where someone had been before. The trees were now large and had a full appearance, unlike our skinny spruce. Many of the plants here were strange to us. Our friendly moss carpet was gone and in its place was dark silt populated with thorny rose bushes and coarse grass. Gone, too, were the blueberry and cranberry. Poplars now formed large trees, and alders grew as thick as my leg and higher than a house in dense hedges along the muddy bars. There were signs of beaver and black bear.

One day the river swept through a gate of high bluffs and spilled onto the Yukon Flats, leaving the mountains behind. We felt a pang of loss as we sped from the Brooks Range into this vast and unfamiliar land. It had been a trip of slow severance and gradual good-byes, but leaving the mountains was hard for all of us. The river itself had changed. It was beautifully clear, emerald in color and deep as it rushed over the gravel, but too big to feel at home. The banks were often fifteen feet high, walls of mud and falling trees above the swirling water. Channels were a hundred yards wide and serious crosscurrents formed where they joined, twining into whirlpools and sheers. If we swamped here it was unlikely we would be able to swim to shore.

The one welcome change was an instant drop in the number of mosquitoes. It was like walking through a door. There were still some, but our lives were no longer about protecting ourselves from them. We didn't choke on them or eat them. There was, however, a plague of no-see-ums, bugs so tiny they made the mosquitoes look big and awkward.

Late one morning we rounded a bend and spotted a flat riverboat against the right shore. Several Gwich'in Indians were in the process of breaking camp. Most were already aboard while a teenage lad held the painter from shore.

"Look! People!" Luke yelled in excitement.

We paddled over and grabbed their gunwale. It was a family of four generations headed into the mountains to pick berries and hunt moose. They were reserved at first until they realized we had been living upriver.

"You been out there all winter?" asked a plump woman in her sixties. She was dressed in pants and her short hair was tied back with a colorful bandanna. She smiled at Luke and reached across to pat him. "Gee, he look just like my grandson. Don't he look just like my Johnny?" she said turning to her son-in-law. Her ancient mother spoke little English and sat quietly beside her, a tiny woman with a straight back, wearing a dark dress and knee-high nylon stockings.

"You don't remember me," her son-in-law spoke up. He was about forty, a sturdy man with an open face. "I give you that dog you took up river last time." It was John Erick Junior, grown middle-aged. The wild youth of my memory was now a responsible father of teenage girls.

"That was a good dog," I told him. "She lived sixteen years."

"You want some Cheetos and Sugar Babies?" the woman asked Luke. She was rummaging through a box of food, pulling out treats for him. His eyes sparkled and she pushed the food into his grubby hands with a look of satisfaction. "You keep them alone in the woods at that age and they talk all the time, don't they?" she turned to me.

"Would you like some dry-meat?" I asked.

Eagerly, they took the offered strips. It is traditionally made without spices or salt and I hoped we hadn't spoiled it for them with too much pepper. In a few minutes we parted, going our separate ways on the river we shared.

❧

LUKE WAS THRILLED AT the prospect of seeing more Indians as we traveled downstream. We were nearing a village and soon spotted occasional riverboats racing up or down the current. He was enthralled with their power and speed, finding our mode of travel sadly inadequate in comparison. In our nightly camps he could not be dissuaded from running out to wave at passing boats, and we were sometimes embarrassed when people stopped to check on our safety after spotting the little figure gesturing wildly from the shore.

It became more difficult to read the map, for numerous braided channels formed vast islands that changed seasonally. The river had been greatly altered by a flood in 1976, and stark vistas of uprooted trees attested to its power. One very hot afternoon we spotted the village on a bluff ahead. Flat-bottomed boats were tied along the bank. We pulled in and secured our canoe to a heavy metal stake driven into the mud. Tying a tarp over our load to conceal the rifles and cameras, we started up the road. This was a place that did not cater to tourists and a white face was not always welcome.

After the flood, the settlement had moved onto the bluff, leaving only a few ghostly remnants of the old village I remembered. It had been a place of small cabins connected with footpaths. The new village was laid out along dirt roads. Most people still walked, but pickups and ATVs had found their way up the river or through the air to this remote place. The cabins were large, airy, and almost identical, built by teams of young men in a effort to provide jobs as well as housing. A community center offered hot showers, washing machines, and chlorinated drinking water (which was still hauled to individual homes). Each cabin had electricity, a refrigerator, satellite telephone, and color television, but all used outhouses.

I found my old friend, Jessie Williams, in the clinic where she still served as the village health aid. She was delighted to see us. She had grown stouter and now wore thick glasses. She still did without dentures. Her husband, Albert, had died and she lived with her sister, Clara. Standing in the spotless new clinic, I felt suddenly grubby in my rubber boots and smoky clothing. Luke's pants had wedges of material enlarging the sides and his face and hands were burned brown. Jessie petted him fondly and remarked on how he had grown since our earlier trip. She rushed out to buy ready-made frozen hamburgers, shoestring potatoes, Tang, gum, and animal crackers from the village store. We gave her dried moose. We heated the burgers in her office microwave and talked while we ate.

It was late afternoon when we headed back toward the river through seeding fields of fireweed and foxtail grass. A wind had picked up, whipping sand off the exposed bars—a headwind, I noticed with a feeling of gloom. We had chosen not to film the village because the Indians are a private people and it didn't feel respectful to point a camera at them, but I wanted to video the deserted cabins along the shore. As I neared the old church, a very large man came down the road on a three-wheeler. With him were two children, one on each fender. He pulled to a stop beside me, his face a dark, quiet mask. I imagined he had come to challenge me about filming the old building.

"Long time no see," he stated. "I heard you was in town and thought I'd come visit. I guess Phil is history, huh?"

"Well, he's making his own history," I answered. I was surprised at how well I was remembered in this village after all these years.

"He sent Jessie some moose when he was up hunting one time," he went on. I nodded. "That sounds like Phil."

"We was up at your old cabin about five years ago. We left you a note. Did you see it?"

"No, must have gotten used for squirrel bedding." Imagine leaving us a note, I thought fondly. We didn't always understand each other, but these people had befriended me. Perhaps the old cabin did serve a purpose after all. It might yet save a life someday.

"Me and Stanley was up there. You know Stanley? He died of a heart attack." The big man seemed sad and thoughtful. We spoke a minute longer and he warned me with oblique politeness to be careful of the wind on the Yukon. "Especially a south wind like this," he went on. "Even Indians with a big boat and engine stay off that river when the wind is up. Lotta guys get drowned."

I thanked him for the advice. He started his little vehicle and headed up the road and I turned for the canoe where Tom and Luke waited.

It was after five when we passed through the slough into the main channel. With that, we committed ourselves to the next long voyage, down to the Yukon and along that mighty river to the only bridge that crossed it in Alaska. Strong gusts of wind pushed us inexorably into the sweepers, forcing us to paddle hard down the broad bends, eyes squinted against the blast. A few miles below town we found a small channel between overgrown banks. Tying the canoe, we forced a way through a tall thicket and onto a forested bench where we gratefully set up camp. As usual, we unloaded the boat and pulled it up between the alders, stashing our belongings under a tarp near the fire.

It was well that we did. Dusk had settled over the land and the mosquitoes were out in numbers when we heard something thump against the hull.

"It's probably just a beaver," Tom said. He was in his nightclothes and bare feet, but he took the pistol and stepped into the thorny rose bushes outside the tent.

"There's an enormous black bear out here!" he breathed. "Oh, no! I think he's headed this way."

There was no place to hide in the flimsy, old tent, but I cowered over our sleeping child and held my breath. My heart was pounding so loudly I was sure the bear could hear it.

"He's going away!" Tom whispered. His voice was almost a groan. A moment later he unzipped the tent and handed me the pistol. He had retrieved his .30-30 from the pile of gear and stood guard before the door for several minutes, oblivious to the mosquitoes and thorns. When he entered, bringing hordes of bugs, his face looked strained in the dim light.

"Pretty stupid, not keeping the rifle in the tent," he muttered. He was trying to find a place for it along his side of the cramped shelter.

"We've gotten lax," I agreed.

"We may as well sleep," he told me, as I lay listening, every nerve alert. He was right, of course, I couldn't stay awake forever, and it was hard to hear anything in the wind. If the bear had gone it was a good sign.

"Black bears are different from grizzlies," I told him. "They tend to skulk around." We were whispering as if the very sound of our voices would attract danger.

"We might as well get used to it," he answered. "The Indians tell me there are lots of black bears from here on."

🦋

BEYOND THE VILLAGE WE left the hot summer weather. Although the sky remained fair, strong afternoon winds often forced us to seek shelter early. The river had become very broad and it took considerable paddling to cross from one side to the other. We would take refuge in the trees, a mixed forest of spruce, poplar, and alder standing deep in prickly rose that was now turning yellow and hanging with red fruit. Piles of dead leaves smelled of autumn and above our heads the wind thundered like a train. Through the branches we could see clouds of sand ripping down the shore across the river.

At one camp we were weather-bound four days. The forest was dense and flat, a place where one could easily become lost. Highbush cranberries were ripe, large red globes that hung like cherries from slender bushes as high as our heads. We collected many quarts and made syrup for pancakes and biscuits. A naked spruce pole projected at an angle from the nearby sandy beach where Luke spent many happy hours balancing as he leaned into the blowing grit. He dug small wells by the mint-colored river and made "mud bombs." He also hailed passing boats and brought in visitors who squatted around our fire, talking above the roar of the wind and leaving gifts of fresh caribou and fish. The Native people enjoy a culture of sharing and they included us. We were awkward at first, not understanding the unspoken rules, but gradually came to realize that to decline a gift was to doubt the generosity of the giver.

Only at night did the wind die down, but it was now too dark to travel safely. As twilight fell and the world stilled, the first full moon of autumn rose golden over the rim of the world. From far away came the wild cries of sandhill cranes, loud and hauntingly beautiful.

※

I WAS SO ANXIOUS to be underway that I woke Tom in the early twilight. The sun was resting on the glassy river and cool damp air wafted from the water. We let Luke sleep as we broke camp about him. Tom gently roused him with a song and I fed him breakfast as the last few items were being stowed aboard the canoe.

Beavers slapped their tails and dove in alarm as we slipped down the teal-green current. The land was very flat, and we could no longer see the mountains. The river had settled into lazy loops, preparing for its marriage with the Yukon. Soon we became aware of open spaces, lakes and swamps behind a sliding fringe of trees. As the day progressed, dark clouds rolled in, dramatically highlighting the shimmering foliage along the bank.

Around noon the current merged with a slough, a muddy channel of the Yukon as large as our own river. The two waters twisted together in a plume of blue and brown. Within a mile all trace of the river was gone. The brown slough now coiled between sloping banks, clothed in waving horsetails and overhung by tall bushes. Behind the dense hedge one could often see spruce forests. Here the trees were far larger than we had known. When the wind rose, we found a sheltered camp back in those big trees and gratefully called it home.

The following day the wind picked up again, forcing us to paddle hard to make headway. We had reached a place where it would be easy to get lost, for channels now joined and diverged, communicating with the big river, unseen ahead. One assumes that water flows downhill and that a canoe could not fail to drift into the Yukon eventually, but there are literally hundreds of wrong turns along this mighty waterway: backwaters and sloughs that go for miles or flow into and out of lakes depending on their level. In some areas a map of the Yukon resembles a plate of spaghetti.

We made little progress that day and camped just before entering the mother river. Across our slough, a forest fire still smoldered, sending showers of sparks and smoke into the sunset sky.

❦

THE MORNING WE GAVE ourselves to the Yukon was a dawn of gray and yellow mirrored in miles of traveling water, so that we seemed to float upon the very sky itself. Where whitecaps had ruled the day before, all was flat and glossy, a dark ribbon of trees separating earth from air. There were times that even this disappeared, and it seemed we were being carried into the sky.

We had planned to hug the land, timidly sprinting between the smaller channels, but now stepped out, following the currents. With geography on such a grand scale, and changing with each breakup, it was difficult to track our progress on the map. Major bends took hours to negotiate and were deceptive in this flat land. We could never see all the river at once and were often surprised to find huge channels plowing back into ours when we had not seen them leave. With the maze of sloughs forming vast islands, the concept of "shore" quite lost its meaning.

When we swung toward the banks we were awed at how high and formidable they were. Most reared twenty or thirty feet above the muddy flow, and the sound of them collapsing into the current carried far out over the water. It was lovely on a sunny morning, but very intimidating when the afternoon squalls kicked up. This river was too big for my comfort. It was difficult to find any place to camp, and we often spent hours paddling across only to discover that a bank that looked inviting from a distance was built on the scale of giants. Everything was enormous here: river, cutbanks, trees, and dense forests of willow. Watching the Yukon devour hundreds of acres of mature spruce—toppling them like so many matches—I felt unimportant and fragile. It was a blunt reminder of how little Nature cares for the individual. This country didn't tolerate us; it didn't even notice us.

We were becoming fatigued. Twice more a bear had come into camp. It was hard to rest in a state of alertness. Tom was cranky and I had started making mistakes. At one point I wanted to stop at an island where hundreds of seagulls had congregated to nest, but Tom was irritated at the delay. Luke and I walked a half mile to the nursery, where the sky filled with wheeling, screaming birds, but Tom stayed with the canoe.

"What's the point of all this hurry," I asked him that evening. "We should enjoy this trip. Years from now Luke will have forgotten most of the Yukon, but he'll remember Gull Island."

"I'm sorry," he sighed. "It's all the packing and hauling. Fewer camps means I don't have to load the canoe as many times."

As we traveled on, the wind became worse and sometimes we paddled continuously all day into big waves. With the challenge of climbing the thirty-foot banks and hauling all our gear up, we now sought refuge among the willows on the trailing end of bars. These were precarious spots, for there was little shelter, but the wind generally dropped at night and it saved us two hours of work. In the golden light of sunset Luke would swim in the muddy shallows while Tom and I made a home.

One such camp we named "Green Lee." Our tent crouched beneath a palisade of willows that rose above the rocky shore. These were nothing like our mountain willows. Roots grew from their trunks like cypress trees, and they were so densely packed that it was difficult to force a way between them. Although a shelter, they exuded a great, green energy that was almost hostile.

I could hear Tom and Luke speaking quietly in the tent as I put away the cooking things for the night. Sunlight twinkled low through the thicket on one side, while miles of water reflected blue sky on the other. The sound of geese and cranes drifted on the calming air, and the back of an occasional migrating salmon broke the muddy water close to shore. In the shallows, a beaver wavered back and forth, seeking the willows but afraid of our camp.

I forced a few steps into the thicket and was soon encased in foliage. Horsetails grew knee-high in the green light that filtered down among the trunks. Insects buzzed somewhere in the leaves overhead. A dense forest of stems disappeared into the gloom on either side. I could imagine dinosaurs here or bears, but not people. There was a primal feeling about the place that seemed to resent my presence, and I backed from the willows onto the open beach. Like

Lake Eugene, here was another mystery. There are elements of Nature that we can never understand, currents that run older and deeper than our own, where we do not belong.

ФФ

OUR LAST CAMP WAS a bivouac of desperation. We had stopped in Stevens Village to buy sugar for preserving quarts of berries. It was a windy day, and we had fought into the blowing sand and high waves for hours to make one bend of the river. At the village we were invited to participate in a funeral potlatch, a very moving experience where our plates were piled with many pounds of boiled moose, caribou, bear, goose, and other food. Guests were expected to carry away what they could not eat.

Luke spent the afternoon romping with the village children. He greeted each person as a friend and I had to warn him that things would be different at the bridge.

"Why is that?" he wanted to know.

"In the village people live as neighbors," I began. "The road that crosses the bridge is connected to the rest of the world. It's sad to tell you that there are people who would harm children, but it's true. You mustn't go anywhere with someone you don't know."

We left the village late in the evening after the wind had dropped. The sun was rapidly sliding into the trees, burning gold beneath clouds lit like embers. As twilight deepened, we searched in vain for a place off the treacherous river. When we reached a shelving bank, it was always a morass of mud. At last we found a wet beach, devoid of anything to burn, where we set up our tent in the horsetails. For the only time that summer, we drove stakes into the mud and tied the loaded canoe nearby, securing a tarp over it to keep out the rain.

It was midnight and the land lay in dark shadow. We crawled into our wet tent out of the falling mist and slept lightly until dawn. By then the clouds had settled and a fine rain blanketed the gray land. Unable to cook breakfast without unloading the canoe into sticky mud, we ate cold moose and bear meat, rolled our soggy tent, and climbed into our dismal craft. It was more of a rout than a homecoming.

As the day progressed, the clouds thickened. Icy rain trickled from our faces and hands as we paddled steadily downstream, adrift in a gray curtain. Luke huddled in his raincoat under the edge of the tarp. Ahead loomed a bank of hills. At length, the mighty Yukon gathered itself into a single channel and funneled between them. The river seemed smaller and more subdued, reduced to a mere three-quarters of a mile in width. Steep rocky outcrops flanked it on either side, herding it along. Already the aspen and birch were a blaze of yellow and the ground had turned to russet with approaching autumn. Eagles chirruped along the cliffs, but above their wild cries could be heard the roar of passing motorboats and the faraway rumble of traffic.

"There's the bridge!" Luke cried, pointing excitedly. Out of the mist ahead loomed the stark girders, a visual metaphor linking our two worlds.

I let my breath out in a sigh. "We've come a long way, guys," I said turning to face my family.

Tom looked sad, his glasses fogged and his hair hanging in wet tendrils. "I wish we could just turn around," he said gazing back in the direction of our arctic home. "Don't you, Luke?"

"Good-bye river!" Luke sang out. "Hi-ho civilization!" He was excited, a grin splitting his glistening, dirty face as he paddled strongly toward a future of friends, technology, and food.

"Too many boats," said Tom.

"I love boats," Luke replied. He was a partner now in our expedition. He had put on fifteen pounds and four inches but, more than that, had matured beyond his seven years. There was a confident spring to his gait and a spark of humor in his eyes.

And me? I was ready for the next step, whatever it brought. There was no point in dragging out the good-byes. I still had my fears, but I was learning to make peace with them. I looked at Tom and Luke. We were a different family from the one that last crossed this bridge. Perhaps we could never really go back to the world we knew. I turned to the ugly structure that spanned this Yukon and wondered what the future would bring.

Mount Laurie.

Tom, Jeanie, Laurie, and Lucas in 2012.

EPILOGUE

And so we arrive at the end of our tale. We hitchhiked back to Fairbanks where Mark and Denise smoothed our transition into the "other world." While Tom set off for Arizona in his little red truck, Luke and I flew north to visit my brothers aboard the blue-and-white Comanche. Cruising at fifteen thousand feet, we gazed down upon the Brooks Range at sunset. Autumn scrolled beneath us, russet and burgundy, laced with winter's first snow. The Arctic Continental Divide formed a jagged wall restraining a press of clouds from the Arctic Ocean. As I watched clouds spill through the high passes like waterfalls, a strange longing arose in my chest to again walk those inhospitable ridges. I knew it was cold and windy down there—not a stick to burn or a bit of shelter—yet already I missed it. Maybe, I thought, when Luke is a little older.

Adjusting to modern life was not as easy as building a home in the wilderness. Noise was a big challenge. It was months before I stopped bolting from sleep at the hum of a Cessna. Shortly after arriving in Arizona I was shopping for school supplies in the towering corridors of Walmart. Crammed into the maze of trinkets with people who treated each other as obstacles, I was suddenly overcome with sadness. I promised myself not to forget the beauty of life. Somehow I would learn to keep my balance and treat those about me with reverence. There must be a way to live in this strange world we have created and not drown in it.

Luke was well prepared for second grade and was put into a gifted program. In the serendipitous unfolding of life, *Reader's Digest* bought rights to my first book, allowing me time to write this one—originally published in 1995. So all of my worry had been for naught. When spring returned to the desert and the white-crowned sparrow passed through our yard headed north with only his small wings and a song, he called this time for Tom. "How many more years can I handle that life?" Tom asked as he packed his little red truck. He would seek any job in Alaska, he told me, just to be near wilderness. Friends looked at me oddly. "Won't you miss him?" they asked. The answer was "Yes," but freedom is the most precious gift we grant one another. Meanwhile, I was back in college, headed for a second degree—this time in nursing.

Tom circled homeward before snowfall. I put Luke on a plane to join him so that they could drive home together—one of many such trips they would make over the coming years. When Luke was nine, we canoed our river and spent three weeks at the cabin. Bears had ripped their way in, and it took us several days to clean up the mess. Luke was thirteen when next we overwintered there. He was already taller than me, a full partner this time in creating our adventures. Wanting to complete her arctic winter, Laurie joined us. We again formed a strong and happy team: building a storehouse and laughing as we hauled logs, put in trails, and played together in the snow. Those fifteen months were integral to the complex, wise, and generous man Lucas would become. Laurie has remained a lifelong friend.

It took Tom and me twenty years to complete our two-hour documentary, companion to this book. Unwilling to relinquish editorial control, we produced and distributed it ourselves. You may see more at www.jeanaspen.com. It gradually attracted a following and now shows on PBS stations across the nation. Lucas received his BSN in nursing, gifting his gentle heart to patients and coworkers alike. When our documentary premiered before the little Alaskan town we now call home, he joined us and shared with the audience what living in wilderness meant to him. Next year, Tom and I plan to film and produce another. Our purpose is to inspire others to live their dreams, create loving community, and honor our sacred Planet.

After more than six decades, I accept that I have little control over events. Worry does not prevent pain, yet surrender to the Journey can bring a strange lightness—even through profound sorrow. In choosing gratitude, I have learned that one can live in joy wherever the river wanders. This is no small Gift and it did not come cheaply. There are no guarantees when you cast off, and you can miss Life's remarkable adventure by playing it too safe. Life never tracks a straight line; its very nature is Mystery—both grander and more terrible than you imagine when you set forth in your little canoe. From the vantage of a mostly completed voyage, I now discern shifting patterns that were not initially apparent. My books and our documentary are the small gifts I leave you from across these trackless miles. As I paddle the last bends, I am thankful that I chose to follow my dreams. I am also deeply grateful to those who traveled with me or supported my trip.

Two decades and more have disappeared down the river since I wrote this book, and an entire lifetime has washed away, leaving only scattered tracks. I had thought it was my life I was completing—for I am ready to leave the river,

Our cabin today, 2013.

as is Tom. Instead, it was our beloved Son, Lucas Foster Irons, who departed our lives a month shy of his twenty-sixth birthday. I had considered myself his teacher, you see, but now I understand he was always a Gift to me. It has humbled me with compassion. Each day, I now realize, is a Sacred pearl. There are no ordinary days.

Tom will soon be seventy, and I am not far behind. We return to our cabin each spring, faithful as sparrows, relinquishing the illusion of security for the wonder of each shining day. We still spend a third of every year walking our beloved valley and listening to the song of running water. My next book, *Trusting the River*, shares the heartbreak and joy of our meandering feet.

Wishing you Beauty, Love, and Wonder,
Jeanie Aspen, December 23, 2013

Books by Jean Aspen

Arctic Daughter: A Wilderness Journey
Arctic Son: Fulfilling the Dream
Trusting the River
A Child of Air (a novel)

Companion documentary to this book

Arctic Son: Fulfilling the Dream, Produced by
Jean Aspen and Tom Irons

Books by Constance Helmericks (Jean's mother)

We Live in Alaska, 1944
We Live in the Arctic, 1947
Our Summer With the Eskimos, 1949
Our Alaskan Winter, 1950
Flight of the Arctic Tern, 1952
Down the Wild River North, 1968
Australian Adventure, 1972

Visit us at www.jeanaspen.com

Printed in the USA
CPSIA information can be obtained
at www.ICGtesting.com
JSHW012022140824
68134JS00033B/2819

9 780882 409207